LINGUISTICS

WORDS, RULES, AND INFORMATION

Chongwon Park   •   William Salmon

University of Minnesota Duluth

Kendall Hunt
publishing company

To my two precious ladies, Bridget and Angela Jean Park
—Chongwon Park

For Jennifer and Joe, the two halves of my heart
—Will Salmon

CONTENTS

PREFACE

Many outstanding textbooks on introductory linguistics are currently available. For that reason, we had to consider whether writing a new book was really necessary. After giving some serious thought to the question, we agreed that our own textbook would benefit our students more.

The course entitled Introduction to Linguistics at the University of Minnesota Duluth (UMD) belongs to the same category as Calculus I, which means that students can replace Calculus I with Introduction to Linguistics. The reason why UMD chose this option is based on the assumption that there is a striking similarity in the course objectives for mathematics and linguistics courses. However, most of the textbooks on introductory linguistics available elsewhere provide only a light sampling of the diverse subfields in linguistics. Though that approach is extremely valuable, we believe that it doesn't fit the need of our Introduction to Linguistics course as both a mathematics course and a required foundational course for linguistics majors and minors. In fact, several other textbooks emphasize only the mathematical nature of linguistics; however, they are generally too difficult to be used as a college freshmen-level textbook.

Our textbook, *Linguistics: Words, Rules, and Information*, deals with traditional theoretical issues. It emphasizes the mathematical and computational nature of human language. We attempted to make our explanations understandable to college freshmen without any background in linguistics by avoiding unnecessary jargon and technical descriptions often found in many other linguistics textbooks. We hope that students will understand the systematic nature of human language after reading this book and why linguistics is considered the science of language. Although this book is written with the UMD freshman in mind, it can be used for any introductory linguistics class that has the same course objectives as ours.

Chongwon Park
William Salmon

ACKNOWLEDGEMENTS

We would like to express our deepest gratitude to the students who took our *Introduction to Linguistics* course at the University of Minnesota Duluth for the past several years. They not only motivated us to finish our project, but they also made helpful suggestions on how to make our book more approachable to absolute novices.

Chongwon would like to thank Bridget, his wife, for her encouragement and support over the course of this project. She was deeply involved in proofreading different versions of the manuscript, which was certainly one of Chongwon's many weaknesses. Dan Turner deserves Chongwon's thanks for the illustrations he created for this book. Chongwon also thanks Debbie Rose who read the page proofs and made many corrections.

Will would like to thank Chongwon Park for inviting him to be part of this project. He also thanks Jennifer Gómez Menjívar, who has been listening to him talk about this for almost a year now. It couldn't have been finished without her support.

Both of us would like to thank Thalia Cutsforth and Jeffrey Huemoeller at Kendall Hunt Publishing Company. Thalia and Jeff have been extremely patient with us from the inception of the project. Without their help, the publication of this book would have been impossible.

Despite all the help from the people mentioned here, we are solely responsible for the mistakes, errors, and incompleteness in our work.

Chongwon Park
William Salmon

CHAPTER 1

Introduction

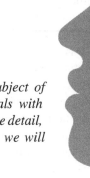

What is linguistics? We assume that most people have heard of the subject of linguistics. We also assume that most people know that linguistics deals with language in some sense. But when people have to explain linguistics in more detail, they might end up saying, "I'm not sure." In this introductory chapter, we will discuss the aims of linguistics in a very general sense.

1.1 Linguistics As A Science

The word *linguistics* is dissected into three parts: *lingu*, *ist*, and *ics*. The first part, *lingu(a)*, literally means "tongue" in Latin, which is often metaphorically interpreted as a language, as in the expression *mother tongue*. You might have heard of the expression *lingua franca*, which means a language adopted as a common language among speakers whose native languages are different. Literally speaking, *lingua franca* means "Frankish language," where *Frankish* is roughly the same as *European* in the modern sense. The second part, *ist*, is a suffix that converts the word to a noun. The third part of linguistics, *ics*, is from Greek. The meaning of *ics* is literally "science." If we combine these individual meanings, we get the meaning of the word *linguistics*: "the science of language." In particular, the third part of linguistics, *ics*, is often found in many other academic disciplines such as mathematics, physics, and statistics, among others. Without difficulty, we understand that these disciplines are all sciences. In many universities, these disciplines belong to the college of science and engineering. But when it comes to linguistics, most people cast doubt on the status of linguistics as a science, although *linguistics* itself means "the science of language." To understand that linguistics is a science, we first have to understand what science is all about.

1.1.1 What is a science?

What is a science, then? We hear the word *science* almost everyday on TV, in newspapers, and in our everyday conversation. We also know that science is everywhere. We often acknowledge that we cannot live without scientific discoveries and scientific revolutions. Nonetheless, we rarely think of the definition of science. The English word *science* comes from the Latin word *scientia*, which literally means "knowledge." As the name itself reveals, science deals with knowledge. However, not every kind of knowledge is qualified to be a topic of a science. Science deals with a very specific type of knowledge. Science organizes knowledge in the form of testable explanations and predictions. Any knowledge that can be built in testable forms falls within a domain of science. To explain the notion of testable explanations, let us consider the following examples.

(1) Sir Arthur Conan Doyle is the best author ever!
(2) The capital of Minnesota is Saint Paul.
(3) Duluth is surrounded by lots of corn fields.

Although many people believe that Conan Doyle is a great writer, (1) is hardly a scientific statement. The notion of the "best author" often depends on the person's subjective opinion. One person might believe that Conan Doyle is the best writer among all the writers in human history, while another person might simply scoff at the first by saying Conan Doyle's writing is "not even close" to the best writing. In either case, it is very hard to prove one person's position because each person's position is fairly subjective. By contrast, (2) is easily provable. To prove that (2) is true, we can go to a library or call a government office, where we can find information on the capital of Minnesota. If the information we gathered confirms the claim, the claim is proved to be true. In this sense, (2) is qualified to be a scientific claim. The last item on the list, (3) exhibits an interesting case. Duluth is a city on the shore of Lake Superior in Minnesota. It has hills and beautiful scenery. In Duluth, you will see lots of birch trees and the gigantic lake, but you will hardly see any corn fields. Anybody who visits Duluth knows that (3) is not true. Nonetheless, (3) is still a scientific claim that we can easily disprove.

As a science, linguistics deals with knowledge in the form of testable explanations and predictions. To illustrate one case of testable explanation, let us consider the imperative sentence in (4) below. Most people know that the subject of (4) must be *you*. But the question is, How can we test it?

(4) Be confident!

To figure out the subject of (4), let us put forth one simple hypothesis called the Y-Hypothesis as in (5).

(5) The Y-Hypothesis
    The subject of imperative sentences is *you*.

Is (5) a scientific claim? The answer is yes because we can test the hypothesis. One prediction of the hypothesis is that, when we add to (4) a *self*-word such as *himself, myself, yourself, themselves*, the *self*-word must be *yourself*. This prediction is made based on the observation that the *self*-word always agrees with its antecedent in person. Here, *antecedent* means "a word that is associated with a *self*-word within a sentence." In general, an antecedent appears before a *self*-word in English. "Person" refers to a grammatical property of the speaker, the hearer, and anything else. For example, *I* (and *my*) is first person; *you* (and *your*) is second person; and everything else is third person, including *he* and *she*. Note that person is a grammatical notion and not a biological property. As a result, an inanimate entity such as *desk* and *book* can have a person property: third person. Examples (6)–(8) illustrate that the *self*-words agree with their antecedents in person.

(6) I love myself.
(7) You should respect yourself.
(8) He kicked himself.

If the *self*-word does not agree with its antecedent in person, the result is not acceptable, as shown in (9)–(11). None of the examples below are acceptable. To illustrate the unacceptability, linguists often use the asterisk symbol (*) as in (9)–(11). Whenever you see the * symbol in front of a sentence or expressions, you have to interpret it as an unacceptable expression or sentence.

(9) * She loves myself.
(10) * I should respect yourself.
(11) * You kicked himself.

Now let us go back to our initial example addressed in (4). If we add *self*-words like *himself* and *itself* as in (12)–(14), the results are not acceptable.

(12) * Be confident in himself!
(13) * Be confident in itself!
(14) * Be confident in themselves!

However, when you add *yourself* to (4), the result is perfectly felicitous, as shown in (15).

(15) Be confident in yourself!

What does this mean? This means that the subject of (4) must be *you*. Otherwise, we cannot explain the acceptability of (15). Similarly, the unacceptability of (12)–(14) is systematically explained by the hypothesis that the subject of (4) must be *you*.

There is an additional test of the hypothesis, if you would like further proof. The Y-hypothesis also predicts that a tag-question of (4) must be (16).

(16) Be confident, will you?

This prediction is made based on the observation that the subject of a sentence must be repeated in a tag-question. In (17)–(19), the tag-question was formed by repeating the subject of the sentence in the pronoun form. In (17), the tag-question *doesn't he* was used because the subject of the sentence is *John*. For the same reason, *won't you* and *aren't I* were used in (18) and (19), respectively.

(17) John studies linguistics, doesn't he?
(18) You will pay my money back in a week, won't you?
(19) I am smart, aren't I?

When the subject of the sentence is not repeated in a tag-question, the result is not acceptable, as shown in (20)–(22). Therefore, the prediction we made in (16) is borne out; the Y-Hypothesis is correct. In (20) and (22), the infelicitous result assumes that the pronouns are the same person as the subject; *you* and *John* are the same person in (20), and *he* and *I* in (22) are the same.

(20) * John studies linguistics, don't you?
(21) * You will pay my money back in a week, won't I?
(22) * I am smart, isn't he?

Throughout this book, we will use the same method repeatedly to test our hypothesis by creating testable explanations and predictions, a method that falls exactly within the definition of science. Although this type of hypothesis testing in relation to language might be unusual to most readers, the method itself is nothing new. Let us recall our science classes in elementary, junior high, and high school. The methods we used in those science classes are exactly the same as the methods we used in this section. The only difference is that the science you learned before is about the natural world, while the science we are doing here is about the human mind.

1.1.2 Prescriptive grammar versus descriptive grammar

To most people, *grammar* is a synonym for "a bunch of rules with do's and don'ts." One of the most well-known rules would be (23).

(23) Do not end a sentence with a preposition!

These kinds of rules are called prescriptive rules or prescriptive grammar. Sometimes, prescriptive grammar is called school grammar because this is the grammar we learn in school. There is a great benefit of prescriptive grammar for students, especially when they learn writing, because writing is a highly conventionalized form of language. Many nonfiction writers observe the conventions in spelling, grammar, and usage.

It must be clarified that prescriptive grammar is *not* the grammar in which linguists are interested. The reason why linguists are not too excited about prescriptive grammar is that prescriptive grammar does not say anything about the workings of the human mind. Linguists try to answer the questions of why and how linguistic expressions are constructed and used. The set of prescriptive directions is not at all related to the questions addressed. Let us use one analogical example to explain prescriptive grammar.

Assume that there is someone who is a putative authority in all kinds of trees in northern Minnesota and that his name is Max. As an authority, Max is proclaiming that every tree in northern Minnesota must look like a birch tree because he believes that the birch tree is an ideal form of all trees. His followers decide to cut down all other trees to make them look like birch trees. Sometimes they have to paint trees white, and sometimes they have to cut trees so that they can be thinner. Other times, they have to make trees taller, which seems to be an extremely challenging task. Although this hard work may make many trees uniform, it does not say anything about the properties of the original trees. More importantly, trees will grow in their own ways, no matter how Max's followers try to change them. Notwithstanding the fact that language can never be the same as trees, the role of prescriptive grammar is somewhat similar to Max's followers. Linguists examine language to understand language as it is, as opposed to controlling language to change it for their own purpose.

The underlying assumption behind prescriptive grammar is that there are some authorities on language. Unfortunately, there are many people who claim to be language authorities. A well-known Harvard linguist, Steven Pinker, mockingly called those people "language mavens." Some other linguists call those people "self-appointed language authorities." No matter what other people call them, the notion of language authority is very odd. Language is a dynamic entity and constantly changing. The English we are using now is not the same as the English Shakespeare used, not to mention the variety that Chaucer used. The *Oxford English Dictionary* attests that almost all English words underwent and undergo some types of changes over time. Many words in English are borrowed from various foreign languages, including, but not limited to, French, Latin, Greek, German, Arabic, and Japanese. Most of the changes just happen over time without direction from the so-called language authorities. Unfortunately, the aforementioned language authorities believe that language change is deterioration, and we have to educate people and thus prevent language from decaying. This is an absurd statement because, once again, language is a dynamic entity that constantly changes. When parents see their children grow, they often say that they don't want their children to mature so fast because they are so adorable the way they are now. However, we have to admit that the children will, should, and do grow. Nobody will say that a child's growth is deterioration. People just grow and change, and so do languages.

When linguists use the word *grammar*, what they mean is descriptive grammar, which is not the same as prescriptive grammar. Descriptive grammar is different from prescriptive grammar because it describes how linguistic expressions are constructed and it explains the structures and meanings of linguistic expressions. For example, let us consider the well-known prescriptive rule (23) again. Different from the "DO-NOT-rule," many people actually do use a sentence that ends with a preposition like (24).

(24) Who do you want to talk to?

Instead of lamenting that people should not use a sentence like (24), linguists attempt to explain how a sentence like (24) arises. Simply put, linguists try to find rules that derive a sentence like (24). We will discuss the derivation of (24) in detail in Chapter 5. Roughly speaking, however, (24) is the result of moving *who* from its original position as in (25). The base sentence of (24) is (25). From (25), (24) is derived by moving *who* to the front position of the sentence. As a result, the preposition ends up appearing in the sentence-final position. Obviously, this process is a bit more complex, and we will take the time to explain the process step by step later. Just know that for every "DO-NOT-rule," linguists have a good explanation of the use in natural language.

(25) Do you want to talk to who?

The same type of explanation then will be extended to other types of sentences in many other languages. By doing this, linguists can reach a generalization that reveals some properties of human language. For example, the said type of *wh*-word (such as *who*, *where*, *what*, etc.) movement is observed in many languages. Because this is so, the movement might be a universal property of human language. If this is a universal property, we are getting closer to understanding human language by discovering this type of movement rule. Throughout this textbook, when we use the term *rule*, it means a descriptive rule just like the *wh*-movement rule we have just discussed. Readers should be aware that the "do and don't" type rules are not the concern of the subject of linguistics, nor of this textbook.

1.1.3 Ungrammatical versus unacceptable

The other distinction we want to make in this chapter is the difference between grammaticality and acceptability. Throughout this book, we will use the term *unacceptable* whenever the speakers reject the linguistic expressions in question for various reasons. For example, most native speakers of English will reject (26). The speakers might have different reasons for the rejection of the sentence, but they might say the sentence is awkward. The awkwardness of (26) is notated by the question mark in front of the sentence.

(26) ? John sleeps violently.

Ungrammatical expressions are particular types of unacceptability. Ungrammatical expressions are ill-formed expressions. Let us take a look at (27), which is unacceptable as well as ungrammatical. Most native speakers will reject (27) because the sentence does not conform to the speakers' grammar in their mind. The speakers' internalized grammar dictates that the copula (*be* verb) does not match its subject *John*. For this particular reason, (27) is treated as an ill-formed sentence and thus is ungrammatical. In this sense, unacceptability is a broader notion than ungrammaticality. From now on, we will use these two terms interchangeably. Nonetheless, the * notation will be used only for ungrammatical linguistic expressions and formulations.

(27) * John aren't smart.

In relation to the discussion on the distinction between prescriptive and descriptive grammars, we need to be clear that judging whether a sentence of English is grammatical is not the same thing as whether the sentence is "proper" or "correct." Although many of us were taught in school that the examples in (28) to (29) are not proper or correct, these are the expressions used by many native speakers of English.

(28) Me and Jenny went to the theater yesterday.
(29) Who would you like to have coffee with?

These expressions are generated by the speakers' internal grammar. As we already discussed, linguists are interested in the grammar that actually exists in the speakers' minds. For the same reason, the notion of grammaticality is not related to whether one expression is proper or not. In other words, when linguists talk about grammatical expressions, they are talking about expressions that native speakers actually speak. If the native speakers actually use the expressions, then the expressions are grammatical. Readers should not be confused between "proper" use of language taught in school and the notion of grammaticality we use in this book.

1.2 Subfields Of Linguistics And Different Approaches In Linguistics

Just like other sciences, linguistics has various subfields and different approaches.

1.2.1 Subfields

Subfields of linguistics include morphology, syntax, semantics, phonology, pragmatics, mathematical linguistics, computational linguistics, sociolinguistics, and psycholinguistics, among others. This textbook focuses on five main subfields: morphology, syntax, semantics, pragmatics, and phonology. The reason we focus on these particular subfields is the organizational nature of natural language. Let us consider the simple sentence in (30).

(30) Jane loves Bill.

To utter the sentence, the speaker first has to choose each word from her mental lexicon, which is a collection of words in the speaker's mind. Selected words must often go through particular types of operations. For example, the verb *loves* in (30) is the result of the combination operation of the verb base *love* plus the suffix *-s*. This type of operation is often treated within the realm of morphology. After finishing the word-level operations, the speaker has to arrange each word in an acceptable order. *Jane loves Bill* is an acceptable order in English, but *Loves Jane Bill* is not. This type of operation occurs at a sentence level. Syntax explains sentence-level operations. When a sentence construction is completed, the result must be interpreted as a meaningful unit to the speaker. For example, when we combine the three words, *Jane, loves, Bill*, in this order, the result has a specific meaning that "Jane loves Bill." Although each word has its own meaning, the meaning of the full sentence is provided when the speaker combines all the words in an acceptable order. The interpretation of a sentence is the role of semantics. Though semantics in this book deals with truth-conditional meanings, there are also non-truth-conditional meanings. For example, if sentence (30) is uttered as a response to the question "Does Bill love Jane?" then the hearer may interpret (30) as "Bill does not love Jane in return." These types of meanings are later discussed in the pragmatics chapters. Finally, the sentence must be uttered by the speaker in sounds. The organization of sound structure is the realm of phonology. Even a simple sentence like (30) exhibits five separate modules of language. These five modules of language interact with each other, however, to produce grammatical expressions. How these five modules interact with each other is explained throughout this book.

1.2.2 Different approaches in linguistics

It is not surprising that there are several different schools of thought in linguistics. Currently there are two mainstream schools of thought in linguistics: the formal approach and the cognitive-functional approach. The formal linguistic approach focuses on the organization of language. The approach is to explain how language works by generating explanations of language out of structure. Therefore, structure-based explanations are treated as legitimate explanations of various linguistic structures. Most formal theories are based on the notion of Universal Grammar, which is the assumption that there are properties that all human languages exhibit. The properties are often equated as grammatical rules. For this reason, many formal linguists attempt to identify rules that can systematically explain linguistic structures across the different languages. The examples of the formal approach include Generative Grammar, Head-driven Phrase Structure Grammar, and Lexical-Functional Grammar, among others. The main difference between the formalist approach and the functionalist approach resides in the question of what counts as an explanation. As we explained, for formalists, structure-based explanations are legitimate explanations. By contrast, functionalists look for their explanations in functions of language. In other words, the functionalist approach views language as a tool, whose forms are adapted to their functions. Functionalists believe that linguistic phenomena can be explained only in terms of their functions, not their forms. The examples of the functionalist approach include Cognitive Grammar, Construction Grammar, and various types of cognitive linguistics, among others.

Although we firmly believe that both approaches are equally valuable, we will adopt the formalist approach to language in this book. This is not because the functionalist approach is inferior to the formalist approach, but because the formalist view fits the purpose of this book better. This book is designed to help students understand the logical nature of language. There is no denying that the functionalist approach can explain the nature equally systematically. Nonetheless, due to the emphasis on the functions of language, as opposed to the formal properties, it might not be easy to see the logical properties of language for readers who do not have enough training in linguistics. The other reason we prefer the formalist approach to the functionalist approach for the purpose of this book is because of its well-formulated framework. For example, the formal approach, such as the generative linguistics framework, is highly structured in terms of mathematical formulation. Although many theories in the functionalist approach (in particular, Langacker's Cognitive Grammar, Goldberg's Construction Grammar, and Croft's Radical Construction Grammar) exhibit a high-level of sophistication in their formulation, mathematically oriented formalism is not their focus. In that sense, our choice of the formal approach over the functionalist approach is driven purely by a specific purpose.

1.3 Noam Chomsky

Although we will try not to discuss particular linguists in this book, we do have to introduce one linguist, whose name is Noam Chomsky. Chomsky is probably the only linguist that most Americans can name off the top of their heads. Chomsky is also known as a leading critic of US foreign policy, which makes him very controversial. Both in linguistics and in politics, the number of books he has authored exceeds 150 as of November 2012 which is an amazingly impressive number. Even though there were many great linguists before Chomsky, it is hard to imagine modern linguistics without him. Certainly, his influence on linguistics and other related fields, such as psychology and philosophy, cannot be emphasized enough. Chomsky is known as the most cited living author, and he is currently an Institute Professor and Professor Emeritus of linguistics at MIT.

Chomsky was born on December 7, 1928, in Philadelphia. After receiving his Ph.D. in linguistics from University of Pennsylvania in 1955, he began to teach linguistics at MIT. His doctoral dissertation was developed into a monograph entitled *Syntactic Structures*, which was published in 1957. In this book, Chomsky challenged the mainstream linguistics at that time, structural linguistics, by introducing a new framework called transformational grammar. One of the most important contributions Chomsky made in his 1957 book and its successor, *Aspects of the Theory of Syntax*, published in 1965, was his claim that human babies are born with the innate ability to acquire language. That innate ability is called language acquisition device (LAD). The reason why other animals cannot acquire a language like human babies is because of the lack of LAD. This assumption naturally led to the notion of Universal Grammar, which is a set of features that defines what the LAD is and what kinds of constraints the LAD provides for all possible human languages. For the past fifty years, Chomsky's theory has been modified and developed into various types of theories called standard theory, extended standard theory, principles and parameters theory, and minimalist program, all of which are often together dubbed generative linguistics. The theory we adopt in this textbook is this type of generative linguistics approach to language. Although not every linguist agrees with Chomsky on the notion of LAD and his approach to language, every one of us must respect Chomsky for his contribution, dedication, and integrity in his research and teaching, which has made us view language from a different angle ignored by earlier linguists.

1.4 What Can Linguists Do?

Before we leave this chapter, we would like to answer one question that is frequently asked by the students of linguistics: What can linguistics majors do? Many people say that, although linguistics is interesting and intriguing, it does not help them to find a job after graduation. We have to admit that linguistics as a discipline has less practicality when it is compared to other fields such as engineering, business, and medicine, among others. Nonetheless, there are lots of things linguists can do. In a general sense, as a science, linguistics helps students develop critical and analytical thinking skills. These skills are probably some of the most important skills for success in modern society. As you will see later in this book, we will deal with lots of problem-solving techniques to explain linguistic phenomena. The problem-solving skills in conjunction with analytical and critical thinking skills will prepare the students for solving the real-world problems they face every day.

In addition to this general benefit acquired from linguistics, there are many other specific benefits of doing linguistics. First, linguistics will help you to be a better professional writer. The most important property of professional writing is the logic and arguments that support your ideas. Linguistics is full of logical arguments to prove and disprove existing hypotheses. Your linguistics training will help you to develop good argumentation skills. Certainly, not all arguments are equally valid. By doing linguistics, you will learn how to evaluate various types of arguments to find the best argument.

Second, if you want to be a foreign language teacher, you will benefit tremendously by majoring in linguistics. The scientific approach to language will provide you with more systematic explanations of language. Students in foreign language classrooms often want to find out systematic accounts of a certain linguistic phenomenon, instead of a set of drills followed by memorizing exceptions. Linguistics will make ready to provide better explanations in foreign language classrooms.

Third, a subfield in linguistics, computational linguistics, is in great demand. Most of you have heard of speech recognition and speech synthesis. These deal with how spoken language can be understood or created using computers. When you call a bigger company these days, you will very possibly have a chance to talk to a machine instead of a real person. Although the experience is usually frustrating to most of us, the machine-answering system is one small achievement of speech recognition and synthesis, which still requires a lot of improvements. The other example of computational linguistics is machine translation, where linguists design a system that automatically translates between languages. In these areas, the linguists' role is very important because, without accurately analyzing linguistic structures and meanings, having computers recognize speech or having computers translate a language into another is impossible. In fact, many of the computer companies that focus on natural language analysis hire linguists every year. Visit www.linguistlist.org to see what kinds of jobs are available for computational linguists.

In sum, there are more benefits than you can imagine from doing linguistics, and we encourage you to explore all the possibilities if you are genuinely curious about human language and the subject of linguistics.

1.5 The Organization Of The Book

This book contains a total of 13 chapters. This chapter (Chapter 1) is an introduction to the book with its brief description of the nature of linguistics. Chapter 2 deals with morphology: word structures and meanings. Chapter 3 reviews English grammar to prepare you for syntax. The following two chapters, Chapters 4 and 5, discuss syntax. Chapter 4 focuses on the standard theory proposed by Chomsky, and Chapter 5 discusses the later development of the theory, called the X-bar theory. Chapter 6 is an introduction to symbolic logic, which is closely connected to its following chapter. Progressing from the understanding of symbolic logic, Chapter 7 discusses semantics, which is a systematic account of natural language meaning. Chapter 8 is also concerned with meaning, but it takes us into the realm of pragmatics, which is the study of the effects that context has on linguistic and speaker meaning. Chapter 8 is thus concerned with how speakers rely on context to convey messages that are above and beyond the semantic meaning of a sentence. The focus of Chapter 9 is both semantic and pragmatic; it focuses on linguistic presupposition and on the way that speakers distinguish between at-issue and background information in an utterance. The final pragmatic topic, the study of speech of act theory, is covered in Chapter 10. Chapter 10 also covers the idea that speakers use language to perform actions. In Chapter 11, we introduce the International Phonetic Alphabet (IPA) to accurately describe English sounds. Chapter 12 then deals with the general organization of natural language sounds, called phonology. The final chapter, Chapter 13, discusses English syllable structures, which is one of the most discussed subjects in phonology.

1.6 Further Reading

The full citations (including specific titles) of the works mentioned here can be found in the Recommended reading at the end of this book. Reaching Chomsky's original works (Chomsky 1957, 1965) will be a challenging but rewarding task. In particular, we highly recommend that you read the first chapter of Chomsky (1965), which clearly explains Chomsky's main assumptions. If you want to compare Chomsky's revolutionary approach to the previous structural linguistics approach, you may refer to Bloomfield's (1933) well-known book. To understand the notion of prescriptive grammar, read Pinker (1994). Pinker used the term *language mavens* in that book. He specifically writes, "The [prescriptive] rules conform neither to logic nor to tradition, and if they were ever followed, they would force writers into fuzzy, clumsy, incomprehensible prose, in which certain thoughts are not expressible at all." Pinker's book is written for general audience, so it is highly readable for people who do not have linguistic training. Lobeck's (2000) textbook precisely explains the difference between prescriptive and descriptive grammars as well. To understand the general trend in linguistic theories in the United States, referring to Newmeyer's (1986) book would be a good idea. This book surveys the history of modern linguistic theories in the United States in a readable fashion, even for beginning students. Readers who are interested in the cognitive-functional approach will benefit by reading various textbooks available on cognitive linguistics, such as Croft and Cruse (2004), Ungerer and Schmid (2006), and Evans and Green (2006). More serious readers may refer to a series of Langacker's books (1987, 1991, 2008). However, Lagacker's books are not easy to read for beginning linguistics students. Radden and Dirven (2007) is a more readable book on Langacker's Cognitive Grammar for the beginning students. Goldberg's (1995, 2006) constructionist approach will be an interesting read for those who want to explore a different type of linguistics than we will discuss in this book.

CHAPTER 2
Morphology

Morphology deals with word structures and meanings. The term morphology *in fact illustrates one example of morphology. Without knowing the etymology of the word* morphology, *most native speakers of English will be able to figure out there are two small parts in the word* morphology. *One is the first part* morph, *and the other* ology *(or* logy*). The first part, morph, is found in other English words such as* amorphous *or* metamorphosis, *and the second part, logy, is used abundantly in English, as in* sociology, psychology, *and* biology, *among others. The first part,* morph, *is originally from Greek, meaning "form," and the second part, logy, is also originally from Greek, meaning "word," which is later extended to "science of" in German. By this short structural analysis of the word* morphology, *we now know the meaning of the word: the science of forms (words). Although this type of analysis of words sounds very simple, the reality is the opposite. We will start this chapter with the question, What is a word?*

2.1 What Is A Word?

Perhaps you might laugh when hearing this question, thinking even elementary school students know what words are. Although we believe we know what words are, defining a word is not an easy task. In this section, we will attempt to define what a word is using four well-known morphological criteria.

2.1.1 Defining word

How many words are in (1) below? Most people's answer for this question would be three: *John*, *loves*, and *Mary*. Even though there are four parts in (1), *John*, *love*, *-s*, and *Mary*, probably nobody would say *-s* is a word. Rather, people might just say *-s* is part of the word *love*. What this means is that we unconsciously apply some criteria in counting the number of words in (1).

    (1) John loves Mary.

The criteria people might have used for (1) would be whether the item in question is free or bound. Here, a free item means a linguistic entity that can stand alone, while a bound item is something that cannot stand alone. A bound item must be attached to another linguistic item. In (1), *John*, *love*, and *Mary* are all free forms because they can stand alone. By contrast, *-s* is a bound form because it cannot stand alone. In particular, this kind of bound form that must be attached to its base is called an affix. This criterion tells us that only free items can be a word.

However, this criterion is far from being perfect. Let us consider (2), where there seem to be four words: *the*, *man*, *loves*, and *Mary*, according to the criterion we used for (1). This seems be an intuitively right solution.

(2) The man loves Mary.

Nonetheless, *the* is not totally free because it can never stand alone in any context. Jane's response to John's question in (3) is not acceptable, because *the* cannot stand alone. Nonetheless, we know that *the* is a word.

(3) John: Which book did you read?
Jane: * The

The opposite is also possible. Some bound elements can stand alone in some contexts. In a highly conversational context like (4), the bound element *non-* can appear as an independent form.

(4) At a restaurant: Smoking or non-?

This observation tells us that the stand-alone criterion is not accurate. In the following four sections, we will introduce four tests for "word-hood."

2.1.2 Criterion 1: Fixed order

The first criterion to test word-hood is a fixed order. Within one word, the order of the sounds must be fixed. In other words, you cannot move around the elements within one word. (5) includes some English items. If you switch the order of the smaller items within the words, the results are not acceptable as shown in (6).

(5) impossible, books, morphology, loves
(6) *possibleim, *sbook, *logymorpho, *slove

This criterion illustrates that all the items listed in (5) are words. Let us compare (5) and (6) with (7) and (8). (8) is a result of moving *yesterday* in (7) to the front position of the sentence, yielding an acceptable result.

(7) He bought the book yesterday.
(8) Yesterday, he bought the book.

This shows that we can move around words within a sentence, but within a word, nothing can change positions. This is a property of word structures and is distinctive from sentence structures.

2.1.3 Criterion 2: Integrity

The second criterion is integrity. If something is a word, the elements within it cannot be separated by moving one of the elements to a different position within a sentence. Let us first consider (9). The original structure of (9) was *It is impossible!* From this, we separated the affix *im-* in *impossible* to move it to the front position of the sentence. The result, of course, is not acceptable.

(9) * Im-, it is possible!

In (10), *greenhouse* is used as one form, yielding an acceptable sentence. By contrast, when *greenhouse* is separated as in (11), the result is not acceptable. What this reveals about word-hood is that a compound like *greenhouse* is actually one word, although we are tempted to say that *greenhouse* is composed of two words.

(10) Which greenhouse did you stop by yesterday?
(11) * Which green did you stop by house yesterday?

Readers might wonder about a case like (12), where *green* seems to be separated from *house*.

(12) the green and blue house.

(12) is not a counterexample of Criterion 2 because *green* modifies *house* to refer to a house painted green, not a place to grow plants. In (12), the compound meaning of *greenhouse* is completely lost.

2.1.4 Criterion 3: Inseparability

The third criterion is inseparability. If something is a word, we cannot separate the word by inserting something between the elements of the word. In the previous section, we saw that the compound *greenhouse* is one word. When we insert the comparative affix, *-er*, between *green* and *house* as in (13), it loses its compound meaning. The meaning of (13) is clearly "a house that is greener than something."

(13) The greener house

This criterion can be naturally applied to simpler forms of words than compounds, as shown in (14) and (15). When we try to insert *-s* inside the words to make the words in (14) plural, the results are all unacceptable, as in (15).

(14) book, table, computer
(15) *boo-s-k, *tabl-s-e, *comput-s-er

2.1.5 Criterion 4: Stress

The fourth and last criterion is stress. This criterion is very useful to distinguish a word from a phrase. We will discuss the notion of phrase in Chapters 3 and 4 in detail. Until then, let us just assume that a phrase is a group of words that functions as one unit. Criterion 4 states that if something is a compound word, the stress falls on the first part of the compound. In (16), *green* is stressed, as notated by the brackets [ ]. When *green* is stressed, the meaning becomes "the glass building in which the plants are grown." When the stress falls both on *green* and *house*, the meaning becomes "a house that is green" as shown in (17). While *greenhouse* in (16) is a word, *green house* in (17) is a phrase, where *green*, as an adjective, modifies *house*.

(16) The [green]house has the vast amount of selections of flowers this year.
(17) I like the [green][house] better than the blue house.

Although a space is often used in orthography for a phrase like *green house*, the space notation is not always useful in identifying a phrase. For example, *Oval Office* is clearly a compound word because it passes the tests we have discussed for a word. Nonetheless, orthographically, a space is used between *Oval* and *Office*. Therefore, readers should not be biased by the orthographical space in identifying a word.

Readers will now be able to figure out the stress pattern of a compound word by using their own intuition. For example, *blackboard*, *White House*, and *black belt* may have two different meanings depending on the stress pattern. Because the answer is trivial, we will leave these for readers' own exercise.

2.2 Types Of Words

Not every word is equal in its grammatical status. For example, the two words *the* and *man* are somewhat different in the sense that *man* seems to have a more concrete meaning than *the*. Similarly, *book* and *books* are different in that *book* seems to be a more basic form than *books*. In this section, we will discuss these four types of words.

2.2.1 Content words versus function words

Words can be subcategorized into content or function words. Simply put, content words are the words that have more concrete meanings than function words. This simple explanation, however, does not say much about the distinction between content words and function words because the notion of "concrete" is not concrete enough. To elaborate this explanation, let us recall our elementary school English class. There we learned about "the little words" of English. Roughly speaking, "the little words" are function words. They are "little" because their role is less important than other words in general communication. Everything that is not one of "the little words" is a content word. We are not claiming that function words are less important than content words. What we are claiming here is that our communication might be largely successful without function words. To illustrate this, let us take a look at (18) and then at (19), where the four words, *a*, *will*, *to*, and *the*, are removed from (18). (19) still makes sense to us, and the intended communication is likely to succeed.

> (18) A knight will come to the town tomorrow.
> (19) Knight come town tomorrow.

Let us compare (19) with (20); as you may recall, (19) is composed of the content words found in (18), whereas (20) is composed of all of the function words from (18). Sentence (20) will not make sense to anyone, much less will it convey the same meaning as (18).

> (20) A will to the.

In general, nouns, verbs, adjectives, and adverbs are content words, while determiners, prepositions, conjunctions, and complementizers are function words. Nonetheless, some nouns act as function words. Similarly, some verbs and adverbs act as function words. The examples of content and function words in relation to their parts of speech are provided in (21). The parts of speech listed here will be discussed extensively in Chapter 3.

(21) Examples of content and function words.

Content words	Function words
Nouns: *book, desk, computer*, and so on. Verbs: *run, sleep, hit, love*, and so on. Adjectives: *pretty, old, green*, and so on. Adverbs: *quickly, probably, randomly*, and so on.	Pronouns: *I, him, her*, etc. Verbs: *am, is*, and so on. Auxiliary verbs: *shall, will, would*, and so on. Determiners: *a, the*, and so on. Prepositions: *at, in, from, above*, and so on. Adverbs: *very, not*, and so on. Conjunctions: *and, or, but*, and so on. Complementizers: *that, for*, and so on.

Content words are often called open class because we can invent new ones. For example, *Facebook* is a recently coined noun for the social-networking site on the Internet. It is now used as a verb as in *Please facebook me today!* In either case, a newly invented word is used as a content word. Function words are often called closed class because the number of function words is limited. Inventing a new function word would be extremely difficult. For example, while we might not find one single preposition recently created, new nouns and verbs are created all the time, like *Facebook*.

2.2.2 Lexeme and word forms

The second categorization of words is lexeme versus word forms. Intuitively, we know that *book* and *books* are related, but how? Both *book* and *books* are concrete word forms that are actually used in sentences. However, there is an abstract form that *book* and *books* share. The abstract form is called a lexeme, which is often denoted in CAPITALS to avoid confusion. Let us assume that the lexeme for both *book* and *books* is BOOK.

The notion of lexeme is not just motivated by a theoretical convenience. There is evidence for the existence of lexemes. Native speakers of English know that the several word forms *walks*, *walking*, and *walked* are all related. When they have to look up the form *walked*, for example, in a dictionary, they will look for the form *walk* instead of *walked*. How do native speakers know the connection among different word forms? The plausible answer is to claim that there is an abstract form of word for all different word forms. As shown in (22), there are four different word forms, but they are connected through one lexeme: WALK.

(22)

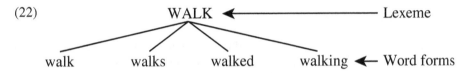

Now let us consider the word *book*. The word has at least two different meanings. One is a noun, and the other a verb. These two different meanings of the word create two different sets of word forms. When *book* is used as a verb, it has the word forms listed in (23). When it is used as a noun, by contrast, it has the word forms in (24).

(23) V: book, books, booked, booking
(24) N: book, books

The forms listed in (23), however, are not related to the forms in (24). Therefore, we have to claim that there are at least two different lexemes for *book*, as illustrated in (25) and (26). In (25), BOOK$_1$ is the lexeme as a verb, while BOOK$_2$ in (26) is the lexeme as a noun.

(25)

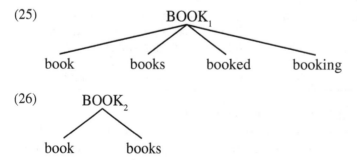

(26)

The word forms related through a lexeme are called inflected forms that a lexeme assumes. That is, in (25), *book, books, booked,* and *booking* are inflected forms that the lexeme BOOK$_1$ assumes. Similarly, *book* and *books* are the inflected forms that the lexeme BOOK$_2$ assumes. The set of all word forms under one lexeme is called a paradigm. For example, *book, books, booked,* and *booking* form one paradigm in (25), while *book* and *books* form one paradigm in (26). It is worth emphasizing that inflectional operations, such as adding *-s, -ed,* and *-ing* to *book* in (25), do not create a new lexeme. The addition of those affixes only creates different word forms under an existing lexeme. In other words, inflectional operations are not lexeme creation operations.

Another example of a noun inflectional paradigm is that of case inflections. Unfortunately, the notion of case is an extremely hard concept for native speakers of English who do not have any foreign language learning experience. As we know, the pronoun *he* has three different forms: *he, his,* and *him.* These three forms are all related, and we can assume that there is one abstract lexeme for all three different word forms. Let us assume that the lexeme is HE, as shown in (27).

(27)

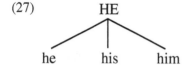

Just like the examples shown in (25) and (26), the three word forms, *he, his,* and *him,* form one paradigm because they are inflected forms that the lexeme HE assumes. This paradigm is particularly interesting because the three forms are used with special grammatical functions called grammatical cases. To explain what we mean here in more detail, let us consider examples (28) to (31), with emphasis placed on the italicized pronouns. In (28), *He* appears in the subject position. When the lexeme HE appears in the subject position, the word form must be *he,* which is called nominative case-marked. (29) shows an example of possession. When the lexeme HE appears as a possessive form, the word form must be *his*, which is called its genitive case-marked form. In (30), *him* is a direct object of the verb *loves*. When the lexeme HE appears in the direct object position, the word form must be *him*, which has a different form due to what is called accusative case marking. Finally, when the lexeme HE appears in the indirect position, as in (31), the word form *him* must be used, which is called dative case-marked. Because these inflected forms are determined based on the position in a sentence, they are called contextual inflection.

(28) *He* loves Jane.
(29) *His* book fell from the table.
(30) Jane loves *him*.
(31) Jane gave *him* the book.

We know that *him* can be two different forms (one with dative case, the other with accusative case), so we have to modify (27) slightly to make it look like (32). For the sake of convenience, we used him_D to refer to the dative case-marked form, and him_A for the accusative case-marked form.

(32)

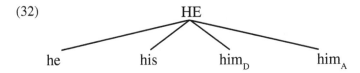

To summarize case inflection in English, a table that shows case inflections of three pronouns, *he*, *she*, and *they*, is provided in (33). Unfortunately, English uses lots of the same forms for different grammatical cases, which might be one of the reasons for many people's confusion. Nonetheless, understanding the notions of case should not be too difficult at this point.

(33) Case in English

	HE	SHE	THEY
Nominative form	he	she	they
Genitive form	his	her	their
Dative form	him	her	them
Accusative form	him	her	them

We have just discussed that grammatical case is an example of contextual inflection. That is, a certain case must be marked in a certain position in a sentence. Let us consider examples (34) to (37), once again with emphasis on the italicized words. If the case inflection is determined based on the position, *John* must be nominative case-marked, although there is no visible case marking. Fortunately, in (35), *John* is shown as genitive-case marked by attaching *'s* to *John*. Similar to (34), both (36) and (37) do use the same form *John*. Nonetheless, *John* in (36) must be accusative case-marked, whereas *John* in (37) must be dative case-marked because of the position of *John* in (36) and (37).

(34) *John* loves Jane.

(35) *John's* book fell from the table.

(36) Jane loves *John*.

(37) Jane gave *John* the book.

Therefore we have to assume that each noun in English has four different word forms, although we do not see the forms overtly in our language use.

2.3 Morpheme

In addition to the notion of word, morpheme is another important notion students in morphology should understand. The term *morpheme* is often defined as the smallest linguistic unit with a grammatical function and/or meaning. Based on this definition of morpheme, we will discuss six subclasses of morphemes.

2.3.1 Stem versus root

Let us consider the word *unhappiness*. This word is composed of three parts. The first part is the affix *un-*, the second is *happi*, and the third is another affix *-ness*. Linguists often use the hyphen when they have to show morpheme boundaries within a word, as in (38). Note that there might be some spelling variations in dissecting a word, but let us ignore them.

(38) un-happi-ness

Each portion of the word *unhappiness* has its function (and meaning). The first affix *un-* changes the meaning of *happy* to negative. The second affix *-ness* makes *unhappy* a noun form. The second part of the word, *happi*, has the base meaning of *unhappiness*. Because all three portions have their own functions (and meanings), they are all morphemes. We intuitively know that *happi* is the base among the three morphemes because the two affixes are attached to *happi*. We have used the term *affix* to refer to a morpheme, which must be attached to its base. There are two types of affixes in English. The first type is prefix, which appears before its base. The second type is suffix, which appears after the base. The base *happi* is also called root. A root is a base unit to which another morpheme is attached. A careful examination tells us that *un-happi* also functions as the base for *unhappiness* because *-ness* is attached to *un-happi*. Although *un-happi* is the base to which the morpheme *-ness* is attached, *un-happi* is not a root. Instead, it is called a stem. The difference between stem and root can be explained as follows: Roots have only one morpheme; stems can have more than one morpheme. As we saw, *un-happi* is morphologically complex because there are two morphemes in *un-happi*. Therefore, *un-happi* is a stem, not a root, although it functions as a base for the word *unhappiness*.

We have just discussed that *un-happi* is a stem because it functions as a base for the word *unhappiness*, and it contains two morphemes. The assumption made in this explanation is that the two morphemes, *un-* and *happi*, are combined first, then *-ness* is attached to the newly formed stem *un-happi*, as shown in (39). In (39), we used a bracket notation to show the morpheme combination process. But how do we know (39) is a correct structure of the word *un-happi-ness*? In other words, why can't we say *happi-ness* is a stem, created by attaching *-ness* to the root *happi*, then the affix *un-* is attached to the stem *happi-ness* to yield *un-happi-ness*, as in (40)?

(39) [$_{stem}$ un-[$_{root}$ happi]]-ness
(40) un-[$_{stem}$ [$_{root}$ happi]-ness]

There is a piece of evidence to claim that (39) is a correct analysis, while (40) is not. In (39), *-ness* is attached to the adjectival stem, while *un-* is attached to a noun stem in (40). If (40) is right, we have to say that *un-* is attached to a noun. Is this true? The words shown in (41), where *un-* is attached to a noun, are all unacceptable. If (40) was a correct structure, the words in (41) must be acceptable, too, because the stems for all the words in (41) are nouns.

(41) *un-destruction, *un-humility, * un-examination

By contrast, (39) shows that *un-* and *happi* must be combined first to form an adjectival stem, and *-ness* is attached to the newly formed stem. If this is correct, we expect other words formed by attaching *-ness* to an adjective to yield a noun, as in (42).

(42) calm-ness, bright-ness, willing-ness, etc.

Although *-ness* cannot be attached to all possible adjectives, attaching *-ness* to an adjective creates a possible English word. For example, if we attach *-ness* to the adjective *beautiful*, the result will be *beautifulness*. Although *beautifulness* is not an actual word in English, most native speakers will admit that *beautifulness* is a possible word they might use in a certain context. By contrast, if we attach *un-* to a noun, the result is not a possible English word. This, again, shows that the analysis provided in (39) is preferred to that in (40).

It is worth mentioning that *un-* attaching to an adjectival stem is not something we can consider to be an absolute rule, but only as a general tendency. The prefix *un-* attaching to an adjectival stem illustrates a productive morphological pattern, though there is certainly another, relatively unproductive morphological process that *un-* could take. Perhaps some readers remember the 7-Up commercial where the novel word *uncola* was coined. In the case of *uncola*, *un-* is attached to a noun, *cola*. Although this type of morphological process is considered to be unproductive, it is observed in particular in advertisements, songs, and poems, all of which require the language users to pay attention and analyze the unique usage. By adopting this atypical usage, advertisers of 7-Up have successfully gained the attention of potential customers. Though these types of *un-* attachment are relatively unproductive, they can be used somewhat successfully when accompanied by sarcastic or comical tones. For example, a student can sarcastically say "This is so un-linguistics" to refer to a poetry class that is devoid of the scientific method. Nevertheless, it is clear that the attachment of *un-* to the adjectival stem is more productive than the other uses of *un-*. In this regard, productivity should be understood as a continuum instead of an absolute value.

2.3.2 Bound versus free morphemes

We already discussed the distinction between bound forms and free forms in section 2.1.1. The distinction also holds true for morphemes. As we described, free forms are the forms that can stand alone, while bound forms cannot. Likewise, free morphemes can stand alone, but bound morphemes cannot. To explain the distinction in more detail, let us take a look at the examples in (43).

(43) computers, national, tranquilizer, linguists

In (43), the word *computers* contains three morphemes: *comput-er-s*. Once again, in analyzing the morphemes, let us ignore some spelling variations. The first morpheme, *comput(e)*, is a root of the word, and it can stand alone as you can see in the usage *Compute the formula*. There are two affixes in the word *computers*: *-er* and *-s*. It is very clear that both morphemes are bound morphemes because they cannot stand alone. Rather, they must be attached to their base. The second example *national* has two morphemes: *nation* and *-al*. As a root, *nation* is a free morpheme, while the affix *-al* is a bound morpheme. How about *tranquilizer*? The word *tranquilizer* contains three morphemes: *tranquil*, *-iz*, and *-er*. In this case, the adjective *tranquil* is the root of the word. As a root, of course, *tranquil* is a free morpheme. The two affixes, *-iz* and *-er*, are bound morphemes. Our last word, *linguists*, is somewhat complicated in analyzing its word structure. In the beginning of this book, we briefly discussed the etymology of *linguistics*. Historically speaking, *linguists* contains three different morphemes: *lingu*, *-ist*, and *-s*. However, it is very hard to tell if *lingu* is a separate morpheme in contemporary English. Many native speakers of English might not identify *lingu* as a separate element, at least not without some knowledge in English etymology and Latin. For this reason, treating *linguist* as one morpheme seems to be reasonable.

The same type of difficulty is found in many other words. Let us take a look at the three words listed in (44). We intuitively know that *cranberry* has two morphemes because *berry* is clearly separable. The same intuition might be applied to *raspberry* and *lukewarm*. Then the question is, What are the meanings of *cran* and *luke*? Are they free morphemes or bound morphemes?

(44) cranberry, raspberry, lukewarm

The questions raised are not easy to answer. One possible answer for these questions is to trace the histories of the words. However, the *Oxford English Dictionary* states that the origins of *cran*, *rasp*, and *luke* are all unclear. We know this is a disappointing answer. However, these examples illustrate that identifying a morpheme is not always straightforward, although it seems to be relatively simple at first glance.

2.3.3 Inflectional versus derivational affixes

As we discussed in section 2.2.2, inflectional operations do not create a new lexeme. Instead, they create different word forms under the same lexeme. For example, the word forms *walk*, *walks*, *walked*, and *walking* are inflected forms of the same lexeme WALK. The inflected forms were created by attaching the affixes, *-s*, *-ed*, and *-ing*, to the root *walk*. These affixes are called inflectional affixes because attaching these affixes to their base creates different word forms.

Another type of affix called derivational affix is different from inflectional affixes. Attaching a derivational affix to its base creates a new lexeme. In (45), *-al* is a derivational affix because when *-al* is attached to its root, *nation*, the result is a new lexeme. This can be seen in an English dictionary as well. Usually, *national* is listed as a separate item in English dictionaries, including the *Oxford English Dictionary*.

(45) nation-al

Attaching a derivational affix often changes the part of speech of its base. In (45), the part of speech of *nation* is a noun. When we attach *-al* to *nation*, the part of speech of *national* becomes an adjective. There are many derivational affixes that change the part of speech of their base. In (46), all affixes are derivational affixes because attaching them to their bases creates new lexemes. All of the affixes also change the parts of speech of their bases.

(46) driv-er, normal-ize, simpl-ify, refresh-ment, comput-ing, and so on

Readers might be confused about *comput-ing* because we discussed that *-ing* in *walking* is an inflectional affix. There are two types of *-ing* morphemes in English. The one is the *-ing* used in the progressive forms as in (47). The other one is the *-ing* that is attached to the verb stem to change it to a noun. The *-ing* in (47) is an inflectional affix, whereas the *-ing* in (48) is a derivational affix. The *-ing* in (48) is a derivational affix because the *-ing* changes the part of speech of its root *comput(e)* from a verb to a noun, by creating a new lexeme.

(47) John is walk-**ing** on the Lake Walk in Duluth.
(48) Comput-**ing** is fun with a Macbook.

Of course, the derivational affix *-ing* can be attached to the root *walk* too, as in (49). In (49), the *-ing* changes the part of speech of *walk* from a verb to a noun, and *walking* becomes a new lexeme.

(49) Walk-**ing** is better than sleeping.

These examples illustrate that the identification of morphemes often cannot be done within an isolated word. In analyzing morphological structures, we often have to see the words in question in a larger context. The next section deals with the issue of how to identify morphemes.

2.4 Identifying Morphemes

We have seen that the identification of morphemes is not always straightforward. Sometimes, we might not know whether one element is a morpheme or not. Other times, one same form might be used as different affixes, just like the case of the English *-ing*. In this section, we will introduce three criteria to identify morphemes. These criteria are discussed in Nida (1949, 1965) and in other textbooks dealing with morphology (Aronoff and Fudeman 2011, among others).

2.4.1 Criterion 1: Repeated occurrence

The first criterion for the identification of a morpheme is a repeated occurrence. If the same form is found in many different words with the same meaning, the form is a morpheme. As shown in (50), the derivational affix *-er* is found in many words in English with the same meaning denoting "a person, animal, or thing that performs a specified action or activity." The function of *-er* in these cases is uniform as well: changing a verb to a noun.

(50) driv-er, play-er, handl-er, work-er, and so on

In (51), *-s* is an inflectional morpheme because the form is repeatedly found in many English verbs to denote a grammatical function, stating the subject must be third person singular.

(51) love-s (as in *John loves Mary*), read-s (as in *John reads the book*), and so on

As we discussed in (44) above, the forms, *cran*, *rasp*, and *luke*, are not found consistently with the same meaning. These limited uses of the forms make it hard to identify whether they are morphemes or not.

2.4.2 Criterion 2: Allomorphs

The second criterion is to identify allomorphs. Allomorphs are different forms for the same morpheme. If two or more linguistic elements have the same meaning with different sounds (and/or different forms), they may be examples of the same morpheme, **if and only if the distribution does not overlap**. This criterion seems to be unnecessarily complicated. But with some relevant examples, it will be clear to readers. Let us take a look the examples in (52). In all three examples in (52), *-s* is an inflectional affix, which creates a plural form. Nonetheless, *-s* has three different sound values in these examples. In (52a), *-s* is pronounced as *s*. However, the *-s* in (52b) is pronounced more like *z*, and the *s* in (52c) is pronounced like *iz*. Although *-s* has three different sounds, they are the same morpheme because their meaning (and function) is identical.

(52) a. cat-s
      b. dog-s
      c. house-s

Now, let us focus on the boldface condition above: if and only if the distribution does not overlap. What does this mean? It means that the three different pronunciations are not interchangeable. The *-s* in (52) can be pronounced neither as *z* nor as *-iz*, and the *-s* in (52b) is not interchangeable with either *s* or *iz*. Similarly, the pronunciation of *-s* in (52c) cannot be pronounced either as *s* or *z*. In other words, each of the three pronunciations occurs in a specific context. The *s* pronunciation in (52) is observed when the *-s* affix is preceded by the *t* sound in this particular case, the *z* pronunciation of *-s* in (52b) is observed when *-s* is preceded by *g*. As a result, the contexts where the three pronunciations are observed do not overlap with each other. In this situation, we may claim that *-s* is just one morpheme with three different pronunciations, and the three different pronunciations are called allomorphs.

To explain the notion of allomorphs more, let us use one analogical example. There is Tobey Maguire's superhero movie called *Spider Man*. In the movie, Tobey Maguire plays two roles: one as Spider Man, and the other as Peter Parker. Naturally, in the movie, whenever Spider Man appears on the crime scene, Peter Parker the photographer disappears. Similarly, whenever Peter Parker talks to his boss, Spider Man can never appear. The reason why the two characters cannot appear at the same time in one scene is more than obvious: The two characters are the same person. The same is true for the three pronunciations of -*s* explained above. When -*s* is pronounced as *s*, the *z* pronunciation is never allowed for the -*s* affix. The same is true for the other two pronunciations. What it reveals is that the three different sound forms must be one entity in disguise, just like Peter Parker is Spider Man in disguise. This identification method is not just limited to the morpheme identifications. Throughout this book, we will use the same method to identify some grammatical properties of English words (Chapters 3, 4, and 5) and some sound properties in English (Chapters 12 and 13).

2.4.3 Criterion 3: Zero-morpheme

The third criterion is to identify an invisible morpheme. A morpheme may have a zero variant as one of the allomorphs. The notion of a zero morpheme might be very unappealing to beginning linguistics students because it sounds somewhat random. However, there are some justifications. As in (53), *fish* and *deer* are used both as singular and plural forms.

> (53) a. fish (singular)—fish (plural)
> b. deer (singular)—deer (plural)

The systematic way to capture this type of plural form formation is to posit an invisible morpheme as an allomorph in addition to the allomorphs discussed in the previous section. For example, we may analyze the plural forms *fish* and *deer* as in (54).

> (54) fish-$\emptyset_{PL}$, deer-$\emptyset_{PL}$

In (54), the invisible plural morpheme, notated by $\emptyset_{PL}$, is attached to the singular bases, *fish* and *deer*, to make the singular forms plural, without attaching any visible affixes.

2.5 A Sample Morphological Analysis: Korean

Now that we have discussed some fundamental concepts of morphology, let us do one morphological analysis in Korean. Beginning linguistics students seem to believe that analyzing a foreign language is an impossible task when they don't know the language. After analyzing some Korean morphological structures, however, you will find out that it's simply not true. Korean is one of the most common languages in the world (eleventh among the existing languages), with approximately 72 million speakers. It exhibits very intriguing morphology, especially for English speakers. Let us take a look at five sentences in Korean. Korean has its own writing system called *Hangul*, but for the sake of convenience, we have transliterated the Korean sentences into the Roman letters. Each Korean sentence is then translated into English within a pair of single quotation marks.

> (55) a. Johni papul mekessta.   'John ate rice.'
> b. Johni papul meknunta.   'John eats rice.'
> c. Billi Katialul ttalyessta.   'Bill hit Katia.'
> d. Katiaka papul mekessta.   'Katia ate rice.'
> e. Katiaka Johnul ttalynta.   'Katia hits John.'

Now, without reading the explanations provided below, let us try to answer the following questions.

(56) Q1: What are the subject (nominative) markers in Korean?
    Q2: What are the object (accusative) markers in Korean?
    Q3: What are the present tense markers in Korean?
    Q4: What is the past tense marker in Korean?
    Q5: What is the root for the word *eat* in Korean?
    Q6: What is the root for the word *hit* in Korean?
    Q7: What is the word for *rice* (without the object marker) in Korean?
    Q8: Are the subject markers allomorphs of the same morpheme?
    Q9: Are the present tense markers allomorphs of the same morpheme?
    Q10: What is the word order in Korean?

We believe readers will be able to answer all the questions listed above without additional help. Nonetheless, let us answer the questions one by one together here. There are two subject (nominative) markers in the given data set as shown in (57). After the words, *John*, *Bill*, and *Katia*, either *-i* or *-ka* is attached to mark them as subjects.

(57) A1: *-i* and *-ka*

Similarly, there are two object (accusative) markers in the given set as in (58). Either *-ul* or *-lul* is attached to a noun to mark it as an object.

(58) A2: *-ul* and *-lul*

There are two present tense forms as in (59). Either *-nta* or *-unta* is attached to a verb root to give the relevant tense information.

(59) A3: *-nta* and *-unta*

There is only one past tense marker in the given data as shown in (60). Same as the present tense markers, the past tense marker is attached to the verb root to give the past tense information.

(60) A4: *-essta*

The root form of *eat* in Korean is *mek-* as shown in (61). We know this by eliminating the tense markers from the examples.

(61) A5: *mek-*

The same method applies to Q6. By eliminating the tense markers from (55c) and (55e), we can successfully isolate the root form of *hit* in Korean.

(62) A6: *ttaly-*

We already know that *-ul* is an object (accusative) maker in *papul*. By eliminating *-ul* from *papul*, we get the correct form for *rice* without the object marker, as in (63).

(63) A7: *pap*

Q8 might be a little complicated. As we answered in (57) already, there are two subject mark-ers in the given data. Are they allomorphs of the same morpheme? The answer is yes because both elements have the same meaning and function, although they have different sounds (and forms). In addition, they appear in different contexts. While -*ka* appears when the root noun ends with a vowel, -*i* appears when the root noun ends with a consonant.

(64) A8: yes

The same is true for the object markers. The two object markers are allomorphs of the same morpheme. They have the same meaning and function, and their distributions do not overlap. The object marker -*ul* is attached to the root noun when the noun ends with a consonant. By contrast, -*lul* is attached to the root noun when it ends with a vowel.

(65) A9: yes

The answer seems to be clear for Q10.

(66) A10: Subject Object Verb

Let us finish this section by asking one question. How do you say *John loved Mary* in Korean? In Korean, the root verb *love* is *salangha*. Readers should be able to figure out the answer without much difficulty at this point.

2.6 Lexeme Creation

We briefly discussed a lexeme creation mechanism called derivation when we discussed two types of affixes in section 2.3.3. In this section, we will discuss two lexeme creation processes: derivation and compounding. In addition to these lexeme creation processes, we will discuss several other lexeme creation mechanisms, which are often treated as nonsystematic mental processes as opposed to systematic morphological processes.

2.6.1 Derivation

The first lexeme creation mechanism is derivation. The basic function of derivation is to enable the speaker to create new lexemes. Newly created lexemes often change the part of speech of their base, as we discussed in section 2.3.3. However, not all derivational processes change the part of speech of the base. Consider the examples in (67). In (67), *like, consider*, and *Christ*, are all roots. To these roots, the affixes, *dis-*, *re-*, and *anti-*, are attached. Neverthe-less, the attachment of these affixes does not change the part of speech of the base. The part of speech of the root *like* is a verb in this case. After attaching *dis-* to the root *like*, the part of speech of the result is still a verb. The same is true for *re-consider* and *anti-Christ*. The at-tachment of *re-* and *anti-* does not change the parts of speech of *consider* (V) and *Christ* (N).

(67) dis-like, re-consider, anti-Christ, etc.

These types of affix attachments are nonetheless derivational processes because *like* is clearly a different lexeme from *dislike*. Similarly, *consider* and *reconsider* are two different lexemes. The pair *Christ* and *anti-Christ* seems to be a more compelling case to show a new lexeme creation resulting from attaching a derivation affix.

2.6.2 Compounding

The other lexeme creation mechanism we will discuss is compounding. Compounds are created by combining two lexemes. Compounding is perhaps the most frequently used lexeme creation mechanism in many languages. We already know lots of compounds in English, and new compounds are created constantly. (68) contains some examples of compounds in English.

(68) greenhouse, blackboard, language skills, industry output, and so on

The difficulty in dealing with compounds is the question of how to distinguish compounds from phrases. We discussed this issue in section 2.1 in detail. Nevertheless, let us reintroduce the distinction methods in (69) and (70).

(69) If the expression [α β] is a compound, α and β cannot be separated either by inserting something between α and β, or moving either α or β to a different position in a sentence.

(70) The stress falls on α if [α β] is a compound. If [α β] is a phrase, the stress falls on both α and β.

Because we discussed *greenhouse* and *blackboard* in section 2.1, let us consider the other two examples, *language skills* and *industry output*. These two examples exhibit clear cases of compounding, because if they were phrases, *language* and *industry* must have been in their adjectival forms. In other words, noun compounds have the structure of [Noun + Noun], whereas a similar noun phrase structure has the structure of [Adjective + Noun]. Because *language* has its adjectival form *linguistic*, the phrasal form of *language skills* must be *linguistic skills*. Similarly, the phrasal form of *industry output* would be *industrial output*. In the case of *industrial output*, the *-al* morpheme intervenes between *industry* and *output*; thus, it violates (69) and hence cannot be a compound. In all examples in (68), the stress falls on the first part of the word, when the word is used as a compound. When they are used as a phrase, the stress falls on both parts.

In fact, the same type of distinction is frequently observed in our everyday language use. In Duluth, Minnesota, there is a sandwich place called Jimmy John's. To promote their quality sandwiches, they display a small sign that reads "We do not sell mystery meat." In the sentence, *mystery meat* is a compound, meaning a certain type of undesirable meat such as cafeteria hamburger meat, which may be more of a "meat product" with several kinds of meat mixed together. A phrasal use of a similar expression is commonly observed too. In one episode in the popular comedy show *It's Always Sunny in Philadelphia*, two characters, Charlie and Dee, try to identify the meat they eat, under the assumption that they ate human meat. To describe the meat, Dee uses the expression *mysterious meat*. Dee's expression *mysterious meat* is clearly a phrase because *mysterious* is an adjectival form. The meaning of *mysterious meat* in Dee's usage is also different from *mystery meat* on the Jimmy John's sign. What Dee meant by *mysterious meat* is "the meat whose source is unknown." Equipped with some linguistic knowledge, readers will hear many similar pairs of expressions when they pay attention to what people say in their everyday conversations.

2.6.3 Other processes: analogy

Derivation and compounding create lexemes in a systematic fashion, either by attaching a derivational affix to its base or by combining two lexemes. However, nonsystematic lexeme creation mechanisms exist. In historical linguistics, these processes are called analogy, which is a mental process, as opposed to a systematic lexeme formation morphology. The first example of analogy is blending. Blending is a combination of two linguistic forms. The forms used in blending are not necessarily morphemes or lexemes. In this regard, blending is different from derivation and compounding. Recall that derivation is the result of attaching derivational affixes to a base, while compounding is the result of combining two lexemes. (71) illustrates some examples of blending. The first two words, *brunch* and *spork*, are well-known examples for most people. The word *brunch* is made by combining the first two letters of *breakfast* and the last four letters of *lunch*. As we know, *br* in *breakfast* is not a morpheme. Similarly *unch* in *lunch* is not a morpheme either. These two nonmorphemic parts are combined to create a new word. The same is true for *spork*, where the nonmorphemic *s* combines with the full lexeme *fork* with some changes in pronunciation.

(71) brunch, spork, chortle, and so on

The word *chortle* was blended by Lewis Carroll in his poem, *Jabberwocky*. Apparently, the blending was made from the two source words, *chuckle* and *snort*. In this case, the two parts, *ch* and *le*, are kept from the word *chuckle*, and only the middle part was taken from the word *snort*. All three examples above illustrate that blending is performed in a nonsystematic way, without principles of formation. Nonetheless, it is clear that blending is a powerful lexeme creation mechanism.

The second and third nonsystematic lexeme creation mechanisms we will discuss are acronyms and alphabetisms, respectively. These two processes are somewhat similar, but there is a clear difference between them. (72) illustrates some examples of acronyms. An acronym is a combination of the first letters of words. In (72), NATO is a combination of the first letters of North Atlantic Treaty Organization. NASA stands for National Aeronautics and Space Administration. In Duluth, Minnesota, the school board recently created a program called PASS, the name was created by combining the first letters of the newly launched program Parents And Students Succeeding. All of these words are pronounced like a word instead of pronouncing them letter by letter. For example, NATO is pronounced as one word, instead of N, A, T, O. This is a property of acronyms.

(72) NATO, NASA, PASS, and so on

Alphabetism is very similar to acronym because it is also a combination of the first letters of words. However, alphabetism is different from acronyms because the individual letter is pronounced in alphabetism. (73) shows examples of alphabetism. CD was made by combining the first letters of *compact disk*. Unlike an acronym, CD is pronounced letter by letter. Both DVD and UMD illustrate the same properties. DVD stands for *digital versatile disk*, and it is pronounced as D, V, D. UMD is an alphabetism of University of Minnesota Duluth.

(73) CD, DVD, UMD, and so on

Clipping is the last nonsystematic lexeme creation mechanism we will discuss in this section. Clipping is a shortening process where one or more syllables of a word are used to create a new lexeme. In (74), *auto* is a clipped form of *automobile*, *bike* for *bicycle*, *fridge* for *refrigerator*, and *exam* for *examination*. Although there are lots of variations when we clip syllables to create a new lexeme, we tend to clip stressed syllables. In (74), the examples are stressed syllables in their original forms.

> (74) auto, bike, fridge, exam, and so on

The same technique is used to create nicknames in English. By clipping a stressed syllable from its original name, we can create nicknames like *Liz* (from *Elizabeth*), Mandy (from *Amanda*), *Katie* (from *Katlyn*) and so on.

> (75) Liz, Mandy, Katie, and so on

Although there seems to be some principle in the process of clipping, there are many clippings that do not follow the patterns we have described. (76) includes some examples of clipping that were made by clipping unstressed syllables in the original forms.

> (76) gym (for gymnasium), info (for information), burger (for hamburger), and so on

For this reason, clipping is not a systematic lexeme creation process like blending, acronym, and alphabetism. All the processes we explained in this section, however, create new lexemes in interesting ways and enrich our dictionaries.

2.7 Morpheme-Based Morphology Versus Lexeme-Based Morphology

In concluding this chapter, let us discuss two theoretically different approaches to morphology. One is called morpheme-based morphology (MBM), and the other is called lexeme-based morphology (LBM).

2.7.1 Morpheme-based morphology (MBM)

The focus of MBM is placed on the analysis of words into their constituent morphemes. The assumption of MBM is that morphemes are minimal linguistic units, and they function as the basic building blocks in forming words. As an example of MBM, let us consider the word *national*. The word *national* is composed of two morphemes: *nation* being the root, *-al* being the derivational affix. As we discussed earlier, the *-al* affix must be attached to a noun root to yield an adjective. In other words, the function of the *-al* affix may be described as in (77). In (77), the *-al* affix has its own category, which refers to adjectival affix, A-*aff*. By attaching it to the noun root or stem, a new adjective is created.

> (77) $[[N_{root/stem}]\text{-}al_{A\text{-}aff}]_A$

In this approach, the complex word can be created by the general mechanism of concatenation, or by combining morphemes in a linear sequence. That is, in the case of *driver*, the root *driv(e)* and the affix *-er* are combined sequentially. The creation of *nationalize* can be explained in a similar fashion. The polymorphemic word *nationalize* is created by applying (77), followed by (78). In (77), we saw that the word *national* is created by attaching the *-al* affix to its noun root to yield an adjective. The result, *national*, now becomes a new stem to which the affix *-ize* is attached, yielding a new verb, as schematically described in (78).

(78) $[[A_{root/stem}]\text{-ize}_{V\text{-aff}}]_V$

The schematic notations we saw in (77) and (78) can be applied to many adjectives derived by attaching *-al* to their bases. Similarly, we can analyze many derived verbs from their adjectival stems by attaching *-ize* to their bases as in (78).

One big challenge that MBM faces is the fact that many morphological operations cannot be accounted for by morpheme concatenations. The past forms of many English irregular verbs are not formed by attaching a past tense morpheme to their bases. The past tense forms of *sing*, *ring*, and *run* are formed by replacing one vowel with another. The past form of *bring* exhibits a more complicated irregular past tense formation.

(79) sing–sang, ring–rang, run–ran, bring–brought

Although the past tense formation like (80) may explain many regular verbs in English, explaining irregular verb forms, as in (79), is not always easy. This is because there is no segmental past morphemes forming a past tense form in the examples given in (79).

(80) $[[V_{stem/room}]\text{-ed}_{V\text{-aff}}]_V$

For this reason, some linguists prefer a different type of morphology called lexeme-based morphology, where the morpheme is not the basic building block of word formation.

2.7.2 Lexeme-based morphology (LBM)

In LBM, the creation of a new word is the result of an extension of the existing pattern of form-meaning relationship. (81) illustrates an analysis of the derivational process achieved by attaching the *-er* affix to its base. In this analysis, which is different from MBM, *-er* does not have its own categorical status. Instead, a pattern shows a relationship between $[X]_V$ and $[X\text{-}er]_N$ with a specified meaning. When this pattern is extended to the verb *catch*, the new noun *catcher* is created to mean "one who catches."

(81) Pattern: $[X]_V : [X\text{-}er]_N$
       Meaning: "one who Vs"

Readers should be aware that LBM does not deny that *catcher* has two morphemes: *catch* and *-er*. What LBM emphasizes is that the morphemes are not the basic building blocks of word formation. In LBM, words and relationships between words are highlighted, giving morphemes a secondary status in lexeme formation.

To explain the past tense verb form formation, let us consider (82). In (82), C stands for a consonant, and *i* and *a* denote the vowels as they are. This pattern shows that a word that is composed of a consonant, the *i* vowel, and another consonant becomes a past verb by replacing the *i* vowel with the *a* vowel.

(82) Pattern: $[CiC]_V : [CaC]_V$
       Meaning: "past V"

Although this is an oversimplified analysis of some of the irregular verbs, it shows that the pattern-based approach to morphology (the LBM approach) may overcome the difficulty left unsolved in the morpheme-based morphology approach.

2.8 Summary

We started this chapter by defining *word*. We discussed various notions such as morphemes, lexemes, word forms, inflection, derivation, compounding, and so on. We also provided morphological analyses of simple Korean examples based on the definitions provided. We then discussed how we create new lexemes. We closed the discussion by comparing two different approaches to morphology. Unfortunately, we have shown that morphological analysis is not always clear-cut because there are many cases where we cannot provide enough evidence for the morpheme status of the given linguistic element. This type of difficulty should not discourage readers, however, because we are discovering the properties of natural language by conducting a scientific study of language instead of providing all definite answers.

2.9 Further Reading

Many outstanding introductory books on morphology are available. Nida's books (1949, 1965) are valuable resources for readers, although they are some of the earliest textbooks on morphology. Katamba's (2006) and Matthews's (1991) introductions will be helpful for readers, as well. Aronoff and Fudeman's (2011) recent textbook is very approachable and informative. Booij's textbook (2007) also provides a great deal of information on current morphology. More serious readers may refer to the reference book by Spencer and Zwicky (2001) to understand what kinds of research topics exist in the field of morphology. Spencer's (1991) in-depth survey of morphological theories will also be beneficial for serious readers in morphology.

CHAPTER 3
English Grammar Review

English grammar is something often regarded as an elementary school topic. It is learned and forgotten, never to be discussed again in future classes. Now that you are beginning your study of linguistics, it will be necessary to review and relearn some of the fundamental grammar concepts. Not only will this make learning linguistics easier, but relearning basic grammar will give you a better understanding of the language that you use on a daily basis. This grammar review is not a comprehensive look at English grammar, but rather a directed review with the intent to provide you with the necessary grammar background for later chapters.

3.1 Clauses

Rather than start on the single-word level, we begin our overview by looking at a sentence as a whole entity. One important thing to note is that the word *sentence* is interchangeable with the word *clause*. Throughout this text, when you see the word *clause*, it will refer to a sentence. Later, we will define exactly what constitutes a clause. A single clause is the most basic kind of clause, such as in (1).

> (1) Lisa sleeps.

(1) is a clause that is composed of only two words. In (1), *Lisa* is the subject of the sentence, and *sleeps* is the predicate of the sentence. In the next section, we will discuss the distinction between a subject and a predicate.

3.2 Subjects And Predicates In Clauses

While many people can identify a clause intuitively, our scientific approach to language mandates that we create a definition from specific criteria. A clause is comprised of a subject and a predicate, the latter of which begins with the verb of a sentence. A subject is defined as everything that comes before the verb. This definition is very rudimentary because there are many examples where the subject is not simply something before the verb. Nonetheless, let us use this rudimentary definition for a while to understand the basic concept of subject and predicate. The verb itself should be an obvious find, even if you have forgotten much of your grammar. In elementary school, *verb* was defined as a word of action or being. Though we will amend that definition throughout our discussion, you can use it for now to find the verb in

(1). In example (1) the subject is *Lisa* because *Lisa* is the only word appearing before the verb *sleeps*. If we were to look at example (2) instead, our subject would be slightly more lengthy.

(2) The girl with the black skirt at Starbucks works at a Chinese restaurant in town too.

In (2), our verb, which begins the predicate part of the sentence, is *works*, so the subject—meaning everything appearing before the verb—would be *the girl with the black skirt at Starbucks*.

It is crucial to mention here that interrogative sentences (questions) are a little different in terms of subject and predicate. Consider the following example of an interrogative clause.

(3) Have you kissed the baby?

Because *have* is a verb, we might think that everything here is actually predicate. After all, subject, as we defined above, is everything before the verb. However, questions function a little bit differently—in the case of all interrogative clauses, it is necessary to find what is called the *base sentence*. This means that the question must be rephrased as a declarative sentence, and this is a relatively instinctive process. Many of you might have already guessed that the base sentence for (3) is *You have kissed the baby*. Once the clause is in its base form, subject and predicate may be determined. In this case, *you* is the subject and *have kissed the baby* is the predicate. The issue of subject-predicate relations only applies to clauses, and as we see in the remainder of the section, both subjects and predicates are composed of phrases.

3.3 Phrases And Phrasal Movement

If our definition of clause is that it is comprised of a subject and a predicate, the latter of which begins with the verb of a sentence, we must now tackle the oft-mentioned notion *phrase*. The word *phrase* is used frequently in general conversation to mean a variety of things. What, then, constitutes a definition of phrase? A phrase is a unit of words in a clause that may be moved together, or replaced with one single word. These criteria help to define any number of phrases we will see throughout our study of linguistics. While this may seem to be a very basic definition of phrase, let us look at how this definition actually works. Example (4) shows a clause, and the italicized portion is a kind of phrase we refer to as a preposition phrase.

(4) David and Ken sit *in the athletic field*.

Looking at the italicized portion, we can tell it is a phrase because it functions as a single unit of words. We know this because *in the athletic field* can be moved to the front of the clause to produce the new clause *In the athletic field sit David and Ken*. This test to determine whether or not something is a phrase is called a movement test. Our other criterion, replacement with a single word, can also be met in this situation. Taking out *in the athletic field* and replacing it with one word, for example, *there*, will yield another logical sentence: *David and Ken sit there*. Because *in the athletic field* meets at least one of the requirements (in this case, it meets both), we can consider it a phrase. These tests for a phrase will be reintroduced in Chapter 4.

Phrases come in many different varieties. For every part of speech, there is a corresponding kind of phrase: verb phrases, noun phrases, and adjective phrases, all of which meet the phrasal criteria mentioned in the above paragraphs. Though these kinds of phrases were not extensively discussed in your English education in elementary or middle school, they are standard concepts in the field of linguistics, and you will surely learn to identify them quickly.

When we break down a clause, we find that it is composed of several kinds of phrases, all of which eventually account for each word in the sentence. When it comes to the number of words in a phrase, there is no real limit as to how many words can comprise a phrase. There are one-word phrases just as there are five- and six-word phrases. The only stipulation is that the phrase must pass the movement and/or replacement tests mentioned above to qualify as a phrase. As you may have already guessed from our previous discussion, subjects often comprise noun phrases, and predicates *must* contain one verb phrase. Let us look at some other examples of phrases: (5) illustrates some examples of noun phrases, (6) verb phrases, (7) adverb phrases, (8) adjective phrases, and (9) preposition phrases, respectively.

(5) John, the destruction, the boy in the red car, and so on
(6) ran to the store, gave the book to Maria, smiled, wore gloves, and so on
(7) very slowly, extremely carefully, and so on
(8) very red, pretty intelligent, and so on
(9) over the fence; to the big, green fence; in a pickle; and so on

How some of the phrases are categorized might not be clear to readers at this point, but it will get clearer in the step-by-step discussion provided below.

3.4 The Breakdown Process: Finding Phrases

One important thing to notice is that some phrases may contain smaller phrases, much like how Russian nesting dolls contain smaller dolls. A bigger doll may contain several smaller dolls, but the bigger doll still exists as one doll entity. Smaller dolls may be exposed later, and each doll may contain smaller dolls as well. See, for example, the noun phrase *the boy in the red car*. *In the red car* is a preposition phrase because it begins with a preposition, *in*, but it is contained within the bigger phrase, which is the noun phrase, *the boy in the red car*. Keep in mind that phrases are phrases because they can be moved to the front of a sentence or replaced with a single word. In the sentence, *Look at the boy in the red car*, *the boy in the red car* is a phrase because it can be replaced with *him*, as in *Look at him*. The phrase *in the red car* can be replaced with a word like *there*. If you look even one step further, *the red car* is actually a noun phrase, and *red* is an adjective phrase within that.

While it may seem very confusing to try to figure out what all the phrases are, the best advice is to take the process one step at a time. For example, break a sentence into a noun phrase and a verb phrase. Then, work onto the next largest units within each until you get down to very basic units that cannot be broken down further: single words. Let's take a look at this process with the sample sentence in (10). In (10), the subject *the man in the bookstore* is a noun phrase (NP), while the predicate *likes funny novels* is a verb phrase (VP). The notation we use in (10) should read like the noun phrase *The man in the bookstore* and the verb phrase *likes funny novels* form a sentence (S).

(10) $\underline{\text{The man in the bookstore}}$ $\underline{\text{likes funny novels.}}$
$\phantom{\text{The man in }}NP\phantom{\text{ the bookstore}}$ $\phantom{\text{likes}}$VP

$\underline{\phantom{\text{The man in the bookstore likes funny novels.}}}$
$\phantom{\text{The man in the book}}$S

Remember that we are starting with the two biggest phrases. Every sentence can be broken into two phrases—a noun phrase and a verb phrase, as mentioned several times above. In this initial stage, we see that the NP in this case is the subject of the sentence, and the VP is the predicate. While you should not confuse the notions of phrases and subject-predicate, for those of you who have taken extensive grammar classes before, you will see how, in this case, the two concepts match up nicely. Everything before the verb (*likes*) is an NP, and everything after (and including) the verb is a VP. How do we know these two phrases are actually phrases? Let us apply the replacement test to each, just to be sure. *The man in the bookstore* can be replaced with *he*, and *likes funny novels* can be replaced with *does*. Note that in this case, the movement test does not yield anything that looks like an acceptable sentence, so we will not apply it. Remember that for a phrase to be a phrase, it has to pass at least one of the two tests we discussed.

Now, let us break the phrases down further. We will begin to break down the NP first. The NP can be broken into a determiner, a noun and a preposition phrase as shown in (11). (11) reads like the determiner *The*, the noun *man*, and the preposition phrase (PP) *in the bookstore* form the noun phrase *The man in the bookstore*.

(11) The man $\underline{\text{in the bookstore}}$
D NPP
$\underline{\phantom{\text{The man in the bookstore}}}$
$\phantom{\text{The man}}$NP

To make sure that *in the bookstore* in (11) is indeed a phrase, you can reapply the phrasal tests. The PP *in the bookstore* can certainly be replaced with one word like *there*, to yield *The man there*. Getting smaller now, we look at the preposition phrase. In (12), within the preposition phrase, *in the bookstore*, there is one preposition (*in*) and a noun phrase. In other words, the preposition, *in*, and the NP, *the bookstore*, form the PP *in the bookstore*.

(12) in $\underline{\text{the bookstore}}$
PNP
$\underline{\phantom{\text{in the bookstore}}}$
$\phantom{\text{in th}}$PP

A careful examination reveals that the NP, *the bookstore*, contains a determiner and a noun, as shown in (13). We are now down to the single-word level because we have broken apart all phrases.

(13) the bookstore
DN
$\underline{}$
$\phantom{\text{th}}$NP

We will do the same thing to the VP. The VP is composed of the verb *likes* and the NP *funny novels*, as analyzed in (14).

(14) 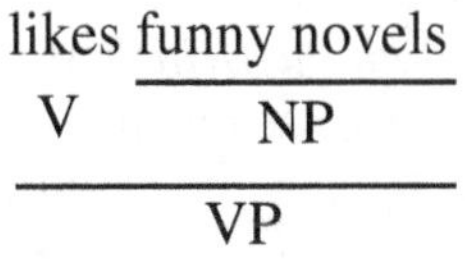 likes funny novels
       V   NP
      ‾‾‾‾‾‾‾‾‾‾‾‾‾‾‾
            VP

In (14), the VP contains the NP *funny novels*. We already know that the NP can be further dissected into the adjective (Adj), *funny*, and the noun, *novels*, as in (15).

(15) 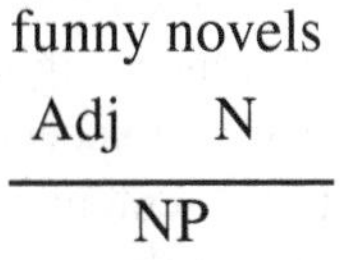 funny novels
       Adj   N
      ‾‾‾‾‾‾‾‾‾‾‾
           NP

Now we have completed our analysis of the sentence *The man in the bookstore likes funny novels*. The final result containing all the analyses shown above would look like (16). To make some distinction among the three NPs in (16), a subscript number has been added to each NP.

(16) 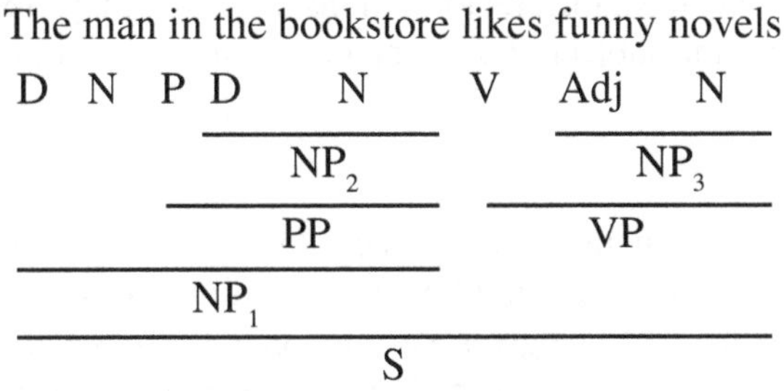 The man in the bookstore likes funny novels.
       D   N   P   D   N   V   Adj   N
                           NP_2 NP_3
                           PP   VP
              NP_1
                              S

(16) might look somewhat complicated. However, the information that (16) conveys is straightforward. That is, (16) shows six different steps of analysis of the sentence *The man in the bookstore likes funny novels*, as illustrated in (17).

(17) **Step 1:** S is composed of NP_1 and VP.
      Step 2: NP_1 is composed of D, N, and PP.
      Step 3: PP is composed of P and NP_2.
      Step 4: NP_2 is composed of D and N.
      Step 5: VP is composed of V and NP_3.
      Step 6: NP_3 is composed of Adj and N.

Let us keep in mind the notions of clause and phrase as we move toward more challenging topics in this chapter.

3.5 Two Important Distinctions: Functions And Categories

As you probably remember from your initial contact with grammar, there are all kinds of word categories: nouns, verbs, adjectives, and adverbs, to name a few. We refer to these categories as *lexical categories* in linguistics; in a traditional grammar classroom, these may be called *parts of speech*. All words belong to a single lexical category in the context of a sentence. Think about the word *house*. In the sentence *Elena walked to her house after school*, the word *house* is a noun. However, if we look at the sentence *Both the British Museum and the Field Museum house large collections of interesting artifacts*, we see that *house* is a verb. To determine the lexical category of any word, we thus have to see the context in which the word appears. Note that, in this particular case, *house* not only is used as a different lexical category for each sentence, but it also has a different pronunciation depending on its lexical category.

Different from lexical categories is the concept of *functions*. Words not only belong to a lexical category, but they also serve a function in the clause. This difference might be confusing to beginning linguistics students. While lexical categories are parts of speech such as noun and verb, functions are just the job a word or phrase carries out in a sentence. A noun, for example, functions as a subject in a sentence when a phrase that contains the noun appears in a subject position. The same noun can function as an object, when a phrase containing the noun appears in an object position. Subject, predicate, direct object, and indirect object are all grammatical functions. A good example of this is sentence (18) below. The three nouns (noun phrases) *Lily*, *Jane*, and *the book*, have different functions, although they are identical in the lexical category of noun. *Lily* is the subject of the sentence, *Jane* is the indirect object, and *the book* is the direct object.

(18) Lily gave Jane the book.

Our analogy is this: lexical category is to function as our name is to our role in different social situations. A person whose name is John can have multiple roles in different social contexts. For example, John is viewed as a linguist when he gives a lecture on linguistics at a university or at a conference. However, he is viewed as the father of his daughter and a husband of his wife at home. Nonetheless, his name does not change: His name is still John. The name John is similar to the notion of lexical category because John's roles as a linguist, as a father, and as a husband are similar to grammatical functions.

3.6 Lexical Categories: An Overview

Now that we have had a brief discussion of categories and functions, it is time to talk about the eight lexical categories in English. We will not include interjections as one of our lexical categories, however.

3.6.1 Nouns

The first lexical category we will discuss is that of *noun*. Often, nouns are the first category discussed by elementary school teachers. Nouns are basic and crucial components of our language and are often found in the subject position of a sentence. They can also be found functioning as either direct or indirect objects in a sentence. Common nouns, which exclude specific names and places, can be modified by a determiner. Here, *determiner* is a lexical category that we will explain later, but it includes words like *the* and *an*. Often, nouns can be identified on sight by specific endings, like *-tion* and *-ity*. Nouns can be pluralized as well, which is perhaps the most distinctive aspect of a noun. We will not extend our definition here to the traditional "person, place, or thing" because this definition proves to be insufficient when looking at language. We will look at why this is so in Chapter 4. Extended discussion on nouns will be provided in section 3.7.1.

3.6.2 Verbs

Nouns are not the only kinds of words suffering from a traditional definition. Verbs too must be redefined before continuing a linguistic analysis of the category because verbs are not simply "action words." Verbs prove to be more diverse than the elementary school definition lets on. Verbs are words that can be inflected for tense in terms of our discussion provided in Chapter 2. In English, verbs may be identified by the suffixes *-ed* or *-s*. Verbs may be *transitive* or *intransitive*, which means they either require an object or not, respectively. One other form of transitive verb is called a *ditransitive verb*, and this kind of verb requires two objects, direct and indirect. While verbs seem more complex now that we have given a rather thorough definition, it is much more accurate to define the verb category this way. Let us consider the example *destruction*. Without difficulty, you will identify the word as a noun. Nonetheless, *destruction* seems to be an action. If this is so, *destruction* must be a verb, following the traditional definition of verbs. Our new definition of verbs can avoid this type of confusion. Because the word *destruction* cannot carry a tense morpheme, as shown in * *destruction-ed*, destruction cannot be a verb.

Below are some examples of the various kinds of verbs we talked about. By reviewing this table, you will be able to better tell the difference between intransitive and transitive verbs. In (19), some examples of these three types of verbs are provided. More detailed discussions on three types of verbs will be provided in section 3.7.2.

(19) Three types of verbs

Examples of intransitive verbs	Examples of transitive verbs	Examples of ditransitive verbs
sneeze, talk, cry, sleep, and so on	satisfy, lock, dissect, hit, and so on	brought, gave, tell, and so on
Anything following these verbs is purely optional.	These verbs need something after them to be understood.	In each of the ditransitive verb situations above, two pieces of additional information must follow the verb for a complete-sounding sentence.
I sneezed, we talked, he cried, and *they slept* are all fine sentences without extra information.	*I satisfied, we locked*, and *they dissected* all sound like they are lacking something if we leave the sentence at that. What they are lacking is the object.	*I brought Mike* sounds funny unless you add something more, like *to the party*.
		I gave Lisa is also odd unless it is completed with something like *the keys*.

3.6.3 Adjectives and Adverbs

The next lexical category we will discuss is that of adjective. Adjectives often describe (or modify) a noun or noun phrase, giving additional information. Adjectives are also the lexical category that undergoes the comparative/superlative phenomenon. This means that some adjectives may be viewed as degrees on a spectrum, like *good, better, best* or *bad, worse, worst.* Adjectives in English often precede the noun they describe or follow the *be* verb, as in examples (20) and (21).

(20) John was *handsome* in his old age.
(21) Kelly and Bud are *unfortunate*.

Functioning similarly to adjectives, adverbs also describe words. In the case of adverbs, however, they describe the *how*, the *when*, the *where*, or the *manner* of a verb. Many times, adverbs end in *-ly*, but this is not always the case, especially considering words like *friendly*, *early*, or *leisurely*, which are adjectives. Adverbs can appear almost anywhere in a sentence, but they are often seen at the sentence initial or sentence final positions. This means, they often begin or end a sentence. Consider examples (22) and (23), where the adverbs are italicized.

(22) *Yesterday*, he came back with the baby.
(23) Wanting to avoid miscommunication, Gina spoke *slowly*.

While adjectives and adverbs are very similar in nature, there is one other major distinction that sets them apart, and this is something you will want to keep in mind as you move through your introduction to linguistics. Other than modifying different phrases or lexical categories in a sentence, how else do they differ? As you will see later on, the position of a word in relation to other words in a sentence is often a big part of what defines its lexical category. Adjectives generally appear right before the nouns they modify, whereas adverbs are a little more free in their position. As stated above, they often begin or end sentences, but can appear elsewhere as well. Consider (24).

(24) Archie *slowly* peered around the corner.

The adverb *slowly* appears, not at the beginning or end of a sentence, but right before the verb. You could also put *slowly* after the verb or at the beginning or end of the sentence. You can never insert adverbs into the middle of a preposition phrase; you must leave *around the corner* intact. Adjectives, however, can be inserted freely into the noun phrases they modify.

Keeping in mind the importance of the position of the word in a sentence, let us take our discussion one step further. Most grammar teachers will say that *careful* is an adjective and *carefully* is an adverb. What, then, is the lexical category of *careful* in (25)?

(25) Drive careful!

There is no doubt that you have heard this sentence countless times when you head out to your car during winter weather. In fact, you probably haven't heard many people say *Drive carefully!* Make no mistake, though. *Careful* in (25) is actually an adverb. We know this because it is in a position that is typical of an adverb, at the end of the sentence. Also, it is easy to see that it does not modify a noun. It tells *how* you should drive, and words that tell the *how* of a verb like *drive* are adverbs. Now, we must face one final question concerning (25). Is this grammatically wrong? Is this incorrect speech? Linguists say no. Getting back to the introduction of this book when we talked about prescriptive versus descriptive grammar, we said that linguists work with descriptive grammar as opposed to prescriptive grammar. That means that anything that a native speaker of a language can say without being questioned is valid. This is why, when asked whether a sentence is grammatical, the linguist can simply reply, "Can you hear it in normal conversation?" If the answer is positive, it is acceptable, and if negative or unsure, probably not. In fact, this is one of the ways that language begins to change. All of a sudden, a so-called improper form is used and it catches on, becoming popularized. Eventually, it becomes part of mainstream language. Remember that we do not speak like Shakespeare did, but our English is no less valuable, intelligible, or proper.

3.6.4 Determiners

As promised, we will revisit the category of determiners here in this section. Determiners are the "little words" that appear before nouns. They never appear without a noun immediately or almost immediately following them, and more than one determiner can never be used at the same time. Often, English word order may reflect the pattern of determiner-noun or determiner-adjective-noun if a determiner is required for a specific noun. Some examples of determiners are *a, an, the,* and so on. Know that many of what we call determiners are called adjectives by grammar teachers, as in *her* in (26).

(26) Her book was on the floor.

How can you tell the difference between a determiner and an adjective? You have the definition of adjective from the section above, and we will draw from some of the above characteristics of determiners to help you figure it out. A word is an adjective if it can be repeated for emphasis, such as in (27).

(27) green, green grass

On the contrary, as we said before, no more than one determiner can appear at one time. (28) is clearly unacceptable, as is (29).

(28) * the, the book
(29) * her, her rice

Obviously, these sound incorrect because they violate the definition of a determiner. This is how we know that determiners and adjectives are two different lexical categories.

3.6.5 Prepositions

One of the most often cited lexical categories after noun and verb is the category of prepositions. Preposition phrases always contain one preposition and one noun phrase, and in that way they are very predictable—more so than other kinds of phrases, which may have countless variations of phrase combinations within them. The italicized portions of (30) and (31) are examples of preposition phrases.

(30) The bag *inside the big green box* is empty.

(31) Yesterday, I went *to the grocery store.*

Prepositions are found directly before a noun phrase, though the entire phrase itself can modify either a noun, as in (30) or a verb, as in (31). In this way, the preposition phrase can function like either an adjective or an adverb. Listen to those around you to hear the various kinds of preposition phrases found in everyday conversation.

Prepositions themselves are words that show a directional relation between two things. Something might be *over* something else. Likewise, something might be *toward* a certain direction. Always, with prepositions there is an explicit location or direction that the preposition serves to describe. *To, from, in, out,* and *within* are examples of various prepositions, but there are many more. In fact, the exact number of prepositions in English hovers somewhere around fifty or slightly higher. When you compare this to the vast number of nouns in the English language, the category of prepositions seems frighteningly small. These words may be small in number, but they are powerful in their role in everyday language.

You may wonder why such a limited category is so powerful in our language. One of the reasons is that prepositions are the verbal representations of the conceptualization of our bodily experiences of time and space. Since the beginning of language, most of our temporal and spatial conceptions have manifested themselves as words right away. Because there are relatively few ways to experience time and space, the addition of a new preposition is unlikely. (32) shows a list of some of the prepositions in English.

(32) English prepositions

English prepositions
about, above, across, after, against, along, among, around, as, at, before, behind, below, beside, between, beyond, by, despite, down, during, for, from, in, into, next, of, off, on, onto, out, outside, over, through, throughout, to, toward, under, until, up, upon, with, within, without, and so on

3.6.6 Coordinators (Conjunctions)

The next category is something you might have already heard about under the name *conjunction*. Examples of conjunctions are *and, or, but,* among others. A coordinated (or conjoined) clause is actually two *independent* clauses linked together with some kind of connector. Remember that an independent clause is what we consider a whole or complete sentence by itself, or as many grammar teachers say, "a sentence that can stand alone." This connective joining of the above-mentioned independent clauses would be one of the coordinators we are now describing. See (33) for an example of a coordinated clause.

(33) Lucy runs in the park *and* Eric buys a hotdog.

The two clauses within the coordinated clause are clearly capable of standing on their own; they are simply coordinated with the word *and* to produce a larger string of words. The beauty of coordinators is that they not only conjoin clauses, but they may also conjoin two like-phrases too. Phrases like *bread and butter* or *eats and sleeps* are examples of conjoined phrases, or phrases that use a coordinator to connect them. These are also commonly used in our everyday speech. Isn't it interesting how often we use coordinators without stopping to think of how important they are? In comparison to some of our bigger lexical categories, the category of coordinators is relatively small, but again, it is often the smaller categories that are more powerful in their usage.

3.6.7 Complementizers

The last category we will talk about in this chapter is that of complementizers. A complementizer is a word that functions similarly to a coordinator in that it connects two clauses. However, complimentizers are slightly more specific in their aim to conjoin because they link a dependent clause to an independent clause, or a clause that cannot stand alone. The complementizer itself is part of the dependent clause. Words like *that, if, whether,* and *for* can function as complementizers in the context of certain sentences. See example (34), where the complementizer is italicized.

(34) Janice believes *that* the store is selling snuggies.

We will come back to complementizers a bit later in Chapters 4 and 5, when you learn to draw tree diagrams. At that point, the whole concept of complementizers will become clearer as you see them in action.

3.7 Nouns And Verbs In Depth

In this section, we will revisit nouns and verbs to discuss their grammatical properties in more detail.

3.7.1 Nouns

As we discussed in previous subsections of this chapter, nouns are a distinct lexical category. Nouns make up a huge portion of our language, and new nouns can be added into our vocabulary at any time. Each year, dictionaries make new entries for the nouns that have been recently popularized. Words like *email, blog,* and *Google* are all words that have been recently defined in the dictionary—we can consider them newborn words because they did not exist even twenty years ago. What makes nouns unique from other lexical categories? In the definition provided to you previously in this chapter, we said that nouns were more than a basic person, place, or thing. Nouns often appear in the subject or object positions, and they can be modified by adjectives or determiners. Nouns can be singular or plural in number, and they can be possessive, meaning that if we add 's to the end of the noun, the noun gains ownership of something. Nouns are indeed more complex entities than you once thought, aren't they? They have so many characteristics that defining them as person, place, or thing seems to pigeonhole them instead of define them.

3.7.1.1 Proper nouns, common nouns, and pronouns

We can also categorize nouns based on more specific characteristics. One interesting distinction is between proper and common nouns.

(35) John has a fountain pen.

As we see in (35), there are two nouns, *John* and *fountain pen*. While the two are indeed both nouns, they differ slightly. The difference is that *John* is a proper noun, whereas *fountain pen* is not. Proper nouns are nouns that describe very specific entities, like places and people's names. They are also words that are capitalized in writing, and they may or may not be modified by a determiner. *Brad Pitt, Toyota Prius, Germany*, and *Doritos* are all examples of proper nouns. Surely you can think of many more. Anything that is not a proper noun is regarded as a common noun(excluding pronouns). Common nouns are exactly that—common. They may or may not be modified by a determiner, and they do not necessarily describe anything specific. *Building, hat, extension*, and *spreadsheet* are all common nouns.

The third subcategory of noun is pronoun. Pronouns, which include *I, he, she*, and *they*, are never modified by a determiner. Pronouns are nouns that usually stand for something else that is commonly understood in the context of a conversation. For example, if you were having a conversation about the famous linguists Chomsky and Langacker, you might use *they* to start a sentence, as in (36). In this case, the pronoun *they* clearly refers to the aforementioned two linguists.

(36) Chomsky and Langacker are respectable figures in the field of linguistics. *They* both put forth novel and intriguing ideas.

3.7.1.2 Number and countablity

Another distinction between nouns is that of number and countability. Some nouns are forever in their singular form and cannot be pluralized. This group of nouns is referred to as singular-only, and they include words such as *harm*, *footwear*, or *nonsense*. Even words that end in an *s* may be considered singular, if the *s* is not a separate morpheme marking plurality (see the chapter Morphology for more details on this). To give you some idea of what nouns might end in *s* but maintain a singular status, a short list follows: *linguistics, italics, news*, and *measles*. To test that they are singular, put them in a sentence and see if you can use the word *is* directly after. If you have to use *are* instead, you are looking at something that is not a singular-only noun. However, if you were able to come up with a sentence such as *The news **is** on channel three* or *measles **is** a terrible ailment*, then your result is clearly a singular-only noun.

Like many nouns that are singular-only, some nouns are plural-only. Words like *cattle, police, belongings*, and *clothes* all belong to this category of plural-only nouns. These are words that do not have a singular form. Again, it is not necessary to get too hung up on the idea that all plural forms must end in an *s*. As you can see, the word *cattle* is in a plural form, and it does not contain an *s* anywhere. If you need to check to see if a word is a plural-only noun, employ the same test as the one above, with a slightly different twist. To see if a word is being used in a plural form, and no other form is available, use the word with *are* in a sentence. An example would be *Cattle are generally best behaved when kept in a large, open pen*. Because *Cattle is…* sounds odd and awkward, we know that what we are dealing with is a plural-only noun. If instead the word required is *is*, then it is likely not a plural-only noun.

One interesting thing that plays into the issue of nouns is that of *count*. Nouns that are count nouns can be modified by a number or quantity, such as *three*, as in *three cats*. Nouns that are not count nouns cannot be modified by a number, such as *rice, water,* or *bread*. It is not likely for someone to use the phrase *one rice* or *many water*. This means that these nouns are noncount nouns. Some noncount nouns are always in singular form, much like we saw with the singular-only nouns. These include words like *furniture, clothing,* and *equipment*. Some noncount nouns are always in a plural form, like plural-only nouns. Some examples of these would be *remains* and *credentials*.

As we have just seen, nouns can be categorized in various ways: common or proper, pronouns, singular-only or plural-only, and count or noncount (within which exist both singular and plural forms). Naturally, this diverse categorization of nouns leads to a wide assortment of possible noun phrases. A noun phrase, as we have previously discussed, can be as simple as a single proper noun, like *John*, or as complex as *The happy girl in the bookstore*, which is a large noun phrase that contains several other kinds of phrases.

3.7.2 Verbs

Verbs are also a major and crucial component to the English language. In fact, without a verb, an English sentence cannot exist. They are so important that speakers of the English language add new verbs to their vocabulary all the time. Think of your conversations now versus those of five years ago. No doubt now, you talk about *twittering*, *googling*, and *skyping*. Five years ago, these activities were just becoming popular and now they constitute valid verbs. The fluidity of natural language, in this sense, is really amazing.

Verbs have several distinctive properties that set them apart from all other lexical categories. One such property is that of tense inflection. When a verb is inflected for tense, its form is changed to reflect tense, a process that many grammarians refer to as *conjugation*. Here, however, we will simply use the term *inflection* to avoid any confusion about technicalities. As we discussed in Chapter 2, when a verb is inflected in various forms, these forms belong to what we call a paradigm. *Walk, walked, walking* are all forms of the verb *to walk*, and as a group of inflected verbs, this paradigm gives us some clues to how the English language functions. For example, one might venture to guess that many past-tense verbs in the English language end in the morpheme *-ed*. This is true, although it does not apply to all cases. Inflection, more often than not, exhibits regular patterns that occur within language, and is usually one of the first things we are taught to memorize when we learn a foreign language.

3.7.2.1 Auxiliary verbs

Verbs, much like nouns, belong to various categories, and a verb may often belong to more than one category at once. As you recall from the brief overview on verbs in this chapter, we have already discussed transitive and intransitive verbs, which form two subgroups of verbs. Another major distinction is made between auxiliary verbs and lexical verbs. Auxiliary verbs are always followed by another verb, and are often regarded by elementary school teachers as helper verbs. These include the commonly used *might, may, could, can, would, will, did,* and *do*. As you can see in the following example, an auxiliary verb is often followed by another verb. In (37), the auxiliary verb is *can*, and the main verb is *fix*.

(37) Belknap Heating can fix the fireplace for $130.

An auxiliary verb is the verb in a sentence that carries tense because it is always the first verb in a series of verbs that carries the tense in English. Of course, not all sentences have an auxiliary verb because lexical verbs can carry tense as well—just not in the presence of an auxiliary verb. In the above example, *can* is clearly in the present tense, whereas the following verb *fix* is left in its non-finite (uninflected) form. On the other hand, the category of lexical verbs comprises everything else. Lexical verbs can be any verbs found in any sentence, provided they are not considered an auxiliary, and may also carry tense marking (inflection) when there is no auxiliary present. While this explanation seems deceivingly simple, it is important to be able to distinguish auxiliary verbs from lexical verbs.

Plain forms are the verb forms that are uninflected. These forms are found in imperatives (commands), to + infinitive constructions as in (38), or after an auxiliary verb. If you have taken a foreign language class, you might already know that the plain form of the verb is the basic starting point before beginning the conjugation process. The plain form of the verb almost always has an identical present tense form in English. Take, for example, the verb *write*. *Write* is the most basic form of the verb, but as you look at the following examples, you will see a difference between the two kinds of *write* used.

(38) I like to write and illustrate novels.
(39) I write several pages a day in my journal.

In (38), the verb *write* is used in its plain form, its infinitive form. We can see that it is uninflected because it follows *to*. By contrast, in (39), *write* is in fact an inflected form, although there is no visible inflectional affix. How do we know this? If you change the pronoun *I* to *he*, the verb would become *writes*. That means, then, that the verb is actually in its inflected form. The pronoun test is a basic and easy way to see if a verb is inflected or not. If the pronoun is changed and the verb changes, then you are dealing with an inflected verb, one that is not in the infinitive form. In short, this means that, even though the forms of the verb in the two sentences look the same, they are actually in two separate forms: one is the plain form, the other plain-present.

One interesting fact about plain form verbs is that almost all of them have an identical plain-present form. Take almost any verb you know and use it to replace *write* in the examples above, disregarding the irrelevant context of novels and journals. There should be two identical forms for every verb you can think of. However, English has one exception to this rule, and it is the most common verb: *be*. If you were to change the above examples, you would not have the two identical examples that you had during your other verb tests, as shown in (40) and (41).

(40) I like to be...
(41) I am...

Let us leave the *be* verb as an exception. In many languages, the more frequently used words are prone to irregularity. Because the English *be* verb is the most frequently used verb in English, this type of anomaly is somewhat expected.

3.7.2.2 Transitivity again

There is one other distinct categorization of verbs that we have already briefly discussed in this chapter. The distinction between transitive and intransitive verbs is an important one because it shows the function of the predicate. We will again cover the difference between transitive and intransitive verbs for further linguistic analysis, but feel free to refer back to the previous section in which we introduced the notion of transitivity.

Intransitive verbs are the proverbial "end of the story." They do not require anything further in the way of the predicate, and they often serve to communicate a simple idea or concept. Like in (42), the predicate will not contain an object.

(42) Jenny sleeps.

As you can see in the above example, the verb *sleeps* requires nothing further. Obviously, it is possible to modify this sentence with a preposition phrase or an adverb to make it more descriptive, but modification does not change the fact that the verb *sleep* is an intransitive verb. Let us consider another example in (43).

(43) Kerry punished the man for his insubordination.

Is *punished* in this sentence also an intransitive verb? We can use a simple test to determine whether it belongs in that category. To do this, we simply create a sentence with a subject and the verb we wish to test. Without adding anything additional, we will determine whether it makes sense. If it does not, then the verb is not intransitive.

(44) ? Kerry punished.

Does the sentence seem like a complete thought to you? In other words, are you satisfied with the completeness, or are you left asking who(m) or what? In this case, the sentence seems lacking because the person interpreting the sentence is left wondering *who* Kerry punished. By asking the question who(m) or what, we can determine that this verb *punish* is actually a transitive verb and requires a direct object.

We have one more kind of transitivity to cover before we end our discussion of verbs. *Ditransitive* verbs are another kind of transitive verb, but instead of requiring a direct object only, they also require an indirect object. To give you a better idea of what a ditransitive verb would be, let us consider the verb *give*. To use the verb *give*, one must provide a *what* and a *to whom*. Consider the example below.

(45) Maria gave Carmen the book.

In (45), we know what is being given (a book) and to whom (Carmen). To see if this verb is truly ditransitive, we need to know if it is possible to use it without the indirect object. Starting with the original test, we try to create the sentence *Maria gave*. We now know, based on the unacceptability of this form, that it is transitive. To test for ditransitivity, however, we need to include an object in the second phase of our test. Does it sound normal if we say *Maria gave the book*? Usually, we would "finish the sentence" by answering to whom or to what Maria gave the book. In other words, our test sentence sounds as incomplete as it actually is. The noun phrase *Carmen* is necessary to complete the thought, meaning *give* is truly ditransitive.

3.7.2.3 Tense

Other than transitivity, which is a fundamental concept in the study of verbs, we must talk about tense. As we have said many times before, a chief characteristic of verbs is that they may take tense. If you have studied any foreign language in a formal setting, you already know that tenses are often formed by adding an ending to a verb stem, or perhaps by adding an additional word or morpheme. In English, you already know that the past tense form is distinctive from the present tense form because it most often adds -*ed*, while the present tense morpheme is usually -*s*. English has a third verb form called the past participle. Often, the past participle is the same as the past tense form, but there are some cases where the participle is a distinctive and unique form of its own. The following examples show the three forms of the verbs *study* and *give*. (48) and (51) are the forms using a past participle and an auxiliary verb, a form of *have*. The fourth and final form, the progressive participle, is seen in (52) and (53). The participle is formed when a verb stem takes the -ing ending. In conjunction with the –*ing* ending, the tense-marked auxiliary verb *be* is used before the participle form, as in *is studying* and *was giving*.

(46) Carla studies linguistics.   (present tense)
(47) Carla studied linguistics.   (past tense)
(48) Carla has studied linguistics.   (past participle)
(49) Carmen gives the flowers to her mother.   (present tense)
(50) Carmen gave the flowers to her mother.   (past tense)
(51) Carmen has given the flowers to her mother. (past participle)
(52) Carla is studying linguistics.   (present tense progressive participle)
(53) Carmen was giving the flowers to her mother.   (past tense progressive participle)

As we see with the verb *study*, the past tense form of the verb is the same as the past participle form. In the case of *give*, however, the past tense form and the past participle form are different.

Before concluding our discussion of verbs, it is necessary to see them as part of a phrase structure. As with nouns, verb phrase structures are diverse and varied. They may consist of simply the verb itself, or the verb and various other phrases, such as noun phrases, prepositional phrases, or adverb phrases. As varied as the possible verb structures are, they are all crucial to forming the predicate of the sentence. Therefore, they are deserving of our attention to detail in our study of verbs here. We have talked about many things: from tense inflection to auxiliary verbs, from plain (infinitive) forms to transitivity. It is safe to say that verbs are complex entities within our language and play a big role in each sentence we speak.

3.8 Summary

In this chapter, we have discussed the fundamentals of the English language. We started with the unit of clause and worked our way through phrases and individual words. We covered grammatical function and how function is different from lexical categories. Then, piece by piece, we examined each lexical category to find its underlying characteristics and tendencies, with a special focus at the end of the chapter on the major building blocks: nouns and verbs. Before you move on to the next chapter, be sure you understand the major concepts and notions in this chapter. Your knowledge of the English grammar discussed in this chapter will set the pace for the rest of your linguistics education.

3.9 Further Reading

Many outstanding reference grammar books are available. Greenbaum (1996) and Quirk et al. (1985) are valuable resources for students who want to learn more about English grammar. Huddelston and Pullum (2002) is an outstanding source too. For readers who want to have a quick overview of Huddelston and Pullum (2002), we recommend Huddelston and Pullum (2005), which is a shorter version of Huddelston and Pullum (2002).

CHAPTER 4

Syntax I

Syntax is the scientific study of sentence structures. As we discussed in Chapter 1, a scientific study assumes a hypothesis formulation followed by testing processes. Let us begin this chapter with three simple case studies of syntax to discuss how we put forth a syntactic hypothesis and test it.

4.1 Three Case Studies

4.1.1 The subject of an imperative sentence

As we already discussed briefly in Chapter 1 of this book, everybody knows that the subject of an imperative sentence, as in (1), is *you*. The question is, *How* do you know what the subject is?

    (1) Work hard!

One way to answer this question is to use a linguistic test called reflexive testing. Recall that the word *reflexive* refers to the *–self* words such as *myself, himself, yourself*, and so on. In English, the reflexives must have appropriate antecedents in the sentence. That is, the reflexive *himself* in (2) must have its antecedent in the same sentence. Because *himself* has its antecedent *John* in (2), the sentence is acceptable. By contrast, (3) is not acceptable because *himself* does not have an antecedent in the given sentence.

    (2) John loves himself.
    (3) * The woman loves himself.

Keeping this in mind, let us go back to the question of the imperatives: How can we justify the claim that the subject of (1) is *you*? Now let us invent another imperative that contains the reflexive *yourself*, as in (4). Although there is no overt antecedent in (4), the sentence is completely acceptable and natural.

    (4) Do not torture yourself by taking linguistics!

At first glance, example (4) seems to be contradictory to (3). We explained the unacceptability of (3) as the lack of antecedent of *himself* in the sentence. If it is true, (4) should be unacceptable too. This contradiction is superficial. We can explain both (3) and (4) systematically without breaking the assumption we made: The reflexives must have an antecedent. Note that imperatives like (4) do not have a visible subject. Nonetheless, the reflexive *yourself* can appear. *Yourself* is the only possible reflexive in imperative sentences. Sentences (5) to (7), where other reflexives are used in imperative sentences, are all unacceptable.

(5) * Do not torture himself by taking linguistics!
(6) * Do not torture myself by taking linguistics!
(7) * Do not torture themselves by taking linguistics!

What does this mean? Although the subject is not clearly visible, there must be *you* in the subject position, which functions as the antecedent of *yourself* in imperative sentences. We thus can prove our claim by creating some test sentences like (5) to (7). This type of testing is often called syntactic argumentation. Another example of syntactic argumentation is syntactic ambiguity.

4.1.2 Syntactic ambiguity

Literally speaking, the word *ambiguity* means "two meanings." But linguists use the word *ambiguity* to refer to "two or more meanings." So if a phrase has multiple meanings, it is still considered ambiguous. Many words in English have more than two meanings. For example, the English word *bank* has at least two distinctive meanings. One is "the land alongside or sloping down to a river or lake" and the other is "a financial institution." In this sense, the word *bank* is ambiguous. This type of ambiguity is called lexical ambiguity because the ambiguity inherently exists in the word. If you look up the word *bank* in a dictionary, you will find the meanings we have just described. This means the meanings exist in the word without respect to the context.

The second type of ambiguity is pragmatic ambiguity. Pragmatic ambiguity arises due to the language use. In other words, the ambiguity must be understood in conjunction with the speaker's intention. The teacher's statement in (8) can be understood in two different ways. The teacher might be just stating that the room is hot today. However, considering all the context and the teacher's looking at Mary, we may interpret the teacher's statement as a request or command that Mary open the windows for him. This will be explained in detail in Chapters 8 and 10.

(8) Teacher: The room is too hot today (looking at Mary who is sitting by the windows).

The third type of ambiguity is syntactic ambiguity. Let us take a look at example (9) below. Every native speaker will agree that (9) has two distinctive meanings. One meaning is "John killed the soldier who had the gun" and the other is "With the gun, John killed the soldier."

(9) John killed the soldier with the gun.

This ambiguity is different from lexical ambiguity because the two different meanings do not stem from different meanings of the words used in (9). The ambiguity must be coming from somewhere else. In this case, we can prove that the ambiguity stems from two different grammatical structures of (9). In one structure, the phrase *with the gun* is related to *the soldier*, but in the other structure, the phrase modifies the verb *killed*. We will explain the structural differences in great detail when we discuss syntactic trees later. Nevertheless, we have to admit that (9) cannot be explained either by lexical ambiguity or pragmatic ambiguity. Then, we can argue that there are two different structures in (9), although there is only one visible sentence.

4.1.3 The part of speech of 'home'

Most students without any linguistics training will identify the part of speech of *home* in (10) as a noun. It is understandable because *home* certainly falls within the school-grammar definition of noun: person, place, or thing. However, as we discussed in Chapter 3, the part of speech must be defined morphosyntactically, based on the word's position in a sentence as well its word structure. If you are not familiar with this information, you will have to go back to Chapter 3 and review. In spite of most people's identification of *home* as a noun, there is clear evidence that *home* is an adverb.

(10) John went home.

As we discussed in Chapter 3, the verb *went* in (10) is an intransitive verb and thus does not require a direct object. Recall that a direct object must appear when a verb is transitive. Because *went* is an intransitive verb, it cannot be followed by a direct object, which is a noun. Therefore, *home* cannot be a noun in this example. Now let us consider other examples illustrated in (11) and (12).

(11) John went quickly.
(12) John went calmly.

Both (11) and (12), where *home* is replaced with the adverbs *quickly* and *calmly*, are acceptable for most (or all) native speakers. By contrast, if you replace *home* with the noun (phrase) *the store*, the sentence is infelicitous to most native speakers, as shown in (13).

(13) * John went the store.

What do these tests reveal about the part of speech of *home*? These tests tell us that the part of speech of *home* is an adverb because *home* can appear in the same position as adverbs, but it is not interchangeable with a noun (phrase). Therefore, we have to conclude that *home* is indeed an adverb in (10) because it is not interchangeable with other adverbs. Note, however, that *home* can be used as a noun in other cases, such as *Welcome to my home!* As you recall from Chapter 3, parts of speech must be determined based on the given word's morphosyntactic properties, which means that a word's part of speech is not bound to the word itself, but rather to the word's position in the sentence, among other factors.

Throughout this chapter, we will introduce similar syntactic arguments to support and test our hypothesis. Because of its hypothesis-testing nature, linguistics is considered a science. We hope readers clearly see the scientific nature of linguistics.

4.2 Lexical Categories And Phrases

In Chapter 3, we discussed eight parts of speech in English, excluding interjection. The eight parts of speech are noun, verb, adjective, adverb, preposition, determiner, conjunction, and complementizer. The parts of speech are also called lexical categories. These lexical categories are independent items because they appear as independent items in a dictionary. They can also be combined to form a larger unit, called a phrase. We will define *phrase* in the following subsection, followed by the discussion of various types of phrases.

4.2.1 Phrase defined

A phrase is a larger grammatical grouping than a lexical item (word). However, not all groupings make a phrase. In (14), most native speakers intuitively know that *to the mountains* forms one unit, yielding a phrase, while *up my eyes* does not, although *to the mountains* and *up my eyes* look very similar superficially.

(14) I lift up my eyes to the mountains.

Linguists use several tests to identify phrases. In this chapter, however, we will introduce only two: movement and replacement. The movement test is defined as in (15). This test is not an ad hoc formulation. Rather it is a very natural proposal. If a group forms one unit, the group must behave like one unit. If the words in the group are one unit, the group of words should be able move together. Our analogy for movement is a set of patio chairs in a hardware store, where chairs are often sold several at a time. As a set, they are usually tied together so that customers realize they cannot be separated and sold individually. Although comprised of many chairs, the set is treated as one unit at checkout. Also, because they are tied together, the set of patio chairs (P) can be moved to the front of the store (S) all at once. This analogy relates directly to the rule stated in (15) below, where a phrase (P) can be moved to the front of the sentence (S). Please note that in the following example, we are using a Greek letter as a variable, instead of the (P) and (S) we use in the prose explanation here.

(15) Movement
      If α is a phrase, α can be moved to the front position of the sentence.

Now, let us apply the movement test to (14) to check the phrasal properties of *to the mountains* and *up my eyes*. If we move *to the mountains* to the front position, the sentence is still acceptable (although there might be a slight meaning change) as in (16).

(16) To the mountains, I lift up my eyes.

By contrast, the movement of *up my eyes* to the front position makes the result unacceptable, as illustrated in (17).

(17) * Up my eyes, I lift to the mountains.

As we see from the examples, *to the mountains* passes our movement test, while *up my eyes* does not. Therefore, we can argue that *up my eyes* does not form one group or set. Now that we applied our first test to the two phraselike expressions, we can further apply the same test to other expressions. That is, we can apply the test to *my eyes*, too, as in (18). The same test can even be applied to *the mountains* as in (19), although many conservative speakers would not accept (19) as a "correct" sentence.

(18) My eyes, I lift up to the mountains.
(19) The mountains, I lift up my eyes to.

The second test we would like to discuss in this chapter is replacement. The replacement test is defined in (20). Similar to the movement test, the replacement test is not just randomly given. A good analogy for the replacement test is the renaming operation in a computer directory. If you open your computer's Documents folder, you will find other folders within. Each folder often contains many files. We can easily change the name of a folder without changing the content. Likewise, if we delete the folder, all of its contents are erased as well. This is possible because the folder is already one unit. If a bunch of files is one unit, it is treated as one entity, and deleting or changing its name is far from being mysterious.

(20) Replacement
      If β is a phrase, β can be replaced with a single lexical item.

Let us now discuss how the replacement test shows the status of a phrase. In the example we used earlier, only certain groups of words could be replaced with one word. (23) is somewhat awkward because the usual word order of (23) is *I lift them up to the mountains* in this context. However, let's ignore the difference in word order for the ease of explanation.

(21) I lift up my eyes to *them* (them = the mountains).
(22) I lift up my eyes *there* (there = to the mountains).
(23) I lift up *them* to the mountains (them = my eyes).
(24) I *raise* my eyes to the mountains (raise = lift up).
(25) I *do* (do = lift up my eyes to the mountains).

As we can see in (21) to (25), several groups of words were replaced with single lexical items. In (21), *them* replaced *the mountains*, and in (22), *there* replaced *to the mountains*, and so on. From this test, we now know that there are many phrases in the sentence *I lift up my eyes to the mountains*.

It is worth noting that it is not necessary that a phrase pass *both* tests to be considered a phrase. That is, a group of words can form one unit to be a phrase when it passes at least *one* of the two tests we discussed. For example, the group of words *lift up my eyes to the mountains* cannot move to the front position in a sentence. The result yields the unacceptable sentence * *Lift up my eyes to the mountains, I*. However, *lift up my eyes to the mountains* is still a phrase because it passes the replacement test, as in (25). For this reason, we can assume that either the movement test or the replacement test sanctions the phrasal status of the group of words in question. Based on this definition of a phrase, we will discuss several types of phrases in the following sections.

4.2.2 *Noun phrases and their rules*

For most people, the term *noun phrase* is somewhat unusual, but it is not hard to grasp the notion intuitively. A noun phrase is a phrase where a noun plays the most important role. Most native speakers agree that the most important word in (26) is *woman* because without *woman*, the phrase is incomplete, as in (27).

(26) a beautiful woman

(27) * a beautiful

More technically speaking, the noun is called the *head* of a noun phrase. The head of any-thing (a department, a corporation, etc.) is considered an integral part of the group it serves, so the term is not difficult to remember. That being said, it follows that every noun phrase must have a noun as its head. Although the notion of noun phrase seems to be simple at first glance, it is far more complex than we have just observed. Noun phrases have several subtypes discussed in the following sections.

4.2.2.1 Proper noun

A proper noun such as *John, Mary, Target*, can be considered a phrase on its own. We know this because the phrase *the man* and *John* are interchangeable. Because *John* can replace the phrase *the man* in any given sentence, *John* by itself must be a phrase too. In this case, the noun phrase *John* has only one word, a noun. To describe this type of structural property in a mathematical rule, linguists often use an arrow notation, as shown in (28). As you may have guessed, NP stands for noun phrase and N stands for noun.

(28) NP $\rightarrow$ N

(28) can be read in prose as "[a particular] noun phrase is composed of a noun." This type of rule is called a phrase structure rule (PS-Rule). The purpose of PS-Rules is to explain how sentences and phrases are constructed. For example, (28) explains a procedure for an English noun phrase, which can be roughly written in English as in (29).

(29) a. Step 1: Take the rule X $\rightarrow$ Y as a basic framework. X and Y are only variables, and we will replace them as we use the framework to formulate something rel-evant to us. Now you can replace the X with NP because your rule will be describ-ing a noun phrase.

   b. Step 2: Now, on the other side of the arrow, write the NP's components. In the case of proper nouns, the rule you will yield will look like (28).

Since (28) gives us an idea on how to rewrite NPs as a mathematical formulation, it is also called a rewrite rule. The rewrite rule we have just discussed can be converted into a tree diagram as illustrated in (30). In a tree diagram like (30), NP is called the mother of N, and N is called the daughter of NP.

(30) NP
       |
       N

Rewrite rule (28) and tree (30) are essentially identical conceptually. If a rewrite rule is given, we can generate a corresponding tree. Similarly, if a tree is given, we can determine a rule that would generate the tree. In the remainder of the following subsections, we will use these rule and tree notations.

4.2.2.2 Determiner + common noun

The second type of noun phrase we will discuss is the one that contains a determiner and a common noun. The example of this type is given in (31) to (34). Recall that, in (31) to (34), *the, a, his, some* belong to the category of *determiner*.

(31) the book
(32) a table
(33) his apron
(34) some problems

The noun phrases listed above all have the same structure, where a determiner is followed by a noun. This structural pattern is formulated as a rewrite rule, as in (35). The rewrite rule provided in (35) reads like "A noun phrase is composed of a determiner and a noun."

(35) NP → D N

Similar to the example illustrated in (30), it is not hard to convert rewrite rule (35) into its corresponding tree diagram, as in (36). In (36), D is called a sister of N and N is called a sister of D, similar to a family tree.

(36)

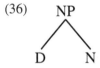

The only difference between (30) and (36) is that the NP in (30) has only one daughter, while the NP in (36) has two daughters. As you might have noticed, it is very straightforward to convert the rewrite rule in (35) into (36), and vice versa.

4.2.2.3 Determiner + adjective phrase + common noun

The third type of noun phrase is the one that contains a determiner, an adjective phrase, and a noun, as in (37) to (39).

(37) the wonderful book
(38) a fabulous story
(39) his beautiful daughter

These examples all illustrate the same type: a determiner, an adjective, and a noun. In other words "A noun phrase is composed of a determiner followed by an adjective phrase followed by a noun." This verbal expression can be formulated into the rewrite rule format, as in (40). In (40), AP stands for Adjective Phrase. Much like one noun can sometimes be a noun phrase, one adjective can sometimes be an adjective phrase as well.

(40) NP → D AP N

The rewrite rule can again be illustrated in a tree diagram format. In this case, the NP mother has three daughters, which is different form the earlier examples.

(41)

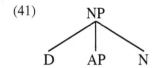

As mentioned before in the previous paragraph, one adjective can sometimes be considered an adjective phrase. As far as notation is concerned, it is best to be as precise as possible when making PS-Rules. The reason why we have to use AP instead of A in formulating the NP rule is because the adjectives used in (37) to (39) all appear in a phrase position. For example, *wonderful* in (37) can be replaced with the phrase *absolutely wonderful,* as shown in (42). Therefore, we can safely assume that the position where *wonderful* appears in (37) is an AP position, instead of A.

(42) the *absolutely wonderful* book
(43) a *tremendously fabulous* book
(44) his *outstandingly beautiful* daughter

One interesting factor concerning APs is that they can be repeated in a noun phrase, as in (45) and (46). Both sentences have two adjectives in a row.

(45) the ugly old house
(46) a round red ball

To capture this type of repetition, we will have to slightly modify the rule we formulated in (40), which is shown in (47). In (47), we have used the + symbol, called Kleene Plus. The meaning of AP+ is simply that AP can be repeated more than once.

(47) NP → D AP + N

Now example (45) can be explained by rule (47), but not by our previous rule, (40). Because there is more than one AP appearing in a noun phrase, rule (40) is not accurate enough. Converting the rule to its corresponding tree diagram is still straightforward. Theoretically speaking, rule (47) states that the number of APs within the NP is unlimited if it is more than one. However, when you generate a tree from the rule, you have to generate an actual tree for the noun phrase in question, instead of a potential tree structure. This is because, when you draw a tree diagram, it reflects the words of an actual sentence and not of a theoretical or potential sentence. For example, tree diagram (48) is generated from rule (47) for the noun phrase in (45).

(48)

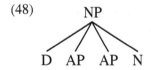

The structure of AP will be explained later in this chapter.

4.2.2.4 Determiner + noun + preposition phrase

The fourth type of noun phrase contains a determiner, a noun, and a preposition phrase. Preposition phrases are explained in section 4.2.4 below. In this section, let us just assume that preposition phrase is a phrase where a preposition appears: more specifically, a phrase where a preposition plays the head role. Examples of preposition phrases are *at the store, for twenty dollars*, and *between the lines*, among others.

A noun phrase can be followed by a preposition phrase, as in (49) and (50).

(49) the man in the black suit
(50) the book with the blue cover

The two noun phrases are explained by the rewrite rule in (51), which reads like "A noun phrase is composed of a determiner followed by a noun followed by a preposition phrase (PP)."

(51) NP → D N PP

The tree generated by the rule in (51) is diagrammed in (52).

(52)

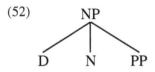

Similar to the case of APs, PPs can be repeated within one noun phrase. Let us take a look at the examples in (53) and (54).

(53) the man in black with a hat
(54) the book of linguistics with a red cover

Now it is obvious that (53) and (54) are not generated by the rule we formulated in (51) because there are two preposition phrases in each example. The remedy for this problem is very straightforward, though. Just like the example of AP, we can use the + symbol to allow a PP to be repeated within a noun phrase, which is shown in (55).

(55) NP → D N PP+

By using (55), a tree diagram for (52) is generated, as illustrated in (56).

(56)

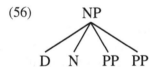

The structure of PP will be discussed in section 4.2.4.

4.2.2.5 Other noun phrases

Thus far, we have discussed four types of noun phrases. Readers should realize, however, that there are many more types of noun phrases. In this section, we will briefly discuss two types of relative clauses. Relative clauses are clauses that begin with a *wh*-word or *that*. Different from regular clauses, relative clauses cannot occur independently. Rather, they must be embedded within a noun phrase.

(57) the person [who she met]
(58) the person [who cries]

Both (57) and (58) are examples of a relative clause. However, (57) and (58) have somewhat different structures. In (57), the relative clause *[who she met]* modifies *the person*, and the function of *who* is an object of the relative clause. In (58), *[who cries]* modifies *the person* too, but the function of *who*, in this case, is the subject of the clause. That is, the original structure of (57) was like (59a). Then, *the person* was replaced with *who*, as in (59b). Next, *who* moved to the front position of the relative clause, yielding the acceptable noun phrase (59c).

(59) a. the person [she met the person]
     b. the person [she met who]
     c. the person [who she met]

Similarly, the original structure of (58) was like (60a). Then, *the person* is replaced with the relative pronoun *who*, as shown in (60b). Finally *who* moves to the front position of the relative clause, yielding (60c). Because *who* is already in the frontmost position in the relative clause, the movement becomes vacuous in this particular case.

(60) a. the person [the person cries]
     b. the person [who cries]
     c. the person [who cries]

In both cases, however, a clause is included in a noun phrase. To capture these types of noun phrases, we will have to formulate a rule like (61), where RC refers to a relative clause.

(61) NP → D N RC

Then tree diagram (62) is generated by (61).

(62)

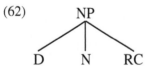

The internal structure of RC is not our concern at this moment. Nonetheless, readers are encouraged to see the difference between a relative clause and a normal clause (sentence). Although both a relative clause and a normal clause are sentences, they must have a different structure because we need an additional spot in the frontmost position of a relative clause to move a relative pronoun there. We will revisit this issue when we discuss sentence rules in section 4.2.6.

4.2.2.6 Optionality

When we formulated NP rules, we always included D (except for the case of proper nouns). This, of course, is not always necessary because noun phrases do not have to contain a determiner. As in (63), a common noun by itself can form a noun phrase without the help of a determiner. Without a determiner, an adjective followed by a common noun can also make a noun phrase, as shown in (64). (65) shows a similar case, where a determiner is still not required to form a noun phrase.

(63) people
(64) busy people
(65) people in black suits

In other words, the appearance of a determiner in a noun phrase is purely optional. This observation can be incorporated in our rewrite rules using the ( ) notation. To explain the use of the ( ) notation, let us consider (66). Superficially, (66) is very similar to the rule we formulated in (35). The only difference between (35) and (66) is the use of ( ). In (66), we simply added ( ) around D.

(66) NP → (D) N

The simple addition of ( ) is extremely useful in explaining several rules at the same time, which is something we do when we try to generalize a set of several sentences. As we know, ( ) means optionality. In other words, what (66) states is, "D might or might not be included in forming an NP." Although there is only one rule formulated in (66), (66) is in fact a shortened form of the two rules in (67a) and (67b).

(67) a. NP → N
b. NP → D N

The adoption of the ( ) notation can further simplify the noun phrase rules we formulated thus far. It is clear that both AP and PP are optional in a noun phrase. Without AP and PP, we can form a legitimate noun phrase. If we make D, AP, and PP all optional, the result would look like (68).

(68) NP → (D) (AP+) N (PP+)

(68) is clearly one rule, but it can be spelled out into a set of possible rules. The expanded forms of (68) are provided in (69a) to (69h). (68) is the result of combining all eight rules, a feat made possible by using the ( ) notation.

(69) a. NP → N
b. NP → D N
c. NP → AP+ N
d. NP → D AP+ N
e. NP → N PP+
f. NP → D N PP+
g. NP → AP+ N PP+
h. NP → D AP+ N PP+

The ( ) notation is a powerful technique, especially when you pursue brevity in formulating rules. As we saw in (69), however, the use of the ( ) might be somewhat confusing. If you add one more optional entity in (68), the number of the spelled-out rules will be 17: $(2 \times 2 \times 2 \times 2) + 1 = 17$. Readers should be aware of the potential complexity of the use of the ( ) notation. If you are not confident about the use of the ( ) notation, you don't have to use the notation when you formulate rules because notation itself does not have any theoretical value. The purpose of the notation is to make the rules "look" simpler.

When we used the ( ) notation in (68), we did not include the RC rule we formulated in (60) for the simplicity of exposition. However, (70) is an acceptable noun phrase to most native speakers, and so a PS-Rule like (71) can be formulated.

(70) the woman at the bookstore who I met
(71) NP → (D) (AP+) N (PP+) (RC)

Nonetheless, if we put (RC) before (PP), as in (72), the result is awkward. Therefore a PS-Rule like (73) must be avoided. Keep in mind that the PP *at the bookstore* modifies the noun *woman*. If you believe (72) is a perfect noun phrase, perhaps you interpreted the PP *at the bookstore* as modifying the verb *met*. If you are not sure about the notion of modification, you should wait until section 4.3, which deals with the notion of modification particularly in the context of tree diagrams.

(72) * the woman who I met at the bookstore
(73) * NP → (D) (AP+) N (RC) (PP+)

We have discussed noun phrases, their rules, and their tree structures in this section. The topic of the next section is verb phrases.

4.2.3 Verb phrases

4.2.3.1 Intransitive verbs

The name *verb phrase* tells us that the most important lexical item (head) in a verb phrase is a verb. Naturally, without a verb, a verb phrase cannot be formed. Similar to a noun phrase, a verb phrase can also be formed by only a single verb. In (74), the verb *went* in itself forms a verb phrase. Recall that a sentence is composed of a subject and a predicate. A subject is a noun phrase and a verb phrase is a predicate. In (74), the subject is *I*, and the predicate is *went*. As a subject, *I* must be a noun phrase in this case. Similarly, as a predicate, *went* must be a verb phrase.

(74) I *went*.

Based on this observation, our first VP rule would look like (75). (75) simply states, "A verb phrase is composed of a verb." Remember that the rule formulated in (75) does not include any subject. This rule only includes the VP (predicate) portion of a sentence.

(75) VP → V

The tree diagram generated by (75) is also very straightforward, as illustrated in (76).

(76)

4.2.3.2 Transitive verbs

The example we saw in (74) is the case of an intransitive verb, a verb that does not need an object. The case of a transitive verb is shown in sentence (77).

(77) John *loves Mary*.

The rule that explains the VP portion of (77), *loves Mary*, is formulated in (78). As we know, *Mary* is a noun phrase. When the verb *loves* is combined with its object *Mary*, the result is a verb phrase.

(78) VP → V NP
(79)

There is a special category of verbs called ditransitive verbs in English. Ditransitive verbs are similar to transitive verbs because they also require an object. Different from transitive verbs, however, ditransitive verbs require two objects. The verb *give* is a proto-typical example of an English ditransitive verb. As seen in (80), *give* requires two objects. The first object, *Mary*, is an indirect object, and the second object, *the book*, is a direct object.

(80) John *gave Mary the book*.

The appearance of two objects is explained by the rule in (81).

(81) VP → V NP NP

Some readers might wonder about the possibility of using the + notation to explain the occurrence of one or two NPs in the VP structure. The rule then would look like (82). This rule, however, does not accurately capture ditransitive verb structures. The + notation is used to explain at least one occurrence of NP. As a result, the rule in (82) can be extended with a theoretically unlimited number of NPs, which is not what we want for the NPs required by a ditransitive verb.

(82) * VP → V NP+

Now, generating a tree from rule (81) is simple. In this case, the mother, VP, has three daughters: V, NP, NP, as shown in (83).

(83)

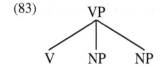

4.2.3.3 Verb + (noun phrase) + preposition phrase

A verb phrase can contain a preposition phrase, too. The italicized part of (84) is one example of a VP that contains a V followed by a PP.

(84) John *went to the store.*

The rule that explains (84) is formulated in (85). We will not show the tree structure here. By now, you can probably guess what it looks like after having seen many in the previous examples.

(85) VP → V PP

A PP can also appear with a transitive verb, as shown in (86), as well as with a ditransitive verb, as in (87).

(86) John *bought the purse at Kohl's.*
(87) John *gave Mary the book in the library.*

This observation enables us to formulate additional rules, like (88) and (89). Here, (88) explains sentences like (86), while (89) explains ditransitive sentences like (87).

(88) VP → V NP PP
(89) VP → V NP NP PP

As we explained in section 4.2.2.6, for the brevity of the rule formation, we might use the ( ) notation, as illustrated in (90).

(90) VP → V (NP) (NP) (PP).

Technically, this shortened form of the rule yields nine individual rules: $(2 \times 2 \times 2) + 1 = 9$. However, because we have two NPs in this particular case, the number of rules yielded by (90) is only six, as spelled out in (91).

(91) VP → V
        VP → V PP
        VP → V NP
        VP → V NP PP
        VP → V NP NP
        VP → V NP NP PP

Once again, if the ( ) notation is confusing, know that you do not have to use this notation. The purpose of the ( ) is to simplify the equation, much like in math class. The equation yields the same result as the extended form and only looks simpler.

The list of six rules in (91) is not an exhaustive list of possible VP structures. For example, PP can be indefinitely repeated within a VP, as shown in (92).

(92) Jane *bought a purse for $20 at Kohl's with the gift card...*

To allow the addition of PPs, we need to slightly modify the rule formulated in (90). This is an easy fix because we already learned about the + notation. The revised VP rule would look like (93).

(93) VP → V (NP) (NP) (PP+)

4.2.3.4 Adverb phrases within a VP

A VP can also contain an adverb phrase as in (94) and (95).

(94) John *went to the store quickly.*
(95) John *sleeps silently.*

To explain the occurrence of an adverb within a VP, we may formulate rules like (96) and (97) for (94) and (95), respectively. Because one adverb can be modified by another, what appears as a sister of V must be an AdvP (adverb phrase), instead of just an adverb.

(96) VP → V PP AdvP
(97) VP → V AdvP

It is worth noting, however, that the position of AdvP is very flexible within a VP, as illustrated in (98) and (99).

(98) John *quickly went to the store.*
(99) John *went quickly to the store.*

For this reason, we may state that an adverb phrase can appear in any position within a VP. However, there is one position where an adverb phrase can never appear within a VP, and that is between the two NPs in a ditransitive verb construction. Clearly, as we see below in (100), the sentence is not acceptable. Except for this one small exception, an adverb phrase can move around freely within a VP.

(100) * John *gave Mary quickly the book.*

To incorporate this observation, we may revise the VP rule in (93) as in (101).

(101) VP → (AdvP) V (AdvP) (NP) (NP) (AdvP) (PP+) (AdvP)

At first glance, the rule formulated in (101) looks very complicated, but what the rule states must be clear to readers at this point. All adverb phrases in (101) are within parentheses because all adverbs are optional.

4.2.4 Preposition phrases

We used PP for both noun phrases and verb phrases. As demonstrated, a PP can be contained within an NP as well as a VP. But the PP itself contains a noun phrase too. As illustrated in (102) to (104), what is followed by a preposition is not just a noun, but a noun phrase.

(102) over the hedge
(103) under the table
(104) for John

This observation makes it possible to formulate a rule like (105). Rest assured that P is followed by NP, not by D and N separately. Therefore, a rule like (106) is not accurate. When we write a rule, we always reflect the biggest units possible, like using NP in (105) as opposed to how D and N are used in (106).

(105) PP → P NP
(106) * PP → P (D) N

We know this because D and N can form one unit called a noun phrase. We also know this by the test for a phrase we discussed earlier. Both D and N can be replaced with one word, as shown in (107) to (109). If they can be replaced by one word, they must form one unit called a phrase.

(107) over where?
(108) under what?
(109) for whom?

The tree diagram generated by (105) would then look like (110).

(110)

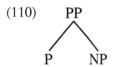

We now know the internal structure of NP, so we can show the full PP structure of the examples we discussed in (102) to (104). The structure of (102), for example, is provided in (111).

(111)

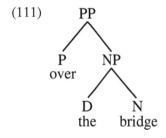

4.2.5 Adverb and adjective phrases

Adverb phrases and adjective phrases behave somewhat similarly. So some scholars choose not to make any distinction between the two phrases. Although there are clear theoretical and empirical justifications for that approach, we will adopt a traditional approach in which adverb phrases are distinguished from adjective phrases.

4.2.5.1 Adjective phrase

Naturally, an adjective phrase must contain one adjective to function as the head of the phrase. One adjective can form an adjective phrase, as in (112) and (113). Note that *changing* is an adjective because it modifies a noun, although it has the *-ing* form, which is often found in verb forms.

(112) a *wonderful* movement
(113) the *changing* situation

(112) and (113) can be explained by the simple rule in (114), where one adjective forms an adjective phrase in itself.

(114) AP → A

Within an adjective phrase, the head (adjective) can be modified by an adverb, as in (115) and (116). It will be clear to readers that *graciously* and *rapidly* modify *wonderful* and *changing*, respectively, in (115) and (116).

(115) a *graciously wonderful* movement
(116) the *rapidly changing* situation

This observation enables us to formulate an additional rule like (117). Because an adverb phrase may be optional in an adjective phrase, we might use the ( ) notation to collapse the two rules (114) and (117) into one shown in (118).

(117) AP → AdvP A
(118) AP → (AdvP) A

The tree diagrams generated by (118) will not be illustrated here because it should now be self-explanatory for readers.

4.2.5.2 Adverb Phrase

Just like the other phrases discussed thus far, an adverb phrase may contain only one adverb. For example, *graciously* and *rapidly* in (115) and (116) form an adverb phrase on their own. An adverb can also be modified by another adverb within one adverb phrase. In (119), the adverb *very* modifies the other adverb *graciously*. Similarly, *extremely* modifies the other adverb *rapidly* in (120).

(119) a *very graciously* wonderful movement
(120) the *extremely rapidly* changing situation

The multiple occurrences of adverbs within an adverb phrase are explained by (121). In (121), one adverb alone can form an adverb phrase, so we used the parenthesis notation to make AdvP optional.

(121) AdvP → (AdvP) Adv

Now using the rule in (121) and other previously formulated rules, let us generate a tree for the noun phrase in (119).

(122)

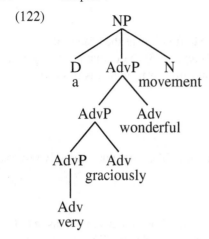

The rule formulated in (121) exhibits one very interesting property of language. In (121), AdvP is being rewritten by using itself. In other words, AdvP contains itself in its rewritten rule. This mechanism is called recursion. A similar type of recursion is found in the definition of factorial. Usually, when we define something, we must avoid using the defined notion in its definition. However, as shown in (123), the notion of factorial is wonderfully defined by using the same notion.

(123) $n! = n \times (n-1)!$

Recursion is a very powerful mechanism in explaining linguistic phenomena. In fact, recursion is everywhere in our language use. In (124), there are five occurrences of the adverb *very*.

(124) Today, I am very very very very very happy.

Theoretically speaking, we can extend (124) by adding the same adverb again and again. There is no maximum number of adverbs allowed in (124). In other words, (124) can be infinitely extended by repeating the adverb again and again. However, it does not mean we need an infinite number of adverb rules to explain the possibility. The infinite possibility is systematically explained by using the same rule we used in generating (122). This is possible because of the power of recursion.

4.2.6 Sentence rules

We have thus far discussed various rules for several phrases. However, none of the rules tell us anything about sentence formation. Although we know that *John* is an NP and *loves Mary* is a VP in (125), we do not have the rule that combines the NP and the VP to form a sentence.

(125) John loves Mary.

The sentence rule we have just addressed is formulated in (126), and the tree diagram generated by (126) for the sentence in (125) is provided in (127).

(126) S → NP VP
(127)

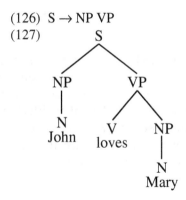

A sentence can contain an auxiliary verb such as *will*, *should*, and so on, right before the main verb, as shown in (128).

(128) John will love Mary.

To explain the occurrence of auxiliary verbs, we need to slightly modify the rule we formulated in (126) by adding Aux (Auxiliary Verb) between NP and VP. Because Aux is optional in a sentence, we can collapse (126) and (129) by using the ( ) notation, as shown in (130).

(129) S → NP Aux VP
(130) S → NP (Aux) VP

The tree diagram generated by the rule in (129) for the sentence in (128) is illustrated in (131).

(131)

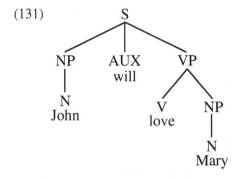

Sentence structures may become complicated when another clause is embedded within a phrase. In (132), the dependent clause *that Mary loves Bill* is embedded in the main clause (more specifically within the VP). To explain this type of embedding, let us take a look at (133), in which clauses are identified within sets of brackets. There are two clauses in (133), as illustrated by two sets of brackets. The bigger clause, called the main clause, is *[John believes…]*, while the smaller one, called the dependent clause, is *[that Mary loves Bill]*. The dependent clause is completely inside the main clause.

(132) John believes that Mary loves Bill.

(133) [John believes [that Mary loves Bill]].

This observation can be formulated as a pair of rules in (134). (134a) states that "VP is composed of a verb followed by S-bar," where S-bar is roughly the same as a dependent clause in our explanation. Although S′ is still a clause, it is different from S because S′ cannot stand alone, while S can stand alone because it is an independent clause. The other difference between S and S′ is that S′ is slightly bigger than S: S′ is composed of *that* + S, as shown in (133). In other words, S′ is composed of a complementizer followed by a sentence. Remember that, as we discussed in Chapter 3, the part of speech of *that* is a complementizer.

(134) a. VP → V S′

b. S′ → C S

When we utilize the two rules formulated in (134a) and (134b) in conjunction with other previously formulated rules, we can generate the tree diagram for (132), as in (135).

(135)

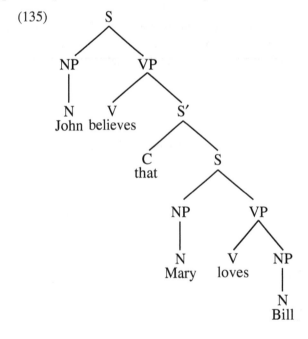

Readers should now realize that the rules we formulated in (134a) and (134b) also deal with recursion. One sentence (S) can contain another sentence (S′) again and again, as in (136)

(136) [John believes [that Mary believes [that Bill believes [that Tom loves Mary]]]].

Without formulating additional rules, (136) is explained by (134a) and (134b) in conjunction with the other rules we discussed.

We briefly discussed relative clauses in section 4.2.2.5. The structure of relative clause is strikingly similar to the S′ structure. Both the relative clauses and dependent clauses shown above are dependent clauses that cannot stand alone. They must be embedded within another phrase or clause. To explain the RC structures, we have formulated a rule like (137). The only difference between RC and S′ is that S′ is embedded within a VP, while RC is embedded in an NP.

(137) NP → D N RC

To capture the similarity between RC and S′, let us use a uniform notation for both S′ and RC by slightly changing the rule in (137) to (138).

(138) NP → D N S′

Then, the tree diagram for the noun phrase containing the relative clause *who she met* is generated as in (140).

(139) the person [who she met]
(140)

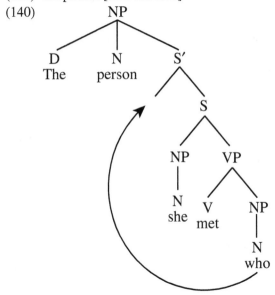

As we briefly explained in section 4.2.2.5, the base structure of (139) is (141a). After replacing *the person* in the dependent clause with *who*, as in (141b), *who* undergoes movement to the front position of the dependent clause, yielding (141c).

(141) a. the person [she met the person]
        b. the person [she met who]
        c. the person [who she met]

4.2.7 The conjunction rules

The last rule we will discuss is the conjunction rule. Here, conjunction includes *and, or, but*, and so on. Conjunction is a symmetric operation, where the left side of a conjunction marker must be the same as its right side. In (142), *but* conjoins the two sentences *John loves Mary* and *Mary loves Bill.* As a result, the left side of *but* is a sentence and the right side of *but* is also a sentence, which is explained in a rule like (143).

   (142) John loves Mary but Mary loves Bill.
   (143) S → S Conj S

   (144) is the tree diagram for (142), generated by (143) in conjunction with other previously formulated rules.

   (144)

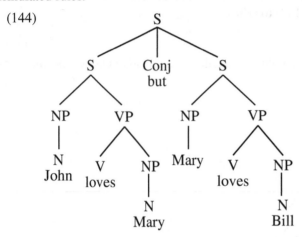

Conjunctions can also combine two noun phrases, as in (145). In (145), *and* conjoins two noun phrases *John* and *Mary.* The structure of (145) looks like (146).

   (145) John and Mary love Minnesota.
   (146)

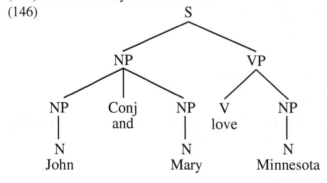

A conjoined phrase is not just limited to noun phrases. In fact, a conjunction can conjoin any phrases if the two phrases are the same type of phrase. (147) shows an example of conjoined verbs, and (148) is an example of a conjoined PP. (149) shows the case where two APs are conjoined.

   (147) John loves Mary or hates Bill.
   (148) John went to the store or to the beach.
   (149) The beautiful and charming lady collects fountain pens.

To explain every possible type of phrasal conjunction, let us introduce a rule with a variable. In (150), X is a variable that can be replaced with any constant that represents a lexical category such as A, N, P, and so on, yielding AP, NP, PP, and so on, respectively. By formulating a rule like (150), we can explain all possible conjunctions that combine two phrases.

(150) XP → XP Conj XP

Conjunctions, however, can combine two lexical items as well. As shown in (151), the conjunction *and* combines two verbs, *loves* and *hates*, instead of two verb phrases. Other lexical items can be conjoined by a conjunction too, as shown in (152) and (153).

(151) John loves and hates Mary.
(152) The pen and pencil set will make a nice gift for John.
(153) She is in and out of the office.

The tree diagram for (151) is provided in (154).

(154)

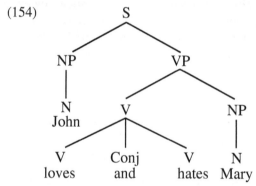

To explain the case of lexical conjunctions like (151) to (153), we can certainly formulate new rules like (155a) to (155c). These individual rules can be explained, however, by using a variable too, like (156).

(155) a. V → V Conj V
      b. N → N Conj N
      c. P → P Conj P
(156) X → X Conj X

Now, using the ( ) notation, we can collapse (150) and (156) into one rule, as in (157). Please note that the parentheses are around P, which in this case means *phrase*. So X can be just X or XP in this equation.

(157) X(P) → X(P) Conj X(P)

(157) states that two identical phrases or lexical items can be combined by a conjunction. The list of all possible conjunction rules then would look like (158).

(158) a. S → S Conj S
      b. S′ → S′ Conj S′
      c. X(P) → X(P) Conj X(P)

(158b) is a new addition, but readers should be aware that an S′ conjunction like (159) is not captured by either (158a) or (158c) because (158a) deals with two sentence conjunction only, and (158c) deals with all possible phrasal conjunctions.

(159) John believes that Mary loves Bill and that Bill loves Mary.

By introducing an additional rule like (158b), we can explain sentences where two S′s are conjoined together.

4.3 Modification And Disambiguation

Although we have discussed the necessary rules to generate many English sentences, it is not always easy to generate trees based on the given rules. For some readers, the difficulty might arise due to the lack of confidence in identifying parts of speech of the given lexical items. If you are still not confident about the identification of parts of speech, you should review the information presented in Chapter 3. The other possible reason for the difficulty is the identification of modification relations in a tree structure. For example, in (160), the PP, *for $1*, modifies the verb *bought*, while the PP, *on gardening*, in (161) modifies *a book*.

(160) John bought a book for $1.
(161) John bought a book on gardening.

How do we explain this modification relation in a tree diagram? This question is not at all easy, in particular for students who are taking linguistics for the first time. To clarify the modification relation, let us define the relation as in (162), using some variables.

(162) If α modifies β, α and β must be directly under γ, which is a mother of α and β.

Now let us illustrate how the definition works. In (160), let us assume that PP is α. Because the PP modifies the verb *bought*, *bought* is β. Because of the modification relation between PP and the verb, both PP and the verb must be directly under the VP, which is the mother of *bought*. (160) is different from (161) because the PP *on gardening* modifies the noun *book*. The same method applies here, though. The PP, *on gardening*, is α and the noun *book* is β because *on gardening* modifies *book*. Due to the modification relation between the PP and the noun *book*, both PP and the noun must be directly under NP, which is the mother of the noun *book*.

With the understanding of the modification relation, let us analyze sentence (163), which has two different meanings. The first meaning of (163) is "Mary killed the soldier and the killing was done by the gun," while the second meaning is "Mary killed the soldier and the soldier had the gun." Readers should keep in mind that these interpretations are two meanings acquired from sentence (163). In other words, the sentence does not change its word order and it does not need any additional words in its structure. The sentence, without any addition or change, has two different meanings. What this means is that sentence (163) has two different syntactic structures.

(163) Mary killed the soldier with the gun.

These two different meanings are systematically accounted for by two different tree diagrams. In (164), the PP, *with the gun*, modifies the verb *killed*. Therefore, the PP must be directly under VP, which is the mother of the verb *killed*. Because the PP modifies the verb, the interpretation of (164) is roughly "Mary killed the soldier and the killing was done by the gun." As you can tell by a simple comparison, the tree structure given in (165) is different from that of (164). (165) shows the case when the PP, *with the gun*, modifies the noun *soldier*. Because the PP modifies the noun *soldier*, both the PP and the noun must be directly under NP, which is the mother of the noun *soldier*.

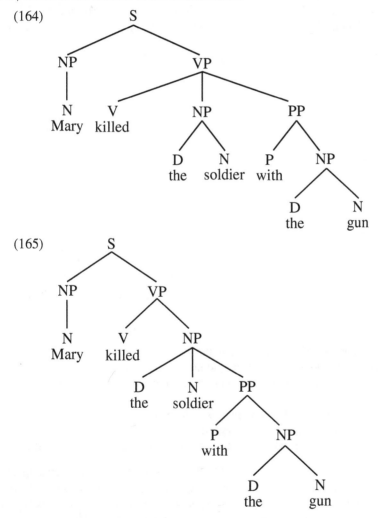

The identification of the modification relation we have just discussed is not just limited to the case of the PP modifications. An adjective phrase modifying a noun can be explained in exactly the same way. Because an AP modifies a noun, both the AP and the noun must be directly under NP, which is the noun's mother. An adverb phrase modifying a verb exhibits exactly the same situation. These cases will not be discussed in detail here, and these modification relations will be left as an exercise for readers.

4.4 Defining Trees

We have seen a number of sentence trees in this chapter. Although there are diverse types of trees, all of them exhibit some uniformity. In other words, only certain types of trees are generated, and not all tree shapes are acceptable. For example, a tree shaped like (166), where there are two mothers for C, is not allowed. A tree like (167), where there are crossing branches, is illegitimate as well. The * mark by the trees below shows that the trees are *not* acceptable.

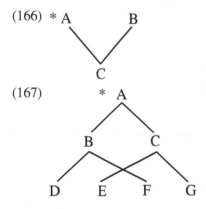

(166) * A   B

              C

(167)   * A

         B   C

      D   E   F   G

The rules we have formulated so far do not say anything about the exclusion of these types of trees. To exclude these types of trees and to generate well-formed trees, we need a solid definition of what a tree is and is not. Trees are defined in terms of two notions: domination and precedence.

(168) Domination
   a. α dominates β if and only if α is higher up in the tree than β.
   b. If α dominates β and β dominates γ, then α dominates γ.
   c. If α dominates β and γ dominates β, then either α dominates γ or γ dominates α.
(169) Precedence
   a. α precedes β if and only if neither α dominates β nor β dominates α.
   b. If α precedes β and β precedes γ, then α precedes γ.
   c. If α precedes β, then all nodes dominated by α precede all nodes dominated by β.

Let us explain these somewhat complicated definitions one by one, using the tree diagram in (170). First, (168a) states that α dominates β if and only if α is higher up on the tree than β. In this tree, the labels such as S_1, NP_1, VP_1, V_1, S', and so on, are called nodes. Now let us assume that the node VP_1 is α and the node S' is β. By definition (168a), VP_1 dominates S' because VP_1 is higher up than S' in (170). Second, (168b) states the transitivity relation in domination. Let us assume this time that S' is α, S_2 is β, and NP_2 is γ. S' dominates S_2 by definition (168a), and S_2 dominates NP_2 by the same definition. By definition (168b), we know that S' dominates NP.

(170)

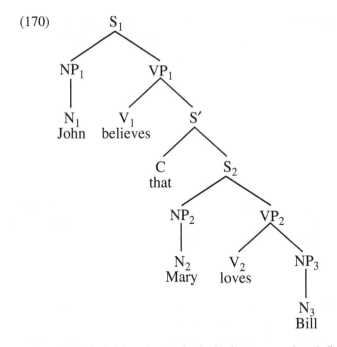

The third definition is particularly important for defining a well-formed tree. Let us assume that S_2 is α, VP_2 is γ, and NP_2 is β. In this case, S_2 dominates NP_3 by definition (168b), and VP_2 dominates NP_3. In this case, because S_2 dominates VP_2, the tree is well-formed. The reason why (168c) is important is because we have to exclude a tree like (171). In (171), β has two mothers: α and γ. Because there is no domination defined between α and γ, definition (168c) is not met. Therefore (171) is not a felicitous tree structure.

(171) An infelicitous tree

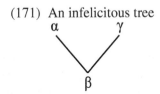

Let us now go over the definition of precedence. First, (169a) states that α precedes β if and only if neither α dominates β nor β dominates α. This means, when α precedes β, α and β must not be in the domination relation. In tree diagram (170), let us assume that NP_1 is α and that VP_1 is β. Because there is no domination relation between α and β, α precedes β. However, S_1 does not precede VP_1 because S_1 dominates VP_1. Definition (169b) explains the transitivity relationship in precedence. Definition (169c) states that if α precedes β, then all nodes dominated by α precede all nodes dominated by β. That is, for example, NP_2 in (170) precedes V_2, NP_3, and N_2. This is because NP_2 precedes VP_2 and VP_2 dominates V_2, NP_3, and N_2. We would like to emphasize the importance of this definition by showing an ill-formed tree structure like (172). In (172), E seems to precede F. However, (172) is illegitimate. Because B precedes C in (172), all nodes dominated by C must be preceded by B too. In this case, however, the node dominated by C (i.e., E) is not preceded by the node dominated by B (i.e., F). In fact, it is the other way around, making (172) an ill-formed tree structure.

(172) An ill-formed tree

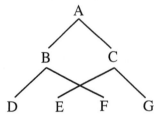

Although the definitions provided above look somewhat complicated, readers should understand why we have to define trees clearly. Trees are not random artistic drawings of sentences. Rather, they are mathematically constrained representations of sentences.

4.5 Sets Of Rules

Now that you have learned about rules and trees, it is time to put your knowledge to the test. As a basic exercise, an analysis of a set of sentences is often required for students who are learning trees and rules. Keep in mind that the word *set* here means that there is given data (generally a list of sentences) and that trees and rules generated from the set must denote all possible trees and rules for that data *only*. This may be hard to picture, so we will imagine that (173) is our set of data for analysis. In an actual set, you can have any number of sentences. For our purposes now, let us use this small set.

(173) a. Janie walks in the crosswalk to the store.
　　　 b. The dog barks at the squirrel.
　　　 c. Her careless brother broke the toy.
　　　 d. Martin ate seven warm cookies from the oven.

The way to begin an analysis of these sentences would be to tree them. Each sentence has its own sentence tree, and each terminal node (the bottommost node for each section with no nodes below it—also, the node that depicts the head of the phrase/part of speech) should have the corresponding word written below it. That way, the sentence can be read across the bottom of the tree (roughly) so you know which tree is which sentence at a glance. The next step is to write a set of rules that applies *only* to that one particular tree. For our case of four sentences, you should end up with four trees and four sets of rules. A set of rules should be all the rules it takes to generate the one particular tree. These sets of rules should *not* include any phrases or parts of speech not seen in that one particular sentence.

Let us make a set of rules for (173a) in (174).

(174) S → NP VP
　　　 NP → N
　　　 VP → V PP+
　　　 PP → P NP
　　　 NP → D N

Now that we have a set of rules for (173a), let us see how we can simplify them. Simplification streamlines the rule process a bit and makes a single equation more powerful and efficient. Note that in your list of rules for (173a), you have two NP rules that are different. By using the notion of optionality (notated by parentheses), you can turn these two NP rules into one rule to describe all NPs *in the given sentence only*.

Keeping in mind that the common factor in each rule is N and only N, that is, the one thing that we may *not* put in parentheses, N is not optional for this set of rules. As you may recall, N is the head of any NP, so therefore it is never optional. However, the point we are trying to make here is that we are generating a set of rules for a particular sentence only, so let us simply assume that any common factor between the two NP rules for (173a) is not optional. So you can simply condense the two rules into one NP rule.

(175) NP → (D) N

Again, if something doesn't appear in *all* the NP rules for a given sentence, it can be considered optional. Obviously, we can extend this kind of simplification process to other kinds of phrases, like VP, PP, and so on.

Now, let us look at the big picture, or rather, our set of four sentences. If we take this simplification process that we used for (173a) and apply it to *all* the rules from (173a) to (173d), we can come up with a set of rules that generates all four sentences. To do this, you need to look at all NP rules for all four sentences at once and note the commonalities. Remember to use parentheses to denote optionality, or rather items that appear in only *some* of the NPs. When you are done with NP rules, move on to VP, PP, and all other rules that apply to at least one of the four sentences. When you are done simplifying the entire set of rules, you should have fewer but more powerful rules that can generate all four sentences. Here is what the set of rules for our data set looks like.

(176) S → NP VP
       NP → (D) N
       VP → V (NP) (PP+)
       PP → P NP

As you can see, each of the rules here has the power to generate the phrases seen in the data set. Note that there is nothing unnecessary listed in the rules. For example, we do not have adverb phrases in our data set, so they do not appear in our rules. Our rules generate *only* our data set—they are not by any means rules to generate general NPs, VPs, and so on. Again, these rules are only for the given set of data.

Before we leave this chapter, it would be prudent to discuss some types of illegitimate PS-Rules. All phrase rules must contain one and only one head, which is directly dominated by its mother. For example, (177) is not an acceptable rule because there is no head, N, which is directly dominated by NP.

(177) * NP → D NP

(178) is not acceptable either because NP contains two heads.

(178) * NP → N N

This property of phrase rules is called endocentricity, which states that every phrase must have its head. For all the phrase rules we have formulated in this chapter, endocentricity was observed. Two sentential (clause) rules that we have provided in (179) and (180), however, do not have heads. This type of structure is called exocentric structure.

(179) S → NP VP
(180) S′ → C S

In Chapter 5, the clause rules will be revised so that endocentricity can be observed in all phrase and clause structures. Until then, readers should remember that endocentricity must be maintained in every phrase in formulating well-formed PS-Rules and trees.

4.6 Summary

We started this chapter by discussing two tests for phrases: movement and replacement. We formulated several rules for noun phrases, verb phrases, adjective phrases, adverb phrases, and preposition phrases. We also formulated rules for clauses, whether they are independent or dependent. In doing so, we discussed a very powerful mechanism called recursion and saw that we can theoretically generate an infinite number of sentences with finite rules because of the power of recursion. The tree generation processes from the rules we formulated have also been discussed. The definitions of trees are provided in the last section to filter out illegitimate tree structures. We will have to revise the rules we have formulated as we go because these rules are far from being complete. This reformulation is a necessary part of scientific reasoning.

4.7 Further reading

There are many well-written textbooks of syntax for beginning linguistics students. Perhaps the two most approachable books are Radford (1988) and Carnie (2007). These two books also deal with the X′ theory in detail, which is the topic of the next chapter of this book. Larson's (2010) book explains fundamental issues in syntax in a very approachable fashion. Readers who are curious about syntactic argumentation may refer to Soames and Perlmutter's (1979) book. This book introduces many interesting syntactic arguments for students of syntax. Napoli (1993) is written for the same purpose as that of Soames and Perlmutter (1979). Carnie's book (2008) on constituent structure will be of great help for students who want to delve into the notion of phrase and/or clause. For students who are interested in lexical categories, we recommend Baker (2003). Baker's book is not written for beginning students, but it contains a great amount of valuable information on lexical categories for many different languages from the formal linguistics perspective.

CHAPTER 5
Syntax II: X' Theory

Students in the college classroom often want to know definite answers for the fundamental questions in the subjects they deal with. When it comes to grammar, they tend to be less patient because answers don't always come easily. As we know, scientists are always formulating hypotheses and testing these hypotheses against a new set of data. They constantly need to revise their hypotheses to find a better explanation for a given phenomenon. Nevertheless, natural scientists don't know everything about nature. There are always new and exciting discoveries! Similarly, linguists don't know everything about language and its rules. We often need to revise what we once thought in order to get the best possible result: an answer that fits better than before. In Chapter 4, we formulated several rules as a way to get our brains to think logically. However, the rules we formulated have some problems. In this chapter, we will identify the problems with our previous rules, and then we will revise them, much like scientists do when testing and analyzing data.

5.1 Intermediate Phrases Within A Noun Phrase

Let us begin this section with one of the NP rules we formulated in Chapter 4. Rule (1) is a rule written for the NP in (2). It states that NP is composed of D, AP, N, and PP. The tree diagram generated by (1) for (2) would look like (3). In (3), you see several triangles. The triangle symbol is often used in a tree diagram to simplify the structure. Because the detailed internal structures of AP and two PPs are not our concern in this tree, we used the triangle symbols to show that the details of the smaller phrases don't matter for our present task. The triangle symbol is used just for the purpose of simplicity of exposition, without having any theoretical significance.

(1) NP → D AP N PP+
(2) the old book of linguistics without the dust jacket

(3)

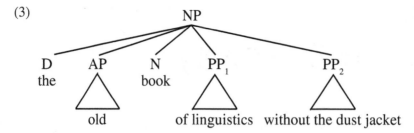

In (3), all five parts, D, AP, N, PP$_1$, and PP$_2$, form one big phrase: NP. In other words, all five parts together make one phrase. Any partial combinations of these components do not form one phrase because they are just parts of the phrase and because it takes *all* parts to make a whole. However, a closer examination shows the somewhat complicated structural patterns of (2). In (4) to (6), *one* replaces *book of linguistics, book of linguistics without the dust jacket*, and *old book of linguistics without the dust jacket*, respectively.

(4) the old *one* without the dust jacket
(5) the old *one*
(6) the *one*

Now, readers should recall one of the two tests for a phrase: replacement. If a group of words is a phrase, it can be replaced with one single lexical item. In examples (4) to (6), three different groups of words are replaced with a single lexical item: *one*. What this means is that *book of linguistics, book of linguistics without the dust jacket*, and *old book of linguistics without the dust jacket* must be phrases too. However, the tree diagram in (3) does not say anything about the three smaller phrases we have just observed within the NP. More technically speaking, this is because there is only one mother that contains all five parts, D, AP, N, PP$_1$, and PP$_2$, as its daughters. This is problematic because, as we have just observed, N, PP$_1$, and PP$_2$ must form one unit, dominated by a separate mother. How can we revise (3) to have a separate mother for N and PP$_1$? At first glance, it seems to be a somewhat difficult task, but it is not that hard if you examine the tree diagram given in (7).

(7)

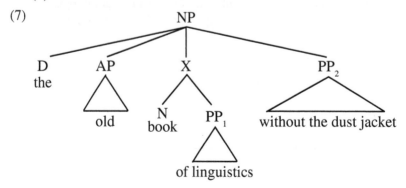

In (7), N and PP$_1$ have a separate mother called X, with X being a variable. Once we explained the case of (4), where N and PP$_1$ have their own separate mother, we can extend the same technique to (5), where N, PP₁, and PP₂ have their own mother. The tree diagram for this case is illustrated in (8).

(8)

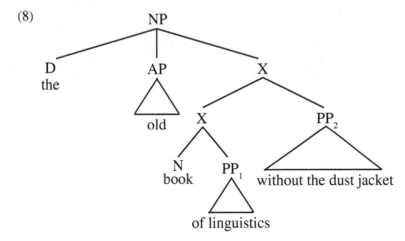

Now, as we saw in (6), AP, N, PP₁, and PP₂ can form one unit too, under their own mother. This observation is explained in a tree diagram like (9).

(9)

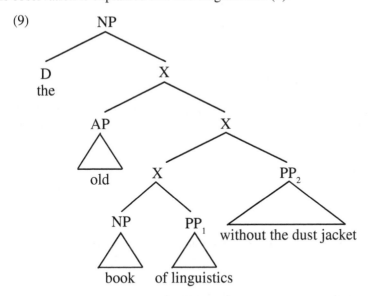

As we can see in (9), the tree diagram for the NP *the old book of linguistics without the dust jacket* has a hierarchical structure as opposed to a flat structure shown in (3) above. The newly provided structure in (9) clearly explains the intermediate phrasal structures of the NP better than our old structure, especially when modification is taken into account. Where PP₁ modifies *book*, the phrases share a mother. Where PP₂ modifies *book of linguistics*, the two phrases share a mother. With this new tree, it is much easier to see this relation. Until now, instead of giving the name of each intermediate phrase, we just used the general symbol X. Now let us give the intermediate phrases the new name N′, which is read N bar. With this new name, the tree diagram in (9) looks like (10). The theoretical reason behind the N′ notation is to provide intermediate space holders. NP is the same as N″ (N double-bar) and N is the same as N^0 (N zero-bar). Because the phrases we have discovered appear between N″ and N^0, it is natural to call the place holders N′. The introduction of the intermediate phrases serves to better show modification relations between phrases using binary branching, or branching that has a maximum of two branches from each node. Later, you will see how this theory takes into account many sentence constructions in English.

(10)

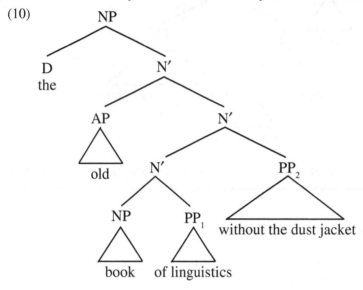

This newly provided structure tells us that there are three different layers in NP: NP–N′–N. As we observed, within one noun phrase, there must be one NP and one N. However, N′ can appear multiple times. The tree provided in (10) is generated by four rules in (11).

(11) a. NP → D N′
     b. N′ → AP N′
     c. N′ → N′ PP
     d. N′ → N PP

Unfortunately, the structure given in (10) has some problems in relation to the category D. This problem will be addressed in section 5.4.1, and its solution will be provided in the same section.

5.2 Intermediate Phrases In Other Types Of Phrases

We have just discovered that there are intermediate phrases, called N′, within a noun phrase. However, intermediate phrases are not just observed in noun phrases. A closer examination reveals that other phrases, such as VP, PP, AP, and AdvP, also have intermediate phrases within them. This is why the theory, X′, was named as such. With X as a variable, it could stand for any one of the lexical categories. In this section, evidence will be provided for the existence of intermediate phrases in phrases other than NP.

5.2.1 Verb phrase

To illustrate intermediate phrases within a VP, let us consider (12). The tree diagram for (12) looks like (13) according to the rules we formulated in Chapter 4.

(12) John studies linguistics at UMD.

(13)

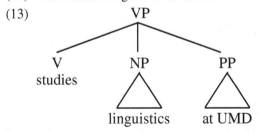

Now, let us extend (12) by conjoining the sentence with another sentence containing *does so*, as in (14). Here, even if *does so* is actually a two-word expression, let us simply assume that *does so* behaves like one word, just like *one* in noun phrase examples. In (14), *does so* replaces the VP, *studies linguistics at UMD*.

(14) John studies linguistics at UMD, and Jane does so, too.

A problematic case is (15), where *does so* replaces only a part of the VP, *studies linguistics*. This is problematic because *studies linguistics* does not form one phrase in our old tree illustrated in (13). The three parts, *studies*, *linguistics*, and *at UMD*, altogether form one big VP. Nevertheless, the observation made in (15) tells us that part of the VP, *studies linguistics*, must be a phrase, too, because it can be replaced with one word *does so*.

(15) John studies linguistics at UMD, and Jane does so at UMTC.

The solution we will adopt here is exactly the same as the one we found in the previous section: We need an intermediate verb phrase. Then the new structure for (12) looks like (16). In this case, X′ theory lets us see the modification relation between the PP, *at UMD*, and the verb, *studies*. As you recall, PPs can modify verbs or nouns. Whatever a PP modifies, it must share a mother with that entity.

(16)

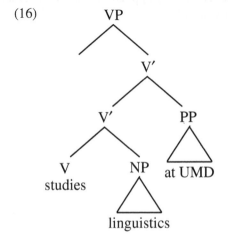

Although (16) is a VP structure, it closely resembles the NP structure illustrated in (10). Let us take a look at the rules that generate (16).

(17) a. VP → V′
      b. V′ → V′ PP
      c. V′ → V NP

Let's compare the rules formulated for VP in (17) and the rules for NP in (11). The two sets of rules exhibit remarkable similarities. First, both sets of rules have only three types of rules. The first type, seen in (11a) and (17a), is the XP → X′ type rule. The second rule is the X′ → X′ type, which is found in (11b), (11c), and (17b). The third is the X′ → X type rule in (11d) and (17c).

Another notable similarity is that a phrase that appears as a daughter of X′ and a sister of X′ is optional. In (11b) and (11c), both AP and PP are optional. Likewise, in (17b), PP is optional. Similarly D is optional in (11a), where D appears as a daughter of NP as well as a sister of N′. However, a phrase that appears as a daughter of V′ and a sister of V is not optional. That is, the PP in (11d) is required. The NP in (17c) is required because (17c) is a rule for transitive verbs. Considering all of these facts, we can provide a generalized set of rules for both NPs and VPs, as provided in (18). In (18), X, Y, and Z are all variables, and both YP and WP are optional, as notated by the ( ) symbol. The X′ → X′ type rule has two possibilities, as we saw in (11b) and (11c). In one case, the optional WP appears on the left side of X′, and in the other case, the optional WP appears on the right side of X′. To explain both possibilities, we simply listed two rules disjoined with *or*.

(18) a. XP → (YP) X′
      b. X′ → (WP) X′ or X′ (WP)
      c. X′ → X ZP

The two tree structures generated by the rules in (18) would look like (19) and (20). In (19) and (20), we have just assumed that both optional phrases, WP and YP, appear. Remember that the two structures given in (19) and (20) are not the only possible tree structures generated by the rules in (18). Because the X′ → X′ type rule can be recursively applied, the possible number of trees generated by the rules in (18) is theoretically infinite.

(19)

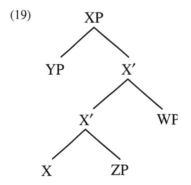

(20)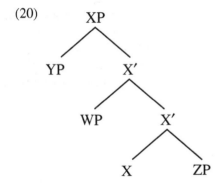

Even if the PP in (11d) and the NP in (17c) are required by their heads, noun and verb, respectively, not all nouns and verbs require PP and NP. For example, a transitive verb requires an NP, but an intransitive verb does not need an NP to form a VP. Similarly, not all nouns need a PP to form an NP. For this reason, we have to say that ZP in (18c) does not have to appear in some situations. To capture this observation, we may propose a maximally generalized version of the rules, as in (21). (21) is identical to (18) except for (21c), where ZP can be optional for certain lexical heads.

(21) a. XP → (YP) X′
     b. X′ → (WP) X′ or X′ (WP)
     c. X′ → X (ZP)

When YP, WP, and ZP above all do not appear, the rules generate a minimalistic tree diagram, as shown in (22). Although (22) looks somewhat odd, it fits the rules we have just formulated perfectly.

(22) 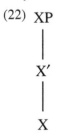 XP

Other phrases also exhibit the same structures, as will be discussed in the following subsections.

5.2.2 Preposition phrase

Preposition phrases exhibit the same properties as both noun and verb phrases. Let us consider (23), where the adverb phrase (AdvP), *right*, modifies the conjoined PP, *before the class and after the meeting*.

(23) Let us meet *right before the class and after the meeting*.

Intuitively, we know this because *right* does not modify only one preposition phrase. Rather, it modifies the combined preposition phrases. One possibility to capture this intuition is to provide a tree structure like (24). As you can guess by the * mark in (24), however, (24) is not an acceptable structure. Recall that the PP → AdvP PP type rule is not acceptable in our old rule system because the mother PP does not contain a head, a single P, directly under it.

(24)

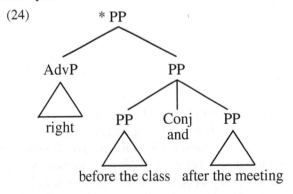

If we adopt the new rule system provided in (21), this problem is resolved without much effort. In (25), *before the class* and *after the meeting* are conjoined to form an intermediate phrase (P′). This intermediate phrase is then modified by the AdvP, *right*, to form a PP. Not only is the structure given in (25) perfectly explained by the newly formulated rules we made in (21), but it also captures our intuition that the AdvP modifies a conjoined PP. Remember that conjunction conjoins two identical categories, yielding the same category. In the case of (25), the conjoined PP is, in fact, the intermediate phrase P′. As a result, the conjoined P′ must have three daughters, where Conj is in the middle, between two P′s.

(25)

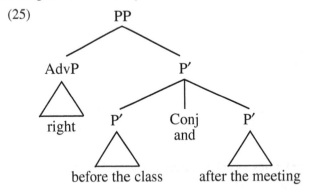

Another piece of evidence can be seen in (26), where the modifier phrase (MP) *three miles* modifies *down the road*, instead of the preposition *down* or the NP *the road*. For the same reason as the unacceptability of (24), the PP → AdvP PP rule is not acceptable because there is no head within the mother PP. When we adopt the new rules in (21), the problem is naturally solved, as shown in (27).

(26) The gas station can be found *three miles down the road*.

(27)

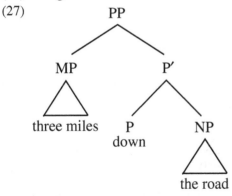

In (27), the MP, *three miles*, modifies the intermediate phrase, *down the road*. The structure generated in (27) also fits the rules formulated in (21) perfectly.

5.2.3 Adjective phrase and adverb phrase

Both adjective and adverb phrases illustrate a very similar problem to the ones we have already discussed. In (28), the adverb phrase *very* may modify the conjoined AP, *good and bad*, although it may modify either *good* or *bad* only in a certain context. Similarly, (29) shows the case where the adverb phrase *very* modifies the conjoined AdvP *wonderfully and graciously*.

(28) The new method might be *very good and bad*.
(29) Your speech was delivered *very wonderfully and graciously*.

This raises the same question we faced in analyzing the sentence in (23). In the case where *very* modifies a conjoined phrase, we need an intermediate phrase that combines two adjective (or adverb) phrases, which is then modified by the adverb phrase *very*. The AP structure of (28) is shown in (30), and the AdvP structure of (29) is shown in (31).

(30)

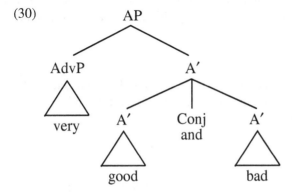

(31)

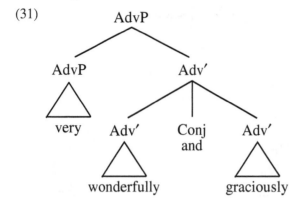

We have shown several supporting pieces of evidence for the X′ rules we formulated in (21). In the following section, we will discuss a set of schemata abstracted as generalized forms of X′ rules.

5.3 X′ Schemata

In this section, we will discuss the generalized X′ schemata that generate well-formed syntactic structures in English. Before we provide the schemata, we will have to discuss the distinction between complements and adjuncts, which is a very important distinction in dealing with the X′ structures.

5.3.1 Complements versus adjuncts

Let us take a look at (32) and (33). For most native speakers of English, (33) is not acceptable because the direct object of the verb *hit* is missing. As a transitive verb, *hit* requires a noun phrase that functions as a direct object. In (32), the direct object *John* is selected by the transitive verb *hit*. When selected by a verb, the selected phrase is called a complement of the verb. In other words, *John* is a complement of the verb *hit* in (32); by selecting the noun phrase *John*, the VP is completed. (33) is not acceptable because there is no noun phrase selected by the verb. Because this particular verb must select a noun phrase to complete the VP, it becomes unacceptable. In other words, a complement is missing in (33), yielding an unacceptable sentence.

(32) Jane hit John.
(33) * Jane hit.

As we all know, not every phrase is required by a verb. Sentence (34) contains the PP, *with the bat*. The PP, however, is not required, as shown in (35), where the PP is missing without affecting the acceptability of the sentence.

(34) Jane hit John with the bat.
(35) Jane hit John.

The PP, *with the bat*, is called an adjunct of the verb *hit*. Unlike complements, adjuncts are not required to complete a VP. Without the adjunct, the VP is still complete. In this sense, we can state that complements are required and that adjuncts are optional.

The distinction between complements and adjuncts is not limited to verb phrases only. Other phrases also exhibit the same type of distinction. For example, the noun phrase illustrated in (36) shows the distinction too.

(36) the student of linguistics from South Korea

In (36), there are two PPs related to the head noun, *student*. However, the first PP, *of linguistics*, is a complement of the noun *student*, while the second PP is an adjunct of the noun. The reason why *of linguistics* is a complement is that the PP explains what the student studies, which is a required piece of information for the noun *student*. By contrast, the PP, *from South Korea*, does not say anything about what the student is studying. The PP is just an additional piece of information about the student. The other piece of evidence for the complement status of *of linguistics* is coming from the clausal paraphrase of (36), as in (37). In (37), *linguistics* is a complement of the verb because the verb *studies* selects the noun phrase, *linguistics*. Once again, in (37), the PP, *from South Korea*, is just additional information about *the student*, without being a required phrase.

(37) The student from South Korea studies linguistics.

Now that we made a distinction between complements and adjuncts in noun and verb phrases, we can extend the same distinction to other phrases. As we identify complements and adjuncts, readers should rely on the criterion we have just used: optionality, for adjuncts.

In (38), the AP, *old*, functions as an adjunct within the noun phrase *old ladies* because the AP, *old*, is not required. Without the AP, we can still make a complete noun phrase. Similarly, in the AdvP in (39), the modifying AdvP, *very*, is not required because, without modification, *wonderfully* can form one adverb phrase.

(38) old ladies
(39) very wonderfully

More detailed properties of complements and adjuncts will be provided in the following section. We hope that readers have a general understanding of the distinction between complements and adjuncts by now.

5.3.2 Complements and adjuncts in X′ structures

In a previous section, we formulated a set of X′ rules in (21). For the sake of convenience, we will reintroduce the same rules below.

(40) a. XP → (YP) X′
      b. X′ → (WP) X′ or X′ (WP)
      c. X′ → X (ZP)

From these rules, we can generate two types of trees, as illustrated in (41) and (42). In both cases, (40a) and (40c) are applied without making both YP and WP optional. In other words, we have simply assumed that everything possible appears in the trees below. The only difference between (41) and (42) is the location of WP. In (41), the second rule of (40b) is applied, and the first part of (40c) is applied in (42). These two generalized tree structures are often called X′ schemata. In (41) and (42), first, YP is generated as a daughter of XP and a sister of X′. Second, WP is generated as a sister of X′ and a daughter of X′. Third, ZP is generated as a sister of X and a daughter of X′. In these configurations, YP is called a specifier, WP an adjunct, and ZP a complement.

(41)

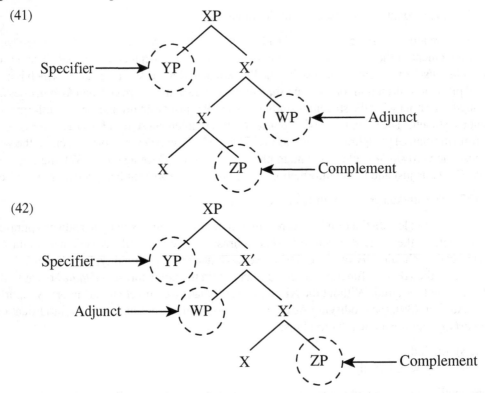

(42)

These structures can be extended by allowing multiple X′ layers, as shown in (43). This potentially unlimited extension is possible because of (40b). In (40b), X′ includes another X′, which allows a recursive extension of the X′ layer. As a result of the X′ extension, (43) has two adjuncts: WP$_1$ and WP$_2$.

(43)

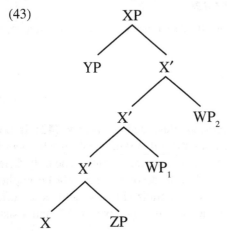

One very interesting property of the X′ structures we can generate from the rules in (40) is that there may be many adjuncts in one tree structure, while there must be only one complement within one phrase, if any. This is because the recursive application of the X′ rule generates multiple positions for an adjunct, while there is only one complement position available in any tree generated by the rules in (40). Based on this observation, we can summarize the properties of complements and adjuncts, as in (44).

(44) Complements versus Adjuncts
    a. Complements are required, while adjuncts are optional.
    b. Complements cannot be repeated in a single phrase, while adjuncts can be.

For beginning linguistics students, the distinction between complements and adjuncts is not always clear-cut. The same expression can often be used as an adjunct in one context, but as a complement in the other. Let us consider (45) and (46) below.

(45) John sleeps on the couch.
(46) John put the wine glass on the couch.

The same PP, *on the couch*, has different functions in (45) and (46). While *on the couch* in (45) is an adjunct, it is a complement in (46). We encourage readers to recall the two properties provided in (44) to identify the PP's function. In (45), *on the couch* is optional. Without the PP, (45) is a fully acceptable sentence, and the VP is complete because of the intransitive verb *sleeps*. By contrast, *on the couch* in (46) is required because the verb *put*, as a ditransitive verb, requires one NP and one PP. In (45), other PPs that modify the verb *sleeps* can be easily added to provide more information to the listener, as in (47). However, any additional PP that modifies the verb *put* yields an unacceptable result, as in (48). Remembering the two properties will be very useful when we draw trees using X′ theory.

(47) John sleeps on the couch in the living room at my brother's house.
(48) * John put the wine glass on the couch on the table on the chair.

5.4 Functional Categories

We have thus far discussed several phrasal structures that include NP, AdvP, AP, VP, and PP. In this section, we will discuss three additional phrases: DP, TP, and CP.

5.4.1 DP

Let us recall the X′ rules we formulated in (21) and (40). Let us also recall the NP structure within X′ theory. There is a clear mismatch between the first X′ rule (XP → (YP) X′) and the NP structure we demonstrated. The structure we used in explaining noun phrases looks like (49), which is the same example as (10) above, just reintroduced. In (49), D is generated as a daughter of NP and as a sister of N′. In other words, D is generated in the YP position in the rule formulated in (40a). Although (40a) states that the specifier of NP must be a phrase, as identified by P in YP, what actually appears in (49) is D, instead of a phrase. In other words, the NP structure provided in (49) does not conform to the rule or the schemata we have discussed so far. We can certainly fix this problem by proposing a structure like (50).

(49)

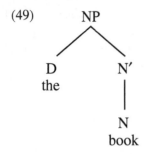

(50)

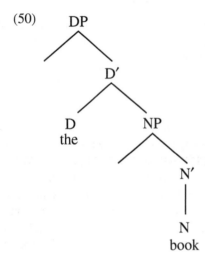

Different from (49), (50) has one more layer on top of NP. (50) also shows that D is actually the head of a higher structure than NP. This solution seems to resolve the issue raised earlier. But the question we have to consider is, Is there any evidence for the structure provided in (50)? Without answering this question, our solution provided in (50) will be unmotivated. In fact, there is some strong evidence for the DP structure we have just posited. As shown in (51) and (52), both *his book* and *the man's book* are acceptable noun phrases in English. However, when we try to use both *'s* and *his*, as in (53), the result is not acceptable. What these examples reveal about the property of *'s* is that *'s* appears in the D position. This is further supported by the example in (54). In previous chapters, to explain this type of property, we used the Spider Man analogy. When Spider Man appears on the crime scene, the photographer, Peter Parker, disappears. When Peter Parker is on the scene, Spider Man cannot be there. This is because Spider Man and Peter Parker are the same person, although superficially they look drastically different.

(51) his book
(52) the man's book
(53) * the man's his book
(54) * the his book

This observation supports the claim that *'s* must be generated under D, as in (55). The modifying DP, *the man*, in (52) then appears in the specifier position of the higher DP.

(55)

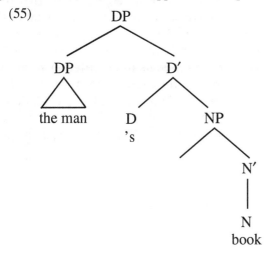

The complicated structure *John's destruction of the city* has the structure shown in (56). In (56), *'s* is generated under D and the DP *John* appears in the specifier position of the higher DP. The noun *destruction* is generated under N, and the PP is generated as a sister of N and as a daughter of N′, making the PP the complement of the noun *destruction*.

(56)

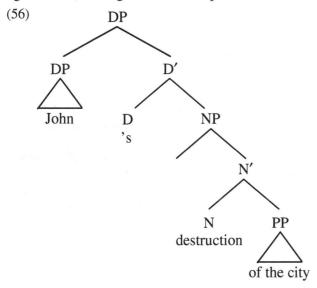

The DP we have just discussed in (56) resembles a clausal structure because *John* behaves like an agent of the destroying action, and the PP *of the city* completes the noun *destruction*. The parallelism between the DP structure in (56) and that of its clausal counterpart *John destroyed the city* gives us some idea that the sentence structure needs to be modified, which is explained in the following section.

5.4.2 TP

As we have just seen, the DP *John's destruction of the city* has a great similarity to its clausal counterpart *John destroyed the city*. In the DP structure, *John* is an agent of the action, and *of the city* is a complement of the head noun *destruction*. In the clausal structure, we know that *the city* is a complement of the verb, and *John* is an agent. Nonetheless, the current tree diagram for the clausal structure seems to be different from (56) except that *the city* is a complement of the verb, as illustrated in (57). In (56), *John* appears in the specifier position of the higher DP, and D is the head of the whole DP. However, *John* in (57) is generated directly under S, as a sister of VP. In addition, there is no head for the clause in (57). This is why our old way of drawing trees, as in (57), needed improvement.

(57)

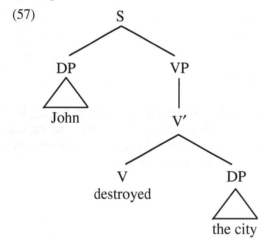

There is a surprising similarity between (56) and its clausal structure, so we may naturally raise the question, Is there any way to capture the similarity between DP and its clausal counterpart? This question is answered by positing another layer called TP (tense phrase) on top of VP, as illustrated in (58), which is completely analogous to the DP solution we provided in the previous section. In (58), *John* is now generated in the specifier position of TP, and the head of the TP is T, which is a tense marking such as *-ed* and *-s* in English. Because we are dealing with a past tense sentence in (58), the head T carries the tense information, which is notated [+past]. The tense morpheme is later lowered to the verb to yield a declarative sentence. The tense-lowering mechanism will be explained in more detail in section 5.5.

(58)

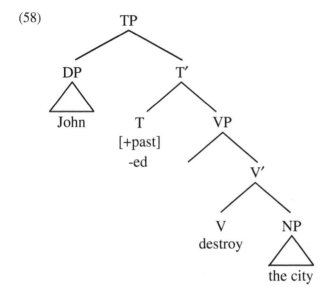

The revised clausal structure not only captures the parallelism between (56) and its clausal structure, but it also fits the generalized X' schemata provided in (41) and (42), without making a sentence structure exceptionally exocentric. In (58), VP is a complement of T, and NP is a complement of V. The subject DP, *John*, is generated in the specifier position of TP, and T is the head of the sentence.

5.4.3 CP

Readers might wonder about the S' structure we discussed in Chapter 4. In Chapter 4, we analyzed *that Mary loves Bill* as an S' structure, which is embedded in the main clause as in (59).

(59) John believes that Mary loves Bill.

The rule we used to explain the S' structure is reintroduced in (60). Now that we are using the notation TP instead of S, we should use (61) instead of (60).

(60) S' → C S
(61) S' → C TP

Unfortunately, (61) does not fit the generalized X' schemata shown in (41) and (42). There is no head in (61), and there is no potential specifier position generated. Fixing (61) to make it conform to the X' schemata is not difficult. Just like the cases of DP and TP, we can posit another layer, called CP, on top of TP. Here, let us say that CP stands for complementizer phrase. Then the tree diagram for the dependent clause *that Mary loves Bill* would look like (62). Just like other phrases we have discussed so far, CP contains a specifier position, which is not saturated by any phrase in this particular case.

(62)

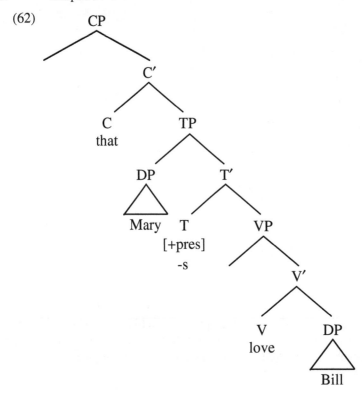

When you embed (62) within a VP, you get the full tree structure for (59), as shown in (63). In (63), the dependent clause *that Mary loves Bill* appears as a complement of V, which is an accurate description of the CP. The CP must be a complement of V because it completes the VP, in this particular case, as a required phrase for the V *believes*. The sentence shown in (63) has two TPs, and hence there must be two Ts that carry a tense marking. Both Ts carry the present tense marking -*s* in this case, and it must be lowered to its corresponding verb to yield an acceptable surface structure.

(63)

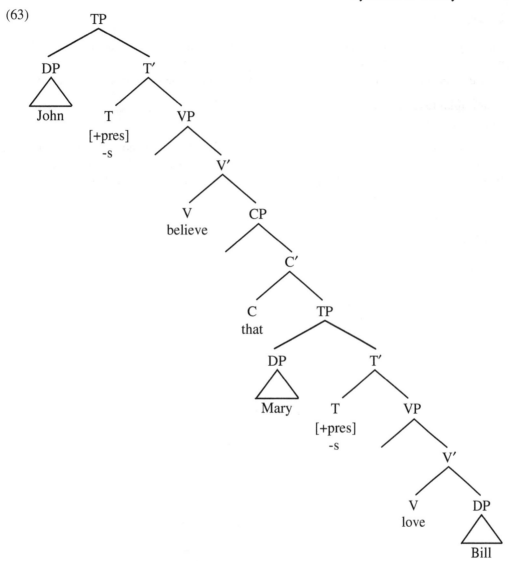

At first glance, the tree diagram illustrated in (63) looks very complicated. However, readers should be aware that the tree is much more systematic than the old trees we used in Chapter 4. First, the tree in (63) is essentially a binary branching tree. Each node has only (or at most) two daughters. Second, all XP structures have three layers: XP–X′–X. In this sense, the tree structure provided in (63) is highly constrained when compared to our old trees introduced in Chapter 4. For this reason, drawing X′ style trees might not be too difficult for readers after some familiarization with the basic schemata and some example structures we have discussed already.

5.5 Deriving Interrogative Sentences

We already know that (64) and (65) are closely related. More specifically, we know intuitively that they share some kind of similarity. In linguistics, we say that they share the same *base structure*. This intuition is now systematically accounted for by the structures we have discussed.

(64) John loved Mary.
(65) Did John love Mary?

First, the base structure for (64) is provided in (66). Although there is no visible C in this particular case, let us assume that the sentence starts with CP instead of TP. The evidence for this will be discussed right after illustrating the interrogative sentence from its base.

(66)

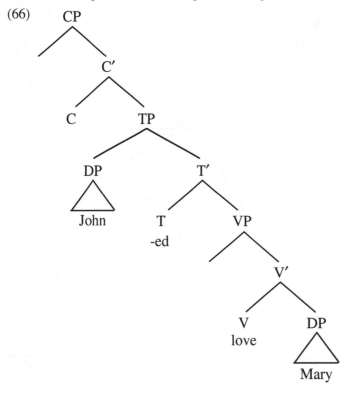

In (66), the past tense morpheme, *-ed*, is generated under T. However, as a bound morpheme, *-ed* must be attached to a verb in English. To fulfill this morphological requirement, the tense morpheme is lowered to the verb, yielding (64). The mechanism is illustrated in (67).

(67)

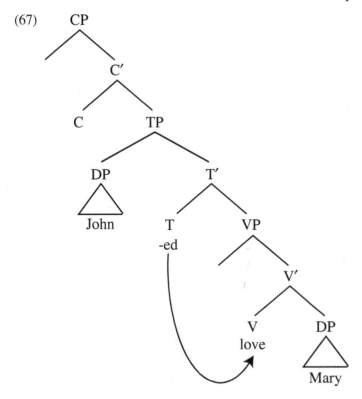

The interrogative sentence in (65) is derived from the same base structure illustrated in (66). Here, the assumption we have to make is that an interrogative sentence is derived from its base by moving the tense morpheme, *-ed*, under T to the empty position under C. When we directly move *-ed* to the C position, however, the result is not acceptable, as in (68). The reason seems to be obvious. As we discussed in Chapter 2, *-ed* is a bound morpheme. Bound morphemes cannot stand alone; they need to attach to a host.

(68) * -ed John love Mary?

The solution to this problem of the bound tense morpheme is to insert some kind of dummy word. In English, *do* functions as a dummy word without having a salient meaning. As illustrated in (69), first, the dummy verb *do* is inserted (a process called *do*-support) to rescue the bound tense morpheme, *-ed*. Second, *do* and the past tense morpheme are combined to yield the irregular verb form *did*. As a result, we acquire a free tense marked morpheme. Finally, we move *did* under T to the empty spot under C to derive the expected interrogative sentence *Did John love Mary?*

(69)

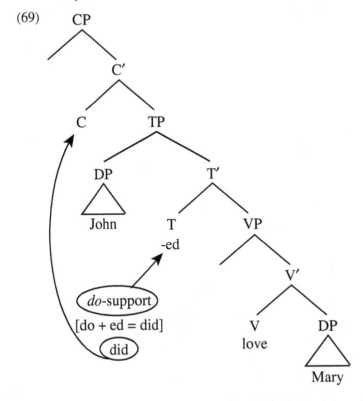

To summarize, the interrogative sentence in (65) is derived from its base, illustrated in (69) by the following three steps.

(70) Interrogative derivation
   Step 1: Insert *do* (*do*-support) to the T position.
   Step 2: Apply morphological operations. ("*do* + tense morpheme" undergoes necessary morphological operations)
   Step 3: Move the result of step 2 under T to the empty position under C.

We have just assumed that all sentences start with a CP instead of TP, although there is no visible element under C or in the specifier position of CP. This choice helped us explain the derivation of an interrogative sentence from its base. Is there other evidence to support the claim that all sentences should start with a CP, whether they have a visible C or not? The answer is yes. (71) shows a case of clausal conjunction, where two sentences are conjoined by *but*. Let's assume that a sentence starts with a TP, when there is no visible C. Then, the first clausal conjunct of (71), *I remembered to lock the door*, is a TP because there is no visible C. However, the second clausal conjunct of (71), *did you remember to lock the window*, clearly requires a CP structure because the position of *did* is under C, as we illustrated above. As we discussed in various places in this book, a conjunction must be symmetric; the two parts being conjoined must be of the same phrase type. If the left conjunct is just a TP, as opposed to a CP, (71) becomes an asymmetric conjunction, as illustrated in (72). Because a conjunction requires two like entities on either side, this is unacceptable.

(71) I remembered to lock the door, but did you remember to lock the window?

(72)

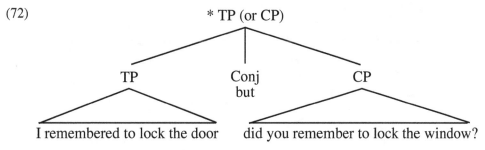

The observations show that positing a CP structure for all sentences is not just a theoretical convenience, but it is also based on empirical justifications.

5.6 Spanish Interrogatives

Although we have generally avoided using data from outside English thus far, now is a good time to briefly discuss the case of Spanish interrogative sentences, which have both similarities and differences to their English counterparts. By discussing some Spanish examples, readers will understand that the interrogative derivation mechanism we have discussed is not just limited to one particular language. Rather, it seems to be a somewhat general rule, which can be applied to many languages. (73) is a Spanish sentence meaning "Juan writes the book," (74) is an interrogative version of (73). When linguists deal with non-English data, they often follow the three-line convention seen below. Take (73), for example. The first line is the target sentence in Spanish. The second sentence is word-by-word translation of the Spanish sentence, called a gloss. The third line is the English translation of the target sentence.

(73) Juan escribe un libro.
Juan writes a book.
Juan writes a book.

(74) ¿Escribe Juan un libro?
write Juan a book
Literal: "Writes Juan a book?" Translation: "Does Juan write a book?"
or "Is Juan writing a book?"

One noticeable difference between English and Spanish in the formation of an interrogative sentence is the existence of the *do*-support mechanism. While English utilizes the *do*-support mechanism to rescue the bounded tense morphemes, Spanish just moves the verb to the C position. To explain this in more detail, let us look at (75), which is the base structure for both (73) and (74). (75) is almost identical to its English counterpart except that there is no specified morpheme under T. Unlike English, it is not always straightforward to identify the present tense morpheme in Spanish because there are many options for various pronouns. As a result, the T position is just provided with the [+pres] information.

(75)

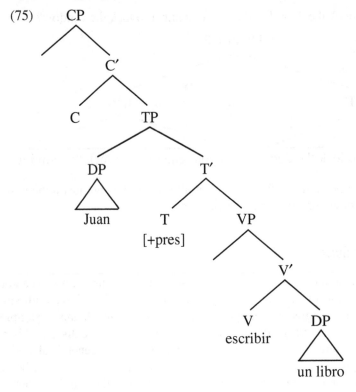

Different from English, however, the infinitive verb *escribir* is raised to the T position to be realized as a present tense third person singular verb *escribe*, as in (76). Recall that the *do*-support mechanism was adopted to rescue the bound tense morpheme in English. Instead of adopting the *do*-support mechanism, the choice made in Spanish is to move the verb directly to the T position. Nonetheless, in both cases, the motivation seems to be clear: The tense morpheme must be combined with the verb. Because there is no visible tense morpheme generated under T, moving the verb directly to the T position seems to be a reasonable choice in Spanish.

(76)

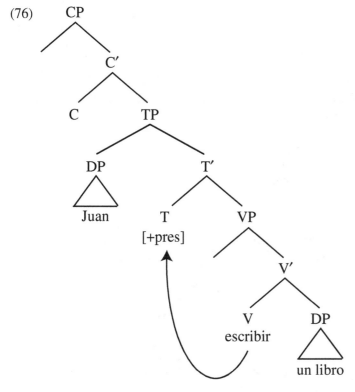

As a result of the V raising to the T position, the fully inflected verb *escribe* now appears in the T position. In the previous section, we assumed that an interrogative sentence is formed by moving everything under T to the C position. We can apply the same assumption to (76). In this case, the present tense marked verb is under T, and we have to move the verb to the C position, yielding the expected interrogative sentence in (74). The final movement of the verb from the T to the C position is depicted in (77).

(77)

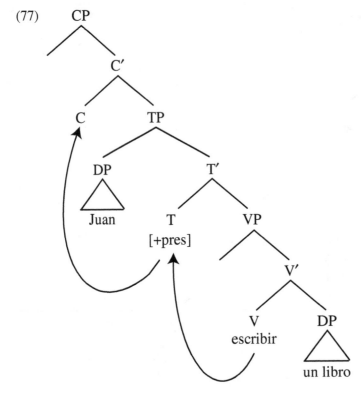

Although there are some differences between English and Spanish in explaining their interrogative sentence formation, we basically adopted the same mechanisms to explain both languages. First, the verb and the tense marking must be combined at the T position (V to T movement). Then everything under T moves to the C position (T to C movement) to make an interrogative sentence. The only difference between English and Spanish is that English adopts the *do*-support mechanism, while Spanish moves the verb directly under V to the T position. The movement mechanism illustrates the interrogative sentence formation in these two seemingly different languages in a uniform way.

5.7 *Wh*-Movement

Another interesting phenomenon concerning a movement mechanism is *wh*-movement, where a *wh*-word such as *what* or *who* moves to the front position of a sentence. In (78), we know that *who* is actually a direct object of the verb *love*. Therefore, it is not hard at all to reconstruct the original position of *who*. The *wh*-word *who* must have been generated as a complement of the verb *love* because a direct object is selected by a transitive verb. If we push *who* back to its original position, the result would look like (79). Here, we also know that *did* is a result of a movement from T to C in order to form an interrogative sentence from its base, which looks like (80).

(78) Who did you love?
(79) Did you love who?
(80) You -ed love who.

Put differently, (80) is the base structure for both (78) and (79). The tree diagram for the base structure, which is illustrated in (81), should not be hard for readers to develop.

(81)

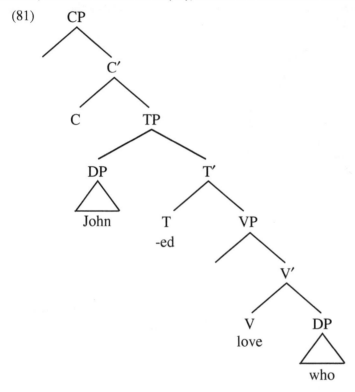

From the base structure in (81), the intermediate interrogative sentence is first derived, as shown in (82). Recall that *do*-support must apply to rescue the bound tense morpheme *-ed* before we move everything under T to the empty position under C. The example in (82) demonstrates the derivation of (79).

(82)

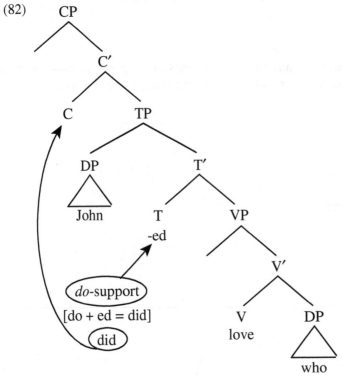

Finally, the *wh*-word, *who*, moves to the specifier position of CP, which is not filled by any element, yielding (78). The derivation processes for (78) are illustrated in (83).

(83)

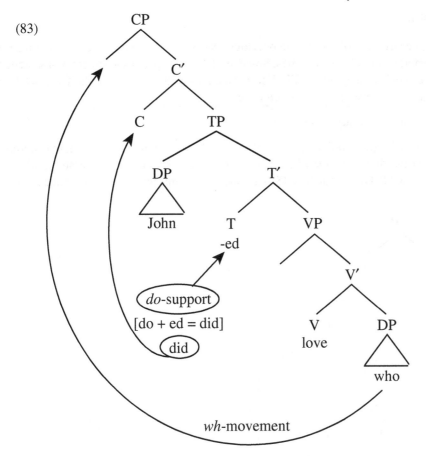

wh-movement

These mechanisms explain the derivation processes of both non-*wh*- and *wh*-question sentences systematically. Nonetheless, we have to answer one question to provide a more solid analysis of interrogative and *wh*-question constructions. The question is, Why do some things move to make question sentences in English? Linguists' answer for this question is intriguing enough: They argue that the C head carries features like [+Q] and [+Wh], which are analogous to magnets in some sense. The former attracts everything under T to make a question sentence, while the latter attracts a *wh*-word from down in the tree structure. The difference between the two features is that the [+Q] feature attracts everything from T to C, while the [+Wh] feature attracts a *wh*-word and has it pass the C position eventually to make it land in the specifier position of CP. These types of explanations are generally understood as mainstream analyses of question sentences and are still adopted with various types of modifications even in the most recent syntactic analyses of interrogative sentences. No matter what the explanations are, readers should be aware that the movement mechanisms we have discussed are not random. The mechanisms are clearly motivated and explainable.

5.8 More On CP

Now we know the structure of CP. In the previous section, we discussed the case when a CP appears as a complement of V. Sometimes, however, CP can appear as a subject of a sentence, appearing in the specifier position of TP. Let us take a look at (84), where the CP *That John loves Mary* functions as a subject of the sentence.

(84) That John loves Mary takes effort.

The structure for (84) would look like (85). (85) seems to be complicated, but there is nothing mysterious about the diagram. Just like a DP subject, the CP subject is generated under the specifier position of TP. Other than this, (85) is exactly the same as the plain sentence *Reading takes effort.*

(85)

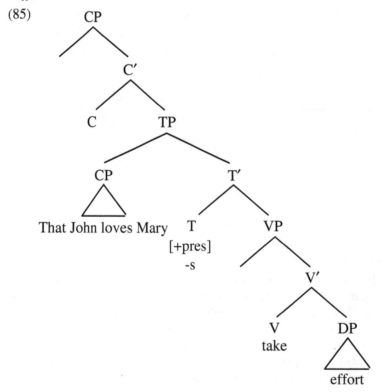

The base structure of the CP subject *That John loves Mary* is illustrated in (86). Obviously, to derive the full clause, the present tense marking *-s* must be lowered to the verb.

(86)

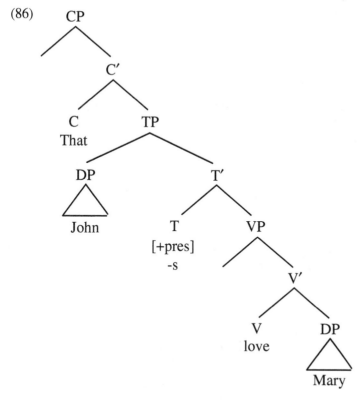

Let us now consider (87), which has a striking similarity to (84). In (87), *for* is a complementizer, and it is generated under C. *John* functions as the subject of the clause *For John to love Mary*, and *Mary* is the complement of the verb *love*.

(87) For John to love Mary takes effort.

The crucial difference between *That John loves Mary* in (84) and *For John to love Mary* in (87) is the appearance of the tense morpheme. While the tense marking, *-s*, appears in *That John loves Mary*, there is no tense marking in *For John to love Mary*. The similarities and differences between these two clauses are systematically captured in a slightly revised CP structure for *For John to love Mary*. (88) is essentially the same as (86) except that T in (88) has [+inf] information instead of [+pres] information, as in (86). The information notated by [+inf] means *to*-infinitive. As we discussed in Chapter 3, *to*-infinitive forms cannot carry a tense morpheme. Because the T position is now specified [+inf], no tense marking can appear here. As a result, the verb *love* cannot have any tense marking attached.

(88)

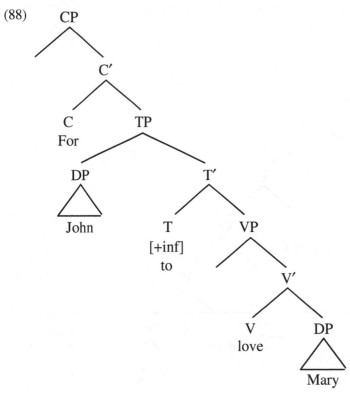

Once again, we have shown that two seemingly different structures like (84) and (87) can be systematically explained in the structures we posited. As readers might have noticed throughout this chapter, many phrases and clauses that we have discussed have similar structures. They are indeed similar because they are generated by the generalized X′ schemata that we discussed.

5.9 Summary

We started this chapter by pointing out some problems with the structures we discussed in Chapter 4. The problems then were fixed by proposing a new set of structures called X′ schemata. As a result, only limited types of rules became acceptable. These generalized schemata have many advantages in explaining English over the PS rules we learned in Chapter 4. After discussing several types of phrases in X′ theory, we discussed DP, TP, and CP. Based on the newly defined phrasal structures, two types of movement mechanisms were discussed. For example, we learned that an interrogative sentence is derived from its base by moving everything under the T node to the empty spot under the C node. We also learned that a very similar mechanism can be applied to Spanish with a slight adjustment due to the difference between the two languages. In conjunction with the interrogative sentence derivation mechanism, we discussed the *wh*-movement mechanism, where a *wh*-word moves to the specifier position of CP. We concluded this chapter by discussing two CP subject constructions. All in all, we learned that the X′ theory explains many linguistic phenomena more systematically than did the old system provided in Chapter 4.

5.10 Further Reading

There are a great deal of textbooks on X′ theory. One of the better books for beginners is Carnie (2007). Carnie's book is written in a very approachable way for undergraduate students who do not have a linguistics background. Radford's (1988) *Transformational Grammar* is a good resource too. It contains an abundance of information and syntactic argumentations valuable for beginning linguistics students. We also recommend Haegeman's (1994) textbook on Government and Binding Theory for students who want to investigate various types of syntactic mechanisms within X′ theory. Naturally, more serious readers will benefit by reading Chomsky's original works. Chomsky (1970) is one of the first works where the general idea of the X′ structures is found. Chomsky's famous book *Lectures on Government and Binding* (1981) will be challenging but definitely worth trying. This book not only discusses technical details of X′-theoretic syntax, but also explains Chomsky's philosophical assumptions, such as human beings' biological endowment for language. More practical discussions on X′ theory are found in Jackendoff (1977), which is also worth trying, even for beginners.

CHAPTER 6
Elementary Logic

Until now, we have focused on the structural properties of language. Without understanding the meaning, however, understanding language is impossible. The subfield of linguistics that deals with the meaning of natural language is called semantics. Modern semantics has relied heavily on mathematical and philosophical logic, which is why we need to discuss some basic notions of logic before we move on to the subject of natural language semantics. For those of you who are already familiar with elementary logic through high school or college logic classes, this chapter will be a review. For the rest of you, this chapter will introduce many interesting concepts that you may not have examined from an academic standpoint.

6.1 The Propositional Calculus

The first topic we will discuss in this chapter is the propositional calculus. To understand what it is, we need to define what a proposition (not *preposition*!) is. Propositions are characterized as being either true or false. In linguistics and logic, we call this concept *truth value*, a value that is either true or false. Propositions are normally expressed by declarative sentences, as shown in (1). In (1), the proposition expressed by the declarative sentence *Saint Paul is the capital of Minnesota* is true. For this reason, some people call the propositional calculus by its alternate term, the sentential calculus. What this means is that the atomic unit in the propositional calculus is a single sentence because a proposition is normally expressed by a declarative sentence.

(1) Saint Paul is the capital of Minnesota.

Other types of sentences such as imperatives and interrogatives do not express propositions because what is conveyed in (2) and (3) cannot be judged either as true or false. Remember, our focus here is the sentence itself, not any potential answers to it.

(2) Go to Cub Foods right now!
(3) Do you like the linguistics class?

However, not all declarative sentences express propositions. Some declarative sentences are hard to judge either as true or false due to their vagueness. In (4), the predicate *is pretty reliable* is not solid enough to provide evidence to make (4) true or false.

(4) My Toyota is pretty reliable.

Keeping in mind the definition of proposition, let us discuss how complex propositions are formed from atomic propositions.

6.1.1 The logical connectives

Conventionally, linguists use the lowercase letters, p, q, r, s, and so on, as variables to refer to propositions. For example, the proposition *John sleeps* in (5) is often notated as p in the propositional calculus. Similarly, the proposition in (6) could be notated as another letter in the Roman alphabet, say, q.

(5) John sleeps.
(6) Mary loves John.

The choice of *p* and *q* is arbitrary because variables are just that: variable. Nonetheless, it would be necessary to use two different letters for the two different propositions to avoid any confusion. These single letters are called atomic propositions because they are the minimum unit for the propositional calculus. Starting from these atomic propositions, we can form more complex propositions by combining them. The first combinatorial operation of the atomic propositions is conjunction.

6.1.1.1 Conjunction

A complex proposition can be constructed by combining two propositions, as shown in (7). In the propositional calculus, the conjunction *and* is denoted as $\wedge$, which is called a connective. As we discussed in the previous section, the proposition *Mary loves John* can be denoted by p, and the proposition *John loves Jane* can be denoted by q. If we combine the two propositions with the conjunction notation $\wedge$, the result is (8). In (8), the complex proposition combined by the connective $\wedge$ appears within a set of parentheses. From now on, we will use the parenthesis notation whenever a new complex proposition is created by a connective.

(7) Mary loves John and John loves Jane.
(8) $(p \wedge q)$

The conjunction of p and q, denoted by $(p \wedge q)$, is true when both p and q are true. Otherwise, it is false. This definition is shown in its standard form in the table format below, in (9). This table is known as a truth table. Read each line across from left to right to understand the outcome of merging two propositions. For example, the first line in the table states the above: When p and q are both true, $(p \wedge q)$ is also true. The second line states that when p is true and q is false, the conjoined $(p \wedge q)$ is false.

(9) Truth table for conjunction

p	q	$(p \wedge q)$
T	T	T
T	F	F
F	T	F
F	F	F

We tend to believe that a conjunction should combine semantically related propositions. (7) is clearly a case where two propositions are semantically related. However, two semantically unrelated propositions can be combined by conjunction to yield a truth value as well. For example, (10) could be logically represented by (p ∧ q) because the proposition expressed in (10) is true when both propositions are true. Here, of course, we're using different sentences with our variables, so p represents the proposition *Mary loves John*, and q represents *Bill is rich*.

(10) Mary loves John and Bill is rich.

Readers should also be aware that *but* is a conjunction too. Although there is a meaning difference between *and* and *but* in natural language use, both of them are treated the same in the propositional calculus. Therefore, the proposition expressed in (11) is also represented by (p ∧ q), where *Mary loves John* is represented by p, and *John loves Jane* is represented by q. Though important, the discussion on the difference between *and* and *but* in language use will be postponed until Chapter 8 (section 8.4.1).

(11) Mary loves John but John loves Jane.

The same truth table (9) can be used in this case too. Just like the *and* examples above, the complex proposition with *but* in (11) becomes true when both *Mary loves John* is true and *John loves Jane* is true. Otherwise, it is false.

6.1.1.2 Disjunction

A complex proposition can be formed by a disjunction connective, which is the same as *or* in English. Let us assume that the proposition *Bill sleeps* is p, while the proposition *Jane snores* is q. Then the complex proposition *Bill sleeps or Jane snores* in (12) is denoted as in (13), where *or* is denoted by ∨.

(12) Bill sleeps or Jane snores.
(13) (p ∨ q)

The conjunction and disjunction truth values are different, resulting in different truth tables. The disjunction truth table is shown in (14). The complex proposition (p ∨ q) becomes true whenever p is true or q is true or both. Otherwise, it is false. This can be seen in the table format below.

(14) Truth table for disjunction

p	q	(p ∨ q)
T	T	T
T	F	T
F	T	T
F	F	F

As readers might have noticed in the truth table in (14), the disjunction we are dealing with in the propositional calculus is the inclusive *or* meaning. In other words, the proposition in (12) is true even when both *Bill sleeps* and *Jane snores* are true. This seems to be somewhat counterintuitive because we believe that A or B means either A or B should be true to make the whole statement A or B true. This is not always the case, even in our ordinary language use. Let's consider (15). Assume that Bill is a US citizen, and he is a linguist. Can he apply for the grant? Of course he can.

(15) To be eligible for this grant opportunity, you must be a US citizen or a linguist.

Although we are not often aware of it, we often use *or* in this inclusive sense in our everyday language use.

6.1.1.3 The conditional

The conditional connective in logic is roughly the same as the *if ~ then* construction in English. In (16), let us assume that the proposition *John loves Mary* is represented by p, and *Boston is in Minnesota* is represented by q. These two propositions can be combined by *if ~ then*, which is denoted by →. The result of this is shown in (17).

(16) If John loves Mary, then Boston is in Minnesota.
(17) (p → q)

The truth value of the conditional (→) is illustrated in (18). The truth table in (18) shows that the complex proposition p → q is false when p is true and q is false. Otherwise, it is true. That means there are three possible scenarios where (16) becomes true. The first scenario is when *John loves Mary* (p) is true and *Boston is in Minnesota* (q) is true. The second one is *John loves Mary* (p) is false and *Boston is in Minnesota* (q) is true. The third one is that both *John loves Mary* (p) and *Boston is in Minnesota* (q) are true. By contrast, there is only one instance that can make the complex proposition in (16) false: When *John loves Mary* (p) is true and *Boston is in Minnesota* (q) is false.

(18) Truth table for the conditional

p	q	(p → q)
T	T	T
T	F	F
F	T	T
F	F	T

It is not hard to explain the case where the proposition (p → q) becomes false. For example, in (19), we know that *All men are mortal* (p) is true, while *Socrates is immortal* (q) is false. As a result, the proposition in (19), which is represented by (p → q), becomes false according to the truth table provided in (18).

(19) If all men are mortal, Socrates is immortal.

The puzzling situation is when p is false, as shown in the last two rows in the table in (18). According to (18), both (20) and (21) must be true. The proposition *1 + 1 = 3* in (20) is false, and *Seoul is in South Korea* is true, yielding the combined proposition being true. In (21), both *1 + 1 = 3* and *Seoul is in Minnesota* are false, also yielding the combined proposition being true.

(20) If 1 + 1 = 3, then Seoul is in South Korea.
(21) If 1 + 1 = 3, then Seoul is in Minnesota.

This might be a somewhat puzzling result for readers, but in fact there is an ample amount of discussion on this logical nature of the conditional from philosophical and mathematical perspectives. We will not discuss this issue in detail because it is beyond the scope of this book. Instead, for the purpose of this chapter, let us just accept the truth table provided in (18) as a logical definition of the conditional.

6.1.1.4 The biconditional

The biconditional is roughly translated in English as *if and only if*, which is notated by $\leftrightarrow$. In (22), the proposition *Jane is smart* is not only a sufficient but also a necessary condition for *I love Jane*. If *I love Jane* is p, and *Jane is smart* is q, the proposition expressed in (22) is represented as in (23).

(22) I love Jane if and only if Jane is smart.
(23) $(p \leftrightarrow q)$

The truth value of the biconditional is provided in the truth table in (23). The biconditional proposition, denoted by $(p \leftrightarrow q)$, is true when p and q have the same truth values. Otherwise, it is false.

(24) Truth table for the biconditional

p	q	$(p \leftrightarrow q)$
T	T	T
T	F	F
F	T	F
F	F	T

Understanding (24) is not difficult. Let us consider our example (22) again. If *I love Jane* is true and *Jane is smart* is true, the proposition *I love Jane if and only if Jane is smart* is also true. If *I love Jane* is false and *Jane is smart* is true, the combined proposition is false because *I love Jane* and *Jane is smart* have different truth values. If *I love Jane* is true and *Jane is smart* is false, the combined proposition is false for the same reason as before. When both *I love Jane* and *Jane is smart* are false, the combined proposition is true because the negation of *Jane is smart* must guarantee the negation of *I love Jane*. For this reason, a biconditional proposition like (23) becomes true when both p and q have the same truth value. Otherwise, it is false.

6.1.1.5 Negation

The last connective operator in making a complex proposition is negation, or the contradiction or denial of something. Negation in a proposition is denoted by ¬, and an example of this is shown in (25). If the proposition *John loves Mary* is represented by p, the complex proposition *It is not the case that John loves Mary* can be represented by (¬p).

(25) It is not the case that John loves Mary.

(26) (¬p)

It is worth noting that only propositions can be negated in the propositional calculus. For example, (27) should be represented as in (28) in the propositional calculus, under the assumption that *Jane loves John* is q. Although the negation *not* modifies the verb phrase *does love John* syntactically, the propositional calculus we are discussing now does not allow us to negate a VP, just the sentence itself. This is because the atomic unit for the propositional calculus is a proposition (or a sentence). Therefore, modifying an internal unit within a sentence is not possible in the propositional calculus.

(27) Jane doesn't love John.

(28) (¬q)

Readers might also be tempted to translate the proposition in (27) into (29) in the propositional calculus by assuming that *Jane doesn't love John* is simply q. This is not accurate in our propositional calculus system because the negation *not* is a connective unit, not an atomic one.

(29) q

In other words, we translate an English sentence into its atomic form when necessary and identify any connectives that might be modifying it. In the case of (27), *not* is a connective, and everything else becomes an atomic sentence. In fact, there are only five connectives in the propositional calculus, as we have discussed thus far. If we remove the connectives from the complex propositions we deal with, we will get atomic sentences. This issue will be discussed with more examples in section 6.1.2.2.

The truth value of negation is provided in the truth table in (30). The truth table in (30) is straightforward and self-explanatory. What it means is the negation of p notated by (¬p) is true when p is false. Otherwise, it is false.

(30) Truth table for negation

p	(¬p)
T	F
F	T

In this section, we have discussed the complex proposition creation mechanism by using the five connectives notated by ∧, ∨, →, ↔, and ¬. Although we discussed each connective individually, one connective can be used with another to form a more complex proposition, which will be discussed in the next section.

6.1.2 The computation of complex propositions

First, let us consider (31), which contains two connectives: ∧ and ¬. The connective ∧ is the representation of *but* in (31); ¬ is the representation of *not* in the second conjunct of the same complex proposition.

(31) John loves Mary but Mary doesn't love John.

How do we translate (31) into the propositional calculus? Let us assume that the proposition *John loves Mary* is p, and *Mary loves John* is q. These assumptions are provided in (32) as a key for the translation of (31) into the propositional calculus. Remember that the propositions used as keys must be atomic propositions. Complex propositions cannot be used in the key because complex propositions are created by combining atomic propositions using connectives in our system.

(32) Key:
 a. John loves Mary: p
 b. Mary loves John: q

The result of the translation of (31) into the propositional calculus form is shown in (33). There are two points we want to clarify in explaining (33). First, both *and* and *but* are notated by ∧ in the propositional calculus. Second, we decided to use the parenthesis notation whenever a new complex proposition is created by using a connective. In (33), the new proposition ¬q is created from q by using the negation ¬. Because ¬q is a newly created complex proposition, we need to put ¬q within a set of parentheses like (¬q) to preserve the unit. Next, the atomic proposition *John loves Mary* and the complex proposition *Mary doesn't love John* are combined by the connective ∧ to yield a more complex proposition, p ∧ (¬q). This is, of course, a complex proposition, so it should be within a set of parentheses, which is shown in (33).

(33) (p ∧ (¬q))

As illustrated, two connectives may interact with each other to form a more complex proposition. However, this is not the end of the story. The number of complex propositions created by the connectives we discussed is infinite, a fact that needs no explanation when you think of how many possible sentences one can create. To clarify how we combine propositions to yield a (more) complex proposition, a highly specific definition of propositions will be provided in the next section.

6.1.2.1 Definition

Most readers who are not familiar with logic and mathematics might not like to see the word *definition* with some kinds of formulas. However, it is necessary to define how propositions are constructed from atomic propositions. By doing so, readers will gain more confidence in translating English sentences into their corresponding propositional calculus forms. The definition of propositions is provided in (34).

(34) Definition 1
 a. The letters such as p, q, r, s, and so on, are atomic propositions in the propositional calculus.
 b. If α is a proposition, then $(\neg \alpha)$ is a proposition too.
 c. If α and β are propositions, then $(\alpha \wedge \beta)$, $(\alpha \vee \beta)$, $(\alpha \rightarrow \beta)$, and $(\alpha \leftrightarrow \beta)$ are propositions too.
 d. Only that which can be generated by (a) to (c) in the above rules is a proposition in the propositional calculus.

Although the definition in (34) looks complicated, what it conveys is straightforward. (34a) states that the atomic propositions are represented by Roman letters such as p, q, r, s, and so on, in the propositional calculus. (34b) defines how to form a complex proposition with the connective ¬. (34c) defines other types of complex proposition formations. (34c) is separate from (34b) because the connectives used in (34c) are all binary operators that require two propositions, whereas the connective ¬ used in (34b) requires only one proposition. (34d) states that there is no other formation except for the three discussed above.

The definition predicts that the propositions in (35) are all well-formed propositions, while the propositions illustrated in (36) are ill-formed and thus unacceptable.

(35) Well-formed propositions: p, q, (p → q), ((¬ (p ∧ q)) ∨ r), (q ↔ (r ∧ s)), (¬ (¬ (¬p))), and so on

(36) Ill-formed propositions: pq, (q ¬ →q), (↔p), (¬pr), and so on

Without additional help, readers will soon be able to explain why the propositions in (35) are well formed and why the propositions in (36) are not.

6.1.2.2 Some practice

Based on the definition provided in the previous section, we will do some practice in translating English sentences into their corresponding propositional calculus forms. Let us consider the three sentences in (37) to (39). These sentences might not make sense to you, but the content is not our concern. Our concern in this section is how to translate the sentences into the propositional calculus forms based on the definition we discussed.

(37) It is not the case that John loves Mary or that Mary loves John.
(38) If John comes to Minnesota, then John loves Mary and Mary doesn't love John.
(39) John majors in linguistics if and only if John loves language or John is obnoxious.

Before we start, we have to figure out which propositions are atomic propositions and which Roman letters will be used for the atomic propositions. In (37), there are two atomic propositions: *John loves Mary* and *Mary loves John*. Let us assume that *John loves Mary* is p, and *Mary loves John* is q, which is provided as keys, as in (40).

(40) Key for (37):
  a. John loves Mary: p
  b. Mary loves John: q

Based on the key in (40), we can translate (37) into (41). In (41), p and q are first combined by ∨, then the newly formed complex proposition (p ∨ q) is combined with ¬ to yield (¬(p ∨ q)).

(41) ((¬p ∨ q))

Now, let us translate (38) into the propositional calculus. In (38), there are three atomic propositions, which are provided in the key in (42).

(42) Key for (38):
  a. John comes to Minnesota: p
  b. John loves Mary: q
  c. Mary loves John: r

The translation of (38) into the propositional calculus is then provided in (43). In (43), first, the proposition *Mary doesn't love John* is translated into (¬r) by adding the connective ¬ to its atomic proposition r. Then, the proposition *John loves Mary* is combined with (¬r), yielding (q ∧ (¬r)). Finally, the proposition *John comes to Minnesota* is combined by the conditional with (q ∧ (¬r)), yielding (43).

(43) (p → (q ∧ (¬r)))

If you understood the translations of (37) and (38), translating (39) into the propositional calculus should not be difficult. There are three atomic propositions in (39), as shown in (44).

(44) Key for (39):
    a. John majors in linguistics: p
    b. John loves language: q
    c. John is obnoxious: r

First, *John loves language* and *John is obnoxious* are combined by ∨ to yield (q ∨ r). Then, this newly formed complex proposition is combined with *John majors in linguistics* by the biconditional as illustrated in (45).

(45) (p ↔ (q ∨ r))

If you still feel unsure of the information presented in this subsection, go back and review the information. Sometimes, students say it takes awhile for the information to "click" with them, and a review of the subsection can help speed up the process.

6.1.2.3 Computation

Now that we learned how to create complex propositions from atomic propositions, let us discuss how to check the truth values of complex propositions. Let us first consider the proposition in (46). The proposition shown in (46) is a well-formed proposition because it can be generated by the definition we provided in (34). We do not need to know the sentence to understand what the variables are telling us here. Let us assume that p is true, q is false, and r is false, as in (47). Given this information, we can check the truth value of the proposition in (46).

(46) ((p ∧ q) → r)
(47) Truth values for atomic propositions for (46)
    a. p: T
    b. q: F
    c. r: F

To check the truth value of (46), let us first write down the truth value under each proposition as shown in (48).

(48) ((p ∧ q) → r)
    T F   F

Then, we can check whether (p ∧ q) is true or false. We already discussed the truth value of conjunction in section 6.1.1.1. When p is true and q is false, the complex proposition (p ∧ q) is false. The result of the computation of the truth value of (p ∧ q) is written down underneath the truth values of p and q, as shown in (49).

(49) ((p ∧ q) → r)
     T F   F

     F

The final step is to compute the truth value of (p ∧ q) and r. As we know, the truth value of (p ∧ q) is false, and the truth value of r is false. According to the definition of the conditional provided in 6.1.1.3, when both α and β are false in the form (α → β), the complex proposition (α → β) is true. Therefore, we can say that the complex proposition ((p ∧ q) → r) is false, given the situation where p is true, q is false, and r is false. It is worth noting that in the form (α → β), α is replaced with (p ∧ q) in this particular case.

Although the computation discussed above might look alien to readers, the concept itself is extremely simple. Look at an example from elementary algebra in (50). We know that (1 + 1) has the priority in computing the formula ((1 + 1) × 2). We also know that the result of (1 + 1) must be multiplied by 2 to yield the result 4. Only this order is accurate because the parenthesis notation denotes the immediacy of the order of operations.

(50) ((1 + 1) × 2)

Keeping this in mind, let us do one more practice exercise of a truth value computation. First, we have to make sure whether or not (51) is a well-formed formula. Although it looks very complicated, (51) indeed is a well-formed formula because it can be generated by the definition in (34).

(51) (¬(p → (q → (r → (s ∨ u)))))

To start the computation of the truth value of (51), we must know the truth values of the atomic propositions. Let's assume the truth values of the atomic propositions as they appear in (52).

(52) Truth values of atomic propositions for (51)
    a. p: T
    b. q: T
    c. r: F
    d. s: F
    e. u: F

Now, let us write down the truth value of each atomic proposition as in (53).

(53) (¬(p → (q → (r → (s ∨ u)))))
       T   T   F   F F

Next, just like the elementary algebraic computation shown in (50), in (53), you now have to figure out where to start the computation. Of course, you have to start your computation from the innermost parentheses, which is (s ∨ u). We know the truth values of s and u, so we know the truth value of (s ∨ u) based on the truth table provided in (14) in section 6.1.1.2. According to the table, when s is false and u is false, (s ∨ u) is false, which is shown in (54).

(54) (¬(p → (q → (r → (s ∨ u)))))
     T   T   F   F F

          F

The next step is to check the truth value of ((r → (s ∨ u)) because ((r → (s ∨ u)) exhibits the next level of immediacy. Referring to the truth table for the conditional in (18) in 6.1.1.3, we get the result in (55).

(55) a. (¬(p → (q → (r → (s ∨ u)))))
      T   T   F   F F

            F

        T

The next step is basically the same as the one shown in (55a). The result would look like (55b).

(55) b. (¬(p → (q → (r → (s ∨ u)))))
      T   T   F   F F

          F

       T

     T

The same type of computation is applied one more time to yield (55c).

(55) c. (¬(p → (q → (r → (s ∨ u)))))
      T   T   F   F F

          F

       T

     T

   T

Now we have one more step remaining, where the truth value of the negation of (55c) must be checked. Keep in mind that ¬ **is** applied to the latest complex proposition (p → (q → (r → (s ∨ u)))) due to the immediacy of the order of operation. As we saw in (55c), the truth value of (p → (q → (r → (s ∨ u)))) is true. When negation is applied to the proposition, the result is false according to the table provided in (30) in section 6.1.1.5. The final step of the computation of the complex proposition in (51) is illustrated in (55d).

(55) d.   (¬(p → (q → (r → (s ∨ u)))))
             T   T   F   F F

                              F

                           T

                         T

                  T

       F

Once again, this might seem somewhat complicated at first glance. If you follow the steps carefully, however, it won't be as difficult as it initially seemed. The computation shown here is made based on the truth tables we provided in previous sections in conjunction with the notion of immediacy of the order of operations learned in elementary school.

6.1.3 Logical equivalence (laws)

Even though the forms might be different, some propositions always have the same truth value. For example, look at (56) and (57). The truth value of the complex proposition (p ∨ p) is always the same as that of the atomic proposition p. Similarly, the truth value of (p ∧ p) is always the same as p. In (56) and (57), we used the symbol ≡ to refer to logical equivalence, which means the same truth value. The type of equivalence shown in (56) and (57) is referred to as idempotent laws. Here, *idempotent* means "an unchanging property when applied to itself." As we saw, when the two connectives, ∧ and ∨, combine two identical propositions, the truth value of the complex proposition is not different from the atomic proposition.

(56) (p ∨ p) ≡ p
(57) (p ∧ p) ≡ p

It is easy to prove that (p ∨ p) has the same truth value as p. As shown in the truth table in (58), the truth value of (p ∨ p) is always the same as p itself.

(58)

p	(p ∨ p)
T	T
F	F

Similarly, the proposition in (57), (p ∧ p), has the same truth value as p, as shown in the truth table in (59).

(59)

p	(p ∧ p)
T	T
F	F

As readers might already know, other laws show logical equivalence among different propositions. Some of the well-known equivalence laws are introduced in (60) to (62). We will not show the equivalences of the propositions in (60) to (62) because showing the truth value for each proposition is fairly mechanical and straightforward.

(60) Associative laws
    a. ((p ∨ q) ∨ r) ≡ (p ∨ (q ∨ r))
    b. ((p ∧ q) ∧ r) ≡ (p ∧ (q ∧ r))
(61) Commutative laws
    a. (p ∨ q) ≡ (q ∨ p)
    b. (p ∧ q) ≡ (q ∧ p)
(62) Distributive laws
    a. (p ∨ (q ∧ r)) ≡ ((p ∨ q) ∧ (p ∨ r))
    b. (p ∧ (q ∨ r)) ≡ ((p ∧ q) ∨ (p ∧ r))

One advantage of understanding the laws is the ease of checking the truth value. Let us consider (63), which seems to be a complicated proposition.

(63) John goes to the store or to the movie and John goes to the store or to the library.

Let us now translate (63) into the propositional calculus based on the key provided in (64). The translation would look like (65).

(64) Key for (63)
    a. John goes to the store: p
    b. John goes to the movie: q
    c. John goes to the library: r
(65) ((p ∨ q) ∧ (p ∨ r))

According to the distributive laws shown in (62), (65) has the same truth value as (p ∨ (q ∧ r)), which means *John goes to the store or John goes to the movie and the library*. When we have to check the truth value of (65), using the formula (p ∨ (q ∧ r)) saves time by reducing the number of connectives.

6.2 The Predicate Calculus

The second topic of this chapter is the predicate calculus. The propositional calculus we discussed earlier has some shortcomings. Let us take a look at (66). We intuitively know that the proposition expressed in (66c) can be deduced by (66a) and (66b). In the propositional calculus, (66a), (66b), and (66c) are represented by Roman letters, such as p, q, and r, respectively.

(66) a. All men are mortal.
    b. Socrates is a man.
    ----
    c. Socrates is mortal.

The result of the translation of (66a) to (66c) would look like (67). In (67), it is impossible to see the connection among the three propositions because p, q, and r are all atomic propositions.

(67) a. p
    b. q
    ----
    c. r

If we modify the structure of the propositional calculus like (68), the deduction shown in (68c) is naturally captured. Because all x's are y and Socrates is an x, Socrates must be a y.

(68) a. All x's are y.
    b. Socrates is an x.
    ----
    c. Socrates is an y.

To overcome this type of difficulty, we will modify the propositional calculus by analyzing the proposition into two parts called a term and a predicate. Roughly speaking, a term is similar to a noun phrase, and a predicate is similar to a verb. The properties of the predicate calculus will be discussed in the next section.

6.2.1 Terms, predicates, constants, variables

Unlike the propositional calculus, a proposition is not the atomic unit for the predicate calculus. Instead, terms and predicates function as the atomic units in the predicate calculus. Let us consider the example in (69). The proposition *John sleeps* is composed of two parts: the term *John* and the predicate *sleeps*.

(69) John sleeps.

The translation of (69) into the predicate calculus would look like (70). Although (70) looks different in form from the propositional calculus, it is still considered a proposition because (70) still has a truth value. In the predicate calculus, the capital letter represents a predicate, and a lowercase letter within parentheses represents a term. Terms that refer to a specific individual are called constants. In (70), S represents *sleeps* and j represents *John*, where j is a constant because it refers to a specific individual.

(70) S(j)

Readers should be aware that an individual does not necessarily mean a person. Any kind of noun expression can be an individual. (71) lists some examples of individuals.

(71) UMD, the number 1, Jane, the United States, and so on

Sometimes, an individual can be unspecified, as in (72). In (72), the term is not specified with any individual. Therefore, (72) cannot have a truth value, making it a propositional function as opposed to a proposition. Nevertheless, (72) can still be denoted in the predicate calculus, as in (73).

(72) x sleeps.
(73) S(x)

In (73), S represents *sleeps* and x represents an unspecified individual. An unspecified individual is simply a variable. The same notion can be extended to a proposition that contains a transitive verb, like (74). In (74), there are two terms, *John* and *Mary*, and there is one predicate, *loves*. Because the two terms are all specific individuals, we need two constants in translating (74) into the predicate calculus form. The translation of (74) into the predicate calculus looks like (75), where the two constants appear within parentheses separated by the comma. The capital letter L represents the predicate *loves*.

(74) John loves Mary.
(75) L(j, m)

Although there are some differences between the propositional calculus and the predicate calculus, they have many common properties. First, in both calculi, propositions are expressed, though in different forms. Propositions can be combined in both calculi by the connectives we discussed earlier. In the next section, we will define well-formed propositions in the predicate calculus.

6.2.2 Definition

As we have just explained, the predicate calculus shares lots of properties with the propositional calculus. The definition provided in (76) for the predicate calculus is indeed reminiscent of the definition of the propositional calculus in (34).

(76) Definition 2
    a. If A is an *n*-ary predicate letter, and each of $t_1, \ldots, t_n$ is a constant or a variable, then $A(t_1, \ldots, t_n)$ is a formula in the predicate calculus.
    b. If α is a formula, then $(\neg \alpha)$ is a formula too.
    c. If α and β are formulas, then $(\alpha \wedge \beta)$, $(\alpha \vee \beta)$, $(\alpha \to \beta)$, and $(\alpha \leftrightarrow \beta)$ are formulas too.
    d. If α is a formula and x is a variable, then $\forall x[\alpha]$ and $\exists x[\alpha]$ are formulas too.
    e. Only that which can be generated by (a) to (d) is a formula in the predicate calculus.

As usual, the definition might look unnecessarily complicated to many readers. However, the reason for providing the definition is to describe accurately which formulas are well-formed in the predicate calculus. Let us take a look at the definition piece by piece.

First, (76a) defines atomic formulas in the predicate calculus. If A is an *n*-ary predicate, then $A(t_1, \ldots, t_n)$ is a formula too, where each of $t_1, \ldots, t_n$ is a constant or a variable. Here, the *n*-ary predicate means the predicate with *n* number of terms. For example, the predicate *sleeps* is a unary predicate, meaning it requires only one term. Therefore, we only need one term, say, t_1.

When we replace A with the letter S that stands for *sleeps*, and t_1 with the variable symbol *x*, what we get from the definition (76a) is (77), which represents *x sleeps*. As defined, each of $t_1, \ldots, t_n$ can be a constant. When we replace A in (76a) with S that stands for *sleeps*, and t_1 with j that stands for *John*, what we get is the formula in (78), which represents *John sleeps*.

(77) S(x)
(78) S(j)

A predicate can also be a binary predicate, where the predicate requires two terms, like in (79). To translate (79) into its predicate calculus form, let us first replace A in the definition (76a) with L, which stands for *loves*. Because the predicate is a binary predicate, we need two terms: t_1 and t_2. Because both *John* and *Mary* are constants, we need to specify them by using constant symbols j and m, which appear within parentheses separated by the comma. The result would look like (80).

(79) John loves Mary.
(80) L(j, m)

If two terms are variables in (79), the result looks like (81). Similarly, if either one of the two terms is a variable, the result is (82a) or (82b).

(81) L(x, y)
(82) a. L(j, y)
      b. L(x, m)

The case of a ternary predicate is explained in the exactly the same way. (83) contains the ditransitive predicate *gave* and this can be translated into (84) by following the definition provided in (76a).

(83) John gave Mary the book.
(84) G(j, m, b)

If all terms in (83) were variables, as in (85), the translation would be (86).

(85) x gave y z.
(86) G(x, y, z)

Similarly, the sentence in (87), where only one term is a variable, is translated as in (88), according to the definition in (76a).

(87) John gave x the book.
(88) G(j, x, b)

Second, (76b) and (76c) define how complex formulas are formed in the predicate calculus. (76b) defines formulas containing negation, and (76c) defines complex formulas with connectives other than negation. According to (76b), if α is a formula, then $(\neg\alpha)$ is a formula too. To explain this with an example, let us consider (89). We now know that (89) is a well-formed formula in the predicate calculus because it can be generated by the definition in (76a). Here, we will use the key (90), which we made based on the formula in (89). What (76b) states is that, if (89) is a formula, then (91) must be a formula too, which means *John does not love Mary* or *It is not the case that John loves Mary.*

(89) L(j, m)
(90) Key
    a. loves: L
    b. John: j
    c. Mary: m
(91) (¬L(j,m))

Similarly, (76c) defines other types of complex formula formations. Let us assume the same key provided in (90). We already know that (89) is a well-formed formula. Under these conditions, we now know that the formulas in (92) to (95) are all well-formed formulas in the predicate calculus because they are generated by the definition in (76c).

(92) (L(j, m) ∧ L(m, j))
(93) (L(j, m) ∨ L(m, j))
(94) (L(j, m) → L(m, j))
(95) (L(j, m) ↔ L(m, j))

If we combine (76a), (76b), and (76c), we can generate more complex formulas, as in (96), where S represents *sleeps*. (96) seems to be very complicated, but it is a perfectly well-formed formula, following the definitions provided in (76a), (76b), and (76c). The meaning of (96) is *It is not the case that if John sleeps, then John loves Mary or Mary loves John.*

(96) (¬(S(j) → (L(j, m) ∨ L(m, j))))

Third, (76d) defines well-formed formulas generated by adding quantifiers. Quantifiers are expressions that convey the information on the quantity of the nouns they modify. There are two representative quantifiers: One is called the universal quantifier denoted by ∀, and the other the existential quantifier denoted by ∃. In section 6.2.1, we discussed a propositional function, which contains a variable and does not function as a proposition. For example, (97), where S represents *sleeps*, is not a proposition because we cannot check its truth value due to the presence of the variable x.

(97) S(x)

There are two ways to convert a propositional function into a proposition. One way is to replace the variable x with a constant, as shown in (98), where j represents *John*. Remember that, when a constant, not a variable, is present, what you see is a proposition.

(98) S(j)

The other way to convert a propositional function like (97) to a proposition is to use a quantifier, as shown in (99) and (100). Both (99) and (100) are well-formed formulas in the predicate calculus because both of them can be generated by the definitions provided in (76). As we know, S(x) is a well-formed formula because it is generated by (76a). If S(x) is a formula, both (99) and (100) must be formulas too, as defined in (76d). Both (99) and (100) are now propositions because we can check their truth values if given a specific context.

(99) ∀x[S(x)]
(100) ∃x[S(x)]

Clearly, (99) and (100) have different meanings. In (99), the universal quantifier ∀ corresponds to the phrases *for each, for all, for every*, and *for any*, while the existential quantifier ∃ in (100) can be paraphrased in English as *there exists, for some, there is at least one*, and so on. In other words, (99) can be paraphrased as (101), and (100) can be paraphrased as (102).

(101) For all x, x sleeps.
(102) For some x, x sleeps.

The last clause in the definition in (76) states that only the formulas generated by (76a) to (76d) are well-formed formulas in the predicate calculus. The formulas that cannot be generated by (76a) to (76d) are ill-formed formulas and are not acceptable in the predicate calculus.

6.2.3 Quantifiers and their scopes

In the previous section, we briefly discussed quantifiers. We will discuss quantifiers in greater detail in this section.

6.2.3.1 Translations of quantifying expressions

Let us first consider the universal quantifier in (103). (103) can be translated into the predicate calculus, as in (104), where M represents the predicate *are mortal*. What (104) means, then, is *For all x, x is mortal*.

(103) All humans are mortal.
(104) * ∀x[M(x)]

A closer examination, however, shows that (104) is not completely accurate because what (103) actually means is *For all x, if x is a human, then x is mortal*. In other words, although there is only one syntactic predicate in (103), we need two predicates to interpret (103) into the predicate calculus. If we directly convert the expression *For all x, if x is a human, then x is mortal* into the predicate calculus form, what we get is (105).

(105) ∀x[H(x) → M(x)]

(105) states that every individual that makes H(x) true also makes M(x) true. If there is an individual that makes H(x) true but makes M(x) false, then (105) becomes false. In (106), we can see this in a Venn diagram form. The Human set is completely inside the Mortal set. As a result, an individual belonging to the Human set automatically belongs to the Mortal set too. Therefore, if an individual belongs to the Human set, then that individual must also belong to the Mortal set in order to make (105) true.

(106)

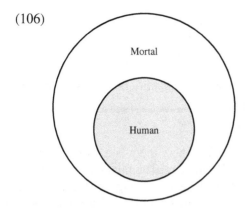

The representation of the existential quantifier is different from that of the universal quantifier. Let us consider (107), which is roughly interpreted as *For some x, x is a linguist and x is obnoxious*. The representation of (107), then, should be like (108), where L denotes *Linguist* and M denotes *are obnoxious*.

(107) Some linguists are obnoxious.
(108) $\exists x[L(x) \land O(x)]$

If we show (108) as a Venn diagram, it would look like (109). To make (107) true, there should be at least one individual that belongs to both sets, Linguist and Obnoxious, at the same time, which is captured by the conjunction notation $\land$ in (108).

(109)

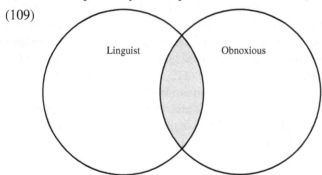

Readers should be aware that the representation of (107) cannot be (110) because (110) produces a different proposition. (110) asserts the existence of at least one individual that, if it is a linguist, then it is also obnoxious. The subtle differences between "and" and "if… then" are important distinctions in the predicate logic.

(110) $\exists x[L(x) \rightarrow O(x)]$

This is not what (107) means, however. Consider the situation where no individual is a linguist. Even in this situation, (110) can be still true because in the form $(\alpha \rightarrow \beta)$, when α is false, the whole formula $(\alpha \rightarrow \beta)$ is true, as we saw in the truth table in (18) in section 6.1.1.3.

Keeping this in mind, let's consider a slightly more complex proposition where both the universal and existential quantifiers are used in one proposition.

6.2.3.2 The scopes of the quantifiers

Let us consider the sentence in (111). In (111), there are two quantifiers: One is the universal quantifier and the other is the existential quantifier.

(111) All men love some woman.

Most people might have interpreted (111) as (112), where there is a particular woman who is loved by all men, which is represented as (113). Some readers might think the formula provided in (113) looks extremely complicated. Nonetheless, figuring out the meaning of (113) is not difficult. We can paraphrase (113) into the English sentence *There is a y that is a woman, and for all x, if x is a man, then x loves y.*

(112) Some woman is loved by all men.
(113) $\exists y[W(y) \wedge \forall x[M(x) \rightarrow L(x,y)]]$

To understand (113), we need to discuss two notions: scope and bound variables. Here, scope is defined as $[\alpha]$ in the formula $\forall x[\alpha]$ and $\exists x[\alpha]$, where α is a well-formed formula. In other words, the scope of $\forall x$ is $[M(x) \rightarrow L(x,y)]$, while the scope of $\exists y$ is $[W(y) \wedge \forall x[M(x) \rightarrow L(x,y)]]$ in (113). The other notion we have to understand is that of a bound variable. A bound variable is a variable that is bound by a quantifier. In (113), the variable x in M(x) and L(x, y) is bound by the universal quantifier $\forall x$ because the universal quantifier carries the same variable. Similarly, the variable y in W(y) and L(x, y) is bound by the existential quantifier $\exists y$ because it carries the same variable. In (113), y in L(x, y) is bound by $\exists y$ outside the scope of $\forall x$. In other words, the variable y is associated with the existential quantifier outside the scope of $\forall x$, yielding the interpretation of *There is a particular woman who every man loves.*

However, (113) is just one possible interpretation of (112). In fact, (112) has two different interpretations. The other possible interpretation is the situation given in (114), where all three men, John, Bill, and Tom, love one particular woman, Katie. (111) can certainly express this situation too. The other possible interpretation of (111) is that the three men all love a different woman; that is, John loves Ashley, Bill loves Mary, and Tom loves Katie. (114) shows who belongs to the set of men and who belongs to the set of women.

(114) Situation
     a. There are three men: John, Bill, and Tom
     b. There are three women: Ashley, Mary, Katie

The situation where three men each love a different woman can be represented as in (115). (115) is clearly different from (113). While $\forall x[M(x) \rightarrow L(x,y)]$ is embedded inside the scope of $\exists y$ in (113), $\exists y[W(y) \wedge L(x,y)]]$ appears inside the scope of $\forall x$ in (115). In other words, the universal quantifier $\forall x$ has a wider scope than that of $\exists y$ in (115). As a result, (115) has the interpretation of *Every man loves some woman, each woman being a distinct individual from the other women* or something similar.

(115) $\forall x[M(x) \rightarrow \exists y[W(y) \wedge L(x,y)]]$

Understanding the notion of scope might not be immediately straightforward to everybody. If you are not confident about your understanding, go back to the beginning of this chapter and review the information discussed.

6.3 Summary

In this chapter, we discussed two elementary calculi: the propositional calculus and the predicate calculus. We provided two sets of definitions to define well-formed formulas for the two types of calculi. We also provided the truth tables for five connectives: $\neg$, $\wedge$, $\vee$, $\rightarrow$, and $\leftrightarrow$. In discussing the predicate calculus, we also discussed the two quantifiers, one being the universal quantifier (denoted by $\forall$), and the other the existential quantifier (denoted by $\exists$). Two different interpretations of the proposition *All men love some woman* was explained by two different formulas where the universal and the existential quantifiers had different scopes.

6.4 Further Reading

Quine (1963) is a classic for students of logic, despite its brevity. The basic formal concepts are clearly explained and are easy to follow. Wall's (1972) introduction to mathematical linguistics is a readable introduction for readers who do not have any background in logic. Partee et al.'s (1990) revision of Wall's book is a great resource for serious readers, although it contains information for advanced students of logic. Finally, Gamut's (1990) introduction to logic is an outstanding resource. Gamut explains the formalism in the propositional and the predicate calculi in a very accessible way, even to beginners.

CHAPTER 7

Semantics

This chapter deals with semantics, which is the study of meaning. Although there are many different approaches to semantics, our approach will be based on the generative approach in syntax (which we discussed in Chapters 4 and 5) and on logic (which we discussed in Chapter 6). We will start this chapter by discussing some preliminaries that we have to understand before we begin our study of meaning.

7.1 Preliminaries

In this section, we will introduce three notions that are necessary for the understanding of semantics: sets, compositionality, and the distinction between reference and sense.

7.1.1 Sets

A set is a collection of objects, and the objects are called members of the set. There are two ways to define a set. First, let us consider set A in (1). Set A is a collection of three objects, a, b, and c, which appear inside the curly brackets. A is the name of the set, and a, b, and c are the members of set A.

    (1) A = {a, b, c}

We can easily define other sets by using the same method. In (2), set B is defined as {d, e, f, g, h}; thus, there are five members in set B.

    (2) B = {d, e, f, g, h}

To explain the membership relation, we often use the ∈ and ∉ symbols. The symbols roughly translate to the phrases *is a member of* and *is not a member of*, respectively. For example, a is a member of set A from (1). Then we may represent the relationship as in (3).

    (3) a ∈ A

By contrast, d is not a member of the same set A, which is represented in (4).

    (4) d ∉ A

The other option in defining a set is to use a variable as in (5), which reads as "the set of all *x* where *x* is a linguist. In other words, (5) defines a set that contains all linguists.

    (5) C = {*x* | *x* is a linguist}

Chomsky is a linguist, so Chomsky is a member of set C defined in (5), notated by Chomsky ∈ C. James Joyce is not a linguist, so James Joyce is not a member of C, which is notated by James Joyce ∉ C.

Two sets might or might not have some overlap in their membership. The sets defined in (6) and (7) have some overlap in their membership: They share two members, members a and b. By contrast, the sets A and B do not share any members, nor do E and B.

    (6) A = {a, b, c}
    (7) E = {a, b}
    (8) B = {d, e, f, g, h}

To explain the overlap in the membership, we use the notation ⊂ and ⊄. The overlapping relation between the sets A and E in (6) and (7), respectively, are represented as (9), which reads as "the set E is a proper subset of A." Know that the set A is not a proper subset of (7) because A contains more members than E, some of which don't overlap. This is notated as in (10). Because there is no overlap between A and B, the relationship between the two sets is represented in (11)

    (9) E ⊂ A
  (10) A ⊄ E
  (11) A ⊄ B, B ⊄ A

Two sets might be equal by having exactly the same members. Set F, defined in (12), is exactly the same as A in (6) because the two sets have exactly the same members. To express this identity relation, we may use the = symbol, as shown in (13). Or we may use the ⊆ symbol, which is a combination of the proper subset symbol ⊂ and the = symbol, as in (14). In (14), A ⊆ F reads as "A is a proper subset of F" or "A is equal to F."

  (12) F = {a, b, c}
  (13) A = F
  (14) A ⊆ F

Because the ⊆ symbol is a disjoint combination of ⊂ and =, we may replace ⊂ with ⊆ in all previous proper subset examples. The notion of proper subset entails the notion of subset.

A new set can be created by two set operations: One is called intersection, and the other is called union. The intersection operator creates a new set that contains only members shared by two arbitrary sets α and β. For example, the intersection operator notated by ∩ in (17) creates the new set {a, b, d, e}, whose members are shared by the sets G and H in (15) and (16), respectively. Keep in mind that the result of an intersection set only has members that are *shared* by parent sets.

  (15) G = {a, b, c, d, e}
  (16) H = {a, b, d, e, f}
  (17) G ∩ H = {a, b, d, e}

The union operator notated by ∪ creates a new set by combining all the members in the arbitrary sets α and β. For example, when the union operator is applied to the sets G and H above, the result is shown in (18).

(18) G ∪ H = {a, b, c, d, e, f}

The last notion we have to discuss is the size of a set. Sets may have any number of members, as seen in (19), where there could be an infinite amount of members. This is because the number of natural numbers is infinite.

(19) N = {x | x is a natural number}

By contrast, sets may contain no element at all, which is called an empty set, notated by ∅. For example, if sets A and B had no overlapping elements, the intersection of A and B would be ∅, as shown in (20).

(20) A ∩ B = ∅

Note that the empty set is still considered a set even when there is no element. For this reason, some people prefer the notation { } to refer to an empty set. Nonetheless, we will use the symbol ∅ for the empty set in this chapter.

7.1.2 Compositionality

In syntax, we discussed that an infinite number of sentences can be generated by a finite number of rules. The same is true in semantics. Let us consider the semantically very odd sentence in (21). It would be surprising if there was a Korean who likes to have cheddar cheese with kimchi broth, much less someone from Norway enjoying this concoction. Due to the oddity of the sentence, it is very unlikely that someone actually used this sentence prior to this instance. Nonetheless, we clearly know what (21) means if we know each word, including *kimchi*, which is fermented cabbage with many other ingredients, such as red pepper powder, garlic, ginger, green onions, and so on.

(21) The blonde woman from Norway likes to have cheddar cheese with kimchi broth.

How do we know the meaning of (21), even if we've never heard the sentence before? The answer for this question is to assume that we utilize some kinds of rules to get the meaning of (21) from its smaller parts. For example, each lexical item (word) has its own meaning in (21). When lexical items are combined, they form a phrase. The meaning of the phrase is coming from the combination of each lexical item. When you combine phrases, you get a sentence, whose meaning is again obtained by combining the meanings of phrases. To show this process in conjunction with syntactic structure, let us consider the fairly simple sentence in (22). We know the meaning of (22), but how do we get its meaning?

(22) John loves Mary.

The meaning of (22) is coming from its smaller parts. As we all know now, (22) has the syntactic structure shown in (23). For the sake of simplicity, let us go back and use the standard theory–based diagram, instead of the X′ theoretic illustration. In (23), each lexical item, *John*, *loves*, and *Mary*, has its own meaning. As shown in the structure, *loves* and *Mary* form one phrase, and that phrase also has its own meaning as a result of the combination of the meanings of *loves* and *Mary*. The noun phrase, *John*, and the VP, *loves*

Mary, combine to yield the sentence *John loves Mary*, where the meaning of the sentence is determined by the meanings of the smaller parts *John* and *loves Mary* by combining them in a certain way.

(23)

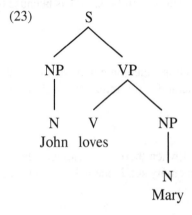

This type of a complex meaning formation method is called compositionality. The principle of compositionality states that the meaning of a complex expression is determined by its parts and the rules that combine the parts. In the example above, we have briefly demonstrated that the meaning of the VP *loves Mary* is determined by its parts, *loves* and *Mary*. Similarly, the meaning of the sentence *John loves Mary* is determined by its parts, *John* and *loves Mary*. When determining the meaning of a complex expression, certain types of rules are used to define what kinds of meanings are combined to yield different kinds of results. Our major concerns in this chapter are the compositional rules of complex linguistic expressions under the assumption of compositionality.

As readers might have noticed already, we will assume that there is a tight connection between the syntactic structure of a sentence and its meaning. Not every linguist agrees with this thought, however. Some linguists also question how close the relation between syntax and semantics is, if there indeed is a relation between the two. Nonetheless, by assuming that there is a tight relation between syntax and semantics, we believe readers will understand the notion of compositionality more easily. It is worth pointing out that compositionality is a methodological assumption in analyzing language rather than an absolute linguistic fact. Consider the idiom *kick the bucket*. This idiomatic expression cannot be explained by compositionality because the idiomatic meaning of *kick the bucket* is "to die," which cannot be understood from the combination of the three words: *kick*, *the*, and *bucket*. Though essential in our language use, idiomatic expressions will not be discussed in this chapter.

7.1.3 *Two types of meanings: reference and sense*

As the final notion of the preliminaries, we would like to discuss two types of meanings. The first type of meaning we will discuss is reference, which is also called denotation. The reference of an expression is what it stands for on a given occasion of its use. For example, the reference of *the morning star* is Venus, and the reference of *the evening star* is Venus as well. In other words, as far as reference is concerned, *the morning star* and *the evening star* have the same meaning. Because *the morning star* and *the evening star* have the same meaning, we should be able to use them interchangeably, without changing the meaning of (24). However, (25), where *the evening star* is replaced with *the morning star*, clearly has a different meaning from (24).

(24) The morning star is the evening star.
(25) The morning star is the morning star.

(24) can be uttered in the situation where one person did not know that *the morning star* was actually the same as *the evening star*. By contrast, (25) does not convey this type of an astronomical discovery meaning. What this reveals is that the morning star and the evening star have different meanings in their senses, although they have the same reference. Here, sense is understood as a concept that enables us to communicate with each other in an objective way. In other words, the notion of concept must not be subjective, which might differ from speaker to speaker. The big difference between (24) and (25) is that *the morning star* and *the evening star* have the same reference, although they have different senses. As a result, (24) is understood as an informative statement. This type of reference-sense discrepancy is not found in (25), yielding (25) as an uninformative statement, unless (25) is used in a certain pragmatic context, such as "The morning star is the morning star; what's so special about it?" Although this type of pragmatic non-truth-conditional meaning is a very important subject in understanding the meaning of natural language, we will not discuss the issue until Chapter 8.

Although the notion of sense plays an important role in various types of modern logic, we will deal with the reference meaning only in this chapter. This will make the topic of semantics more approachable to readers. Simply put, the reference of an individual name such as *John* is the designated object by the individual name. The reference of a sentence is a truth value. Remember that both reference and denotation are used interchangeably throughout this chapter. Based on these simple assumptions and preliminaries, we will discuss how we get the meaning of a complex expression from the meanings of its parts in the following sections.

7.2 Semantic Computation: Intransitive Verbs

7.2.1 A case of a simple sentence

The first sentence we will analyze is (26), where the predicate is an intransitive verb.

(26) John sleeps.

The syntactic structure for (26), as we know, is (27). In (27), the meaning of the NP, *John*, is the person designated by the name *John*, which is notated by $[John]^v$. What exactly $[John]^v$ means is "the semantic value of *John* in the certain circumstance v," where v is a situation or a specification of the relevant facts. Similarly, the meaning of the VP, *sleeps*, is notated by $[sleeps]^v$, which is a set of individuals, notated by $\{x \mid x \text{ sleeps}\}$. The sentence S is true when *John* is a member of the set $\{x \mid x \text{ sleeps}\}$ in the given circumstance.

(27)

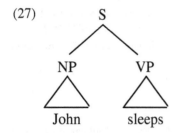

Now, consider the following situation called v_1, where the denotation of *John* is John and the denotation of *sleeps* is the set {John, Bill, Tom}, meaning people in that particular set *sleep*.

(28) a. $[\![John]\!]^{v1} = John$
      b. $[\![sleeps]\!]^{v1} = \{John, Bill, Tom\}$

In this particular circumstance, sentence (26) is true because John is a member of the set {John, Bill, Tom}. The calculation of this sentence is shown in (29).

(29) $[\![John\ sleeps]\!]^{v1} = true$ because John $\in$ {John, Bill, Tom}

Now, we can explain this in relation to the structure provided in (27), which is reintroduced with a number for each node in (30).

(30)

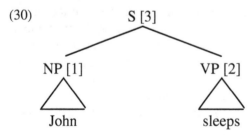

Then the semantic composition of (30) is illustrated in (31).

(31) a. $[\![1]\!]^{v1} = John$
      b. $[\![2]\!]^{v1} = \{John, Bill, Tom\}$
      c. $[\![3]\!]^{v1} = true$ because John $\in$ {John, Bill, Tom}

From now on, we will use the same numbered notations for the semantic interpretations of the nodes in the syntactic structure of a given sentence.

7.2.2 A case of a conjunction

Now that we know how to provide the semantic interpretation of a simple sentence with an intransitive verb, let us consider a conjoined sentence, as in (32). The syntactic structure of (32) is provided in (33) with numbers.

(32) John sleeps and Mary snores.

(33)

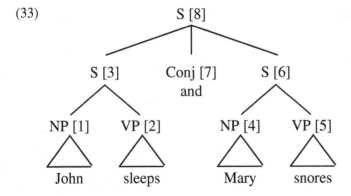

Let us evaluate (32) in the particular situation called v_2, provided in (34).

(34) a. $[\text{John}]^{v2} = \text{John}$
  b. $[\text{Mary}]^{v2} = \text{Mary}$
  c. $[\text{sleeps}]^{v2} = \{\text{John, Bill, Tom}\}$
  d. $[\text{snores}]^{v2} = \{\text{John, Bill}\}$

The step-by-step illustration of the semantic interpretation of (33) is provided in (35).

(35) a. $[1]^{v2} = \text{John}$
  b. $[2]^{v2} = \{\text{John, Bill, Tom}\}$
  c. $[3]^{v2} = \text{true because John} \in \{\text{John, Bill, Tom}\}$
  d. $[4]^{v2} = \text{Mary}$
  e. $[5]^{v2} = \{\text{John, Bill}\}$
  f. $[6]^{v2} = \text{false because Mary} \in \{\text{John, Bill}\}$

To combine $[3]^{v2}$ and $[6]^{v2}$, we have to know the denotation of $[7]^{v2}$, which is a conjunction. When two sentences are combined by *and*, the denotation of the conjoined sentence is defined in (36). This might not make sense to some, but if you don't understand just yet, remember that we will come back to (36) after discussing the meaning of *and*.

(36) $[\text{S1 and S2}]^{v} = [\text{and}]^{v}(<[\text{S1}]^{v}, [\text{S2}]^{v}>)$

The denotation of *and* in circumstance v is provided in (37). (37) explains that the denotation of *and* is a function that maps ordered pairs of truth values onto truth values. This explanation sounds complicated, but what it means is essentially the same as the truth table for *and*, which we discussed in Chapter 6. In (37), $< T, T >$ means an ordered pair of T and T. In other words, what $< T, T >$ means is that the first proposition of the conjoined proposition is true, and the second proposition is true as well. If the input of this function is $< T, T >$, then the output of the function must be T, which is notated by $< T, T > \rightarrow T$.

(37) $[\text{and}]^{v} = \begin{bmatrix} < T, T > \rightarrow T \\ < T, F > \rightarrow F \\ < F, T > \rightarrow F \\ < F, F > \rightarrow F \end{bmatrix}$

Now, let us apply (36) and (37) to the interpretation of $[\![8]\!]^{v2}$. As defined in (36), $[\![8]\!]^{v2}$ is illustrated as in (38).

(38) $[\![8]\!]^{v2} = \begin{bmatrix} <T, T> \rightarrow T \\ <T, F> \rightarrow F \\ <F, T> \rightarrow F \\ <F, F> \rightarrow F \end{bmatrix} (<[\![3]\!]^{v2}, [\![6]\!]^{v2} >)$

Because we know the truth value of $[\![3]\!]^{v2}$ and $[\![6]\!]^{v2}$, we can replace them with their truth values, as shown in (39). According to (39), $[\![8]\!]^{v2}$ is false because among the truth values, the selected pair is the ordered pair $< T, F >$, which is false, as noted by $< T, F > \rightarrow F$ in (39). The selected truth value $< T, F > \rightarrow F$ within the matrix [ ], and the ordered pair $< T, F >$ of the truth values of $[\![3]\!]^{v2}$ and $[\![6]\!]^{v2}$ are shaded for you to see.

(39) $[\![8]\!]^{v2} = \begin{bmatrix} <T, T> \rightarrow T \\ <T, F> \rightarrow F \\ <F, T> \rightarrow F \\ <F, F> \rightarrow F \end{bmatrix} (<T, F >)$

We have shown the semantic interpretation of a conjoined sentence by *and*. The same technique can be extended to the interpretation of a disjoined sentence by *or*, which is the topic of the next section.

7.2.3 Disjunction

In Chapter 6, we discussed the logical difference between *and* and *or*. Although both *and* and *or* share a great syntactic similarity, they have different semantic values, as we illustrated by using truth tables. Keeping in mind the truth table of *or*, let us consider the sentence in (40). The structure of (40), which is shown in (41), is identical to (33) except that *or* (instead of *and*) appears under the node [7] in (41).

(40) John sleeps or Mary snores.

(41)

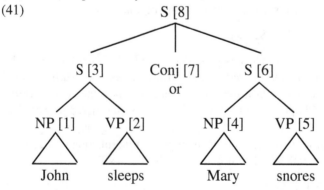

To compare the denotation of (40) with that of (32), let us assume the same situation v_2. For convenience, we will reintroduce the denotations of *John, Mary, sleeps,* and *snores* under the situation v_2, as in (42).

(42) a. $\llbracket \text{John} \rrbracket^{v2} = \text{John}$
    b. $\llbracket \text{Mary} \rrbracket^{v2} = \text{Mary}$
    b. $\llbracket \text{sleeps} \rrbracket^{v2} = \{\text{John, Bill, Tom}\}$
    c. $\llbracket \text{snores} \rrbracket^{v2} = \{\text{John, Bill}\}$

Before we start our step-by-step computation of (41), let's define the denotation of *or* in a certain circumstance *v* as in (43), which is almost identical to the case of *and*. What (43) tells us is that the meaning of *or* is a function that contains four inputs and their corresponding four outputs. In this function, four ordered pairs composed of two truth values such as $< T, T >$ are inputs, and four truth values are outputs, which are the result of the *or* operation applied to the ordered pairs. Although the presentation of (43) is different from that of the truth table for *or* that we discussed in Chapter 6, what (43) conveys is exactly the same as the truth table for *or*.

(43) $\llbracket \text{or} \rrbracket^{v} = \begin{bmatrix} < T, T > \rightarrow T \\ < T, F > \rightarrow T \\ < F, T > \rightarrow T \\ < F, F > \rightarrow F \end{bmatrix}$

Similar to the case of *and*, the denotation of $\llbracket S1 \text{ or } S2 \rrbracket^{v}$ is then defined as in (44). In other words, the denotation of the disjoined sentence *S1 or S2* is the truth value selected from the truth table for *or* based on the truth values of S1 and S1.

(44) $\llbracket S1 \text{ or } S2 \rrbracket^{v} = \begin{bmatrix} < T, T > \rightarrow T \\ < T, F > \rightarrow T \\ < F, T > \rightarrow T \\ < F, F > \rightarrow F \end{bmatrix}$ $(< \llbracket S1 \rrbracket^{v}, \llbracket S2 \rrbracket^{v} >)$

Armed with these necessary definitions, the step-by-step computation of the disjoined sentence in (41) is provided in (45).

(45) a. $\llbracket 1 \rrbracket^{v2} = \text{John}$
    b. $\llbracket 2 \rrbracket^{v2} = \{\text{John, Bill, Tom}\}$
    c. $\llbracket 3 \rrbracket^{v2} = \text{true because John} \in \{\text{John, Bill, Tom}\}$
    d. $\llbracket 4 \rrbracket^{v2} = \text{Mary}$
    e. $\llbracket 5 \rrbracket^{v2} = \{\text{John, Bill}\}$
    f. $\llbracket 6 \rrbracket^{v2} = \text{false because Mary} \in \{\text{John, Bill}\}$

    g. $\llbracket 7 \rrbracket^{v2} = \begin{bmatrix} < T, T > \rightarrow T \\ < T, F > \rightarrow T \\ < F, T > \rightarrow T \\ < F, F > \rightarrow F \end{bmatrix}$

    h. $\llbracket 8 \rrbracket^{v2} = \begin{bmatrix} < T, T > \rightarrow T \\ < T, F > \rightarrow T \\ < F, T > \rightarrow T \\ < F, F > \rightarrow F \end{bmatrix}$ $(< \llbracket 3 \rrbracket^{v2}, \llbracket 6 \rrbracket^{v2} >)$

Now, in (45g), we know the truth values of $\llbracket 3 \rrbracket^{v2}$ and $\llbracket 6 \rrbracket^{v2}$, which are true and false, respectively. As a result, our final step of the computation looks like (46), which yields the value T for the sentence *John sleeps or Mary snores*.

$$(46) \quad \llbracket 8 \rrbracket^{v2} = \begin{bmatrix} <T, T> \rightarrow T \\ <T, F> \rightarrow T \\ <F, T> \rightarrow T \\ <F, F> \rightarrow F \end{bmatrix} \quad (<T, F>)$$

Thus far, we have discussed examples of sentential conjunction and disjunction, where two sentences are combined by *and* or *or*. As we discussed in earlier chapters, phrases can be combined by *and* or *or*, too. Phrasal conjunction and disjunction are the topics of the next section.

7.2.4 Phrasal conjunction

In this section, we will discuss the semantic interpretations of a sentence that contains a conjoined VP, as in (47).

(47) John sleeps and snores.

As the first step, we need to know the syntactic structure of (47), which is provided in (48). As usual, each node is provided with a number for the sake of exposition.

(48)

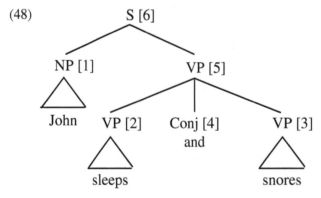

Although the structure provided in (48) is somewhat similar to (33), (48) is clearly different from (33) because the conjunction *and* combines two VPs in (48), whereas it combines two sentences in (33). What is the denotation of the conjunction *and* in this case, then? Is it the same as the *and* that combines two sentences? It cannot be because the *and* in (48) combines two VPs, and the denotations of the VPs cannot be a truth value because VPs are not propositions.

Recall that only propositions can have a truth value as their reference. We can think of the denotation of *and* in this VP conjunction case carefully now. As we discussed in section 7.2.1, the meaning of a VP (or a V) is a set of individuals. In other words, the denotation of *sleeps* is a set of individuals in a certain circumstance. Similarly, the meaning of *snores* is a set of individuals in a certain circumstance, too. Therefore, the *and* in (48) combines two sets, yielding a new set. The operation that the *and* performs in this case is to create a new set that is an intersection of the denotation of *sleeps* and the denotation of *snores*.

It is not hard to understand why the denotation of *and* is intersection when it combines two sets. Let us consider (49), which is often used in our ordinary conversation. Jane is taking two classes, one being a linguistics class and the other a mathematics class. The linguistics class is a set that contains many students. Similarly, the mathematics class is a set that contains many students, too. Because Jane is taking both linguistics and mathematics, Jane belongs to the two sets at the same time, which is exactly the meaning of intersection.

(49) Jane is taking linguistics and mathematics.

If this is the case, we need to redefine the denotation of *and* when it combines two VPs, which is provided in (50). What (50) states is that the denotation of the conjunction of VP1 and VP2 in the certain circumstance v is the intersection of the denotation of VP1 and the denotation of VP2, where the denotations of VP1 and VP2 are sets of individuals. In this case, the denotation of *and* itself is simply the intersection operation, as shown in (51).

(50) $[\![\text{VP1 and VP2}]\!]^v = [\![\text{VP1}]\!]^v \cap [\![\text{VP2}]\!]^v$
(51) $[\![\text{and}]\!]^v = \cap$

If we apply this definition to (48), the denotation of [5] is the intersection of $[\![2]\!]$ and $[\![3]\!]$, where the intersection operation is performed by the set operator *and* denoted by $\cap$.

Based on the definition of *and* provided in (50) and (51), let us provide the semantic interpretation of (48) under the circumstance v_3 provided in (52).

(52) $[\![\text{John}]\!]^{v3} = \text{John}$
$[\![\text{sleeps}]\!]^{v3} = \{\text{John, Mary, Lily, Tom}\}$
$[\![\text{snores}]\!]^{v3} = \{\text{Mary, Tom, Jane}\}$
$[\![\text{and}]\!]^{v3} = \cap$

The step-by-step semantic interpretation of (48) is illustrated in (53).

(53) a. $[\![1]\!]^{v3} = \text{John}$
b. $[\![2]\!]^{v3} = \{\text{John, Mary, Lily, Tom}\}$
c. $[\![3]\!]^{v3} = \{\text{Mary, Tom, Jane}\}$
d. $[\![4]\!]^{v3} = \cap$
e. $[\![5]\!]^{v3} = \{\text{John, Mary, Lily, Tom}\} \cap \{\text{Mary, Tom, Jane}\} = \{\text{Mary, Tom}\}$
f. $[\![6]\!]^{v3} = \text{false because John} \notin \{\text{Mary, Tom}\}$

As we saw, the denotation of *and* is the intersection set operator when *and* syntactically combines two VPs. Not surprisingly, the disjunction *or* is also used as a set operator when it combines two VPs, which will be discussed in the next section.

7.2.5 Phrasal disjunction

The denotation of *or* when it syntactically combines two sentences is a function that contains four ordered pairs with their corresponding outputs. However, this is not the only meaning of *or*. Let us consider (54), where two VPs are combined by *or*. Just like the case of the conjunction *and*, *or* combines two VPs in (54). Therefore, the denotation of *or* cannot be the same as the *or* that combines two sentences. This is because a VP cannot have a truth value; only propositions can be true or false.

(54) John sleeps or snores.

Before we show the semantic interpretation of (54), let us show its syntactic structure, which is essentially identical to (48), except for the use of *or* instead of *and*. The structure is given in (55) below.

(55)

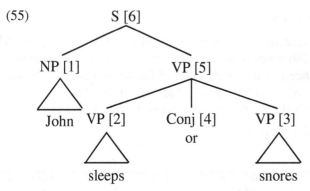

Because the definition of *or* as a sentential disjunction does not work for this case, we need a new definition for *or* that combines two VPs. The denotation of a disjoined VP by *or* in a certain circumstance *v* is defined in (56). What (56) defines is that the denotation of a disjoined VP by *or* is the union of the two sets denoted by VP1 and VP2, where the denotation of *or* is the union operation, as shown in (57).

(56) $[\![\text{VP or VP2}]\!]^v = [\![\text{VP1}]\!]^v \cup [\![\text{VP2}]\!]^v$
(57) $[\![\text{or}]\!]^v = \cup$

Although some readers might be puzzled by the denotation of *or* in this case, explaining (56) and (57) is straightforward. Consider (58), where two VPs are disjoined by *or*. Once again, the linguistics class Jane is taking is a set that contains many students. The mathematics class is a set that contains many students as well. Let's assume that we are not sure exactly which class Jane is taking between the two, but we know for sure that Jane is taking at least one of them. To make the proposition in (58) true, Jane must belong to at least one set created by the linguistics and the mathematics classes. In other words, if Jane belongs to the set that is a union of the two sets (the linguistics and mathematics classes), then the proposition in (58) becomes true. In this sense, the denotation of *or* as a union is very intuitive.

(58) Jane is taking linguistics or mathematics.

Now that we know the denotation of *or* when it combines two VPs, let us start our step-by-step computation of (55) under the same circumstance v_4, provided in (59). The step-by-step illustration is given in (60).

(59) $\lceil$John$\rceil^{v4}$ = John
$\lceil$sleeps$\rceil^{v4}$ = {John, Mary, Lily, Tom}
$\lceil$snores$\rceil^{v4}$ = {Mary, Tom, Jane}
$\lceil$or$\rceil^{v4}$ = $\cup$

(60) a. $\lceil 1 \rceil^{v4}$ = John
 b. $\lceil 2 \rceil^{v4}$ = {John, Mary, Lily, Tom}
 c. $\lceil 3 \rceil^{v4}$ = {Mary, Tom, Jane}
 d. $\lceil 4 \rceil^{v4}$ = $\cup$
 e. $\lceil 5 \rceil^{v4}$ = {John, Mary, Lily, Tom} $\cup$ {Mary, Tom, Jane} = {John, Mary, Lily, Tom, Jane}
 f. $\lceil 6 \rceil^{v4}$ = true because John $\in$ {John, Mary, Lily, Tom, Jane}

We have discussed two types of *and* and two types of *or*, depending on the syntactic structure of a sentence. If you understand these distinctions, you can now provide the semantic interpretation of a more complex proposition, like (61), under the circumstance v_5 given in (62).

(61) John sleeps or snores and Mary runs or walks.
(62) $\lceil$John$\rceil^{v5}$ = John
$\lceil$Mary$\rceil^{v5}$ = Mary
$\lceil$sleeps$\rceil^{v5}$ = {John, Mary, Jane, Bill}
$\lceil$snores$\rceil^{v5}$ = {John, Bill}
$\lceil$runs$\rceil^{v5}$ = {Mary}
$\lceil$walks$\rceil^{v5}$ = {Jane}

The best way to show the step-by-step semantic interpretation of (61) is to start from its syntactic structure. You should first draw a tree for (61), giving each node a number. Then provide a semantic interpretation for each node. In doing so, you have to remember that there are two types of *and* and *or*, whose denotations are not provided in (62) above. If you are not sure about them, you should review the definitions of *and* and *or* that we discussed in this section. Although (61) is more complex than the examples we have dealt with thus far, you should be able to calculate the correct answer by reviewing the steps and working carefully.

7.3 Semantic Computation: Transitive Verbs

So far, we have focused on the semantics of intransitive verbs. In this section, we will deal with the semantics of transitive verbs, which is a bit more complicated. Look at the sentence in (63), which contains the transitive verb *loves*. It is not hard to see that the verb *loves* shows a relation between *John* and *Mary*, which is different from an intransitive verb, where the verb shows a relation to its subject only.

(63) John loves Mary.

In other words, the denotation of a transitive verb must be some kind of relation between the two noun phrases, one being the subject, the other the object. Let us define the denotation of the transitive verb *loves* in the certain circumstance v_5 as in (64). The denotation of *loves* in the circumstance v_5 is a set that contains ordered pairs as its members. As the name suggests, in an ordered pair, if the order changes, it has a different meaning. For example, < John, Mary > and < Mary, John > are two different expressions. In other words, what (64) shows is that the denotation of *loves* in the circumstance v_5 is the three pairs: *John loves Mary, Mary loves John*, and *Bill loves Mary*.

(64) $[\text{loves}]^{v5}$ = {< John, Mary >, < Mary, John >, < Bill, Mary >}

The denotation of the VP, $[\text{loves Mary}]^{v5}$, is defined in (65). What (65) means is that the denotation of *loves* in the circumstance v_5 is the ordered pair that has *Mary* as its second member and that is a member of the set $[\text{loves}]^{v5}$. That is, the denotation of *loves Mary* in the circumstance v_5 is the set { < John, Mary >, < Bill, Mary > }. This is because, among the three ordered pairs in the set $[\text{loves}]^{v5}$, only < John, Mary > and < Bill, Mary > have *Mary* as their second member. These two ordered pairs are also members of the set {< John, Mary >, < Mary, John >, < Bill, Mary >}, which is the denotation of *loves*.

(65) $[\text{loves Mary}]^{v5}$ = {x | < x, $[\text{Mary}]^{v5}$ > ∈ $[\text{loves}]^{v5}$ } = {< John, Mary >, < Bill, Mary >}

The generalized definition of a VP that contains a transitive verb is provided in (66), where VP_t stands for a VP that contains a transitive verb, and NP_o stands for an object NP.

(66) $[\text{V NP}_o]^v$ = {x | < x, $[\text{NP}]^v$ > ∈ $[\text{V}]^v$}

The whole sentence $[\text{John loves Mary}]^{v5}$ is then true when there is an ordered pair that has John as it first member. Because the set {< John, Mary >, < Bill, Mary >}, shown in (65), has the ordered pair < John, Mary >, where John is the first member of the ordered pair, the truth value of $[\text{John loves Mary}]^{v5}$ is true. A more general definition of the denotation of a sentence that contains a transitive verb is provided in (67), which states that a proposition that contains a transitive verb is true in the certain circumstance *v* if and only if the ordered pair < $[\text{NP}_s]^v$, $[\text{NP}_o]^v$ > is a member of the set $[\text{VP}_t]^v$, where NP_s stands for a subject NP.

(67) $[\text{NP}_s \text{ VP}_t]^v$ = 1 if and only if < $[\text{NP}_s]^v$, $[\text{NP}_o]^v$ > ∈ $[\text{VP}_t]^v$

Let us explain this with our example in (63) under the specific circumstance v_5. As we explained in (65), the meaning of the VP_t, *loves Mary,* in the circumstance *v5* is the set of ordered pairs {< John, Mary >, < Bill, Mary > }. In (63), *John* is the subject NP (NP_s), and its denotation is John. In the sentence, *Mary* is the object NP (NP_o), and its denotation is Mary. Therefore, the ordered pair of < $[\text{NP}_s]^{v5}$, $[\text{NP}_o]^{v5}$ > is < John, Mary >. Because < John, Mary > is a member of the denotation of VP_t, { < John, Mary >, < Bill, Mary > }, the sentence becomes true.

Now, let us go back to the sentence in (63) to provide its semantic interpretation. The structure for (63) is provided in (68) with a number for each node.

(68)

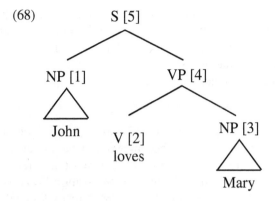

The situation v_5, against which we will evaluate the truth value of (68), is given in (69).

(69) $\llbracket \text{John} \rrbracket^{v5} = \text{John}$
$\llbracket \text{Mary} \rrbracket^{v5} = \text{Mary}$
$\llbracket \text{loves} \rrbracket^{v5} = \{ <\text{John, Mary}>, <\text{Bill, Mary}>, <\text{Tom, Jane}> \}$

Given the definitions and the situation v_5, the step-by-step semantic interpretations of (68) are illustrated in (70).

(70) a. $\llbracket 1 \rrbracket^{v5} = \text{John}$
b. $\llbracket 2 \rrbracket^{v5} = \{ <\text{John, Mary}>, <\text{Bill, Mary}>, <\text{Tom, Jane}> \}$
c. $\llbracket 3 \rrbracket^{v5} = \text{Mary}$
d. $\llbracket 4 \rrbracket^{v5} = \{ <\text{John, Mary}>, <\text{Bill, Mary}> \}$
e. $\llbracket 5 \rrbracket^{v5} = \text{true because} <\text{John, Mary}> \in \{<\text{John, Mary}>, <\text{Bill, Mary}>\}$

Although the semantic interpretations of transitive verbs are more complicated than those of intransitive verbs, we have used the same principle to show them. That is, the meaning of the sentence that contains a transitive verb is determined by the meanings of its parts: NP_s, VP_t, V_t, and NP_o. To account for the semantic computation, we have used somewhat complex-looking formalisms. However, they are only superficially complex-looking because, when you understand the notion of compositionality and the preliminaries we discussed earlier in this chapter, understanding these formalisms shouldn't be difficult. For readers who do not have any previous experience with this type of formalism, we recommend that they go back to the preliminaries provided in section 7.1 and subsequent sections and carefully review the information presented by checking all steps in each semantic computation.

7.4 Semantic Computation: Quantifiers

The last topic of this chapter is the semantic interpretations of quantifiers. We will deal with four quantifiers in this section, which include *every*, *some*, *no*, and *most*. The semantics of English quantifiers is a very complicated topic, and a great amount of research has been conducted on their nature. To discuss the semantics of English quantifiers in their entirety, we would need to discuss detailed formal mechanisms that go far beyond of the scope of this book. Interested readers may refer to other textbooks that focus on semantics only; some are listed in section 7.6 as further reading. In this section, we will see what kinds of roles English quantifiers play in determining the truth value of a sentence. The formalism provided here, therefore, is extremely simplified to show the general functions of the quantifiers only.

7.4.1 Every

We will start by first defining the denotation of the proposition in (71) as in (72). In a certain situation v, the sentence that contains *every* as in *every α β* becomes true when the denotation of α is a subset of the denotation of β. Here, both α and β are variables that refer to a noun and a verb phrase, respectively. In other words, in explaining the proposition *Every man runs*, α will be replaced with *man*, and β will be replaced with *runs*. We already know that the denotation *runs* is a set of individuals. As we saw in Chapter 6, *man* as in *every man* also behaves like a predicate, having the denotation of a set of individuals. Therefore, what (72) means is that a sentence like (71) becomes true when the denotation of the subject noun phrase is a subset of the denotation of the VP.

(71) Every man runs.
(72) $[\![$every α $\beta]\!]^v$ is true if and only if $[\![\alpha]\!]^v \subseteq [\![\beta]\!]^v$

To explain this definition with an example, assume the specific situation v_6 in (73).

(73) $[\![$man$]\!]^{v_6}$ = {John, Bill, Tom, Mike}
      $[\![$runs$]\!]^{v_6}$ = {John, Tom}

As we know, the first thing we have to do to check the truth value of (71) is to draw a tree diagram, which is given in (74) with a number for each node, as usual.

(74)

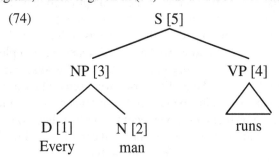

Then the step-by-step semantic interpretation of (74) is provided under the circumstance given in (73), as in (75). In (75), the denotations of [1] and [3] are not provided to simplify the explanation. Let us just assume that the denotation of *every* is $\forall x$, and the denotation of *every man* is something like $\forall x[\text{man}(x)]$, which reads like *for all x, x is a man*. As illustrated in (75), [5] in (74) is false because the condition to make [5] true is not met. (75c) illustrates that [5] in (74) is false because the denotation of *man* (all the members of the set) is not a subset of the denotation of *runs*.

(75) a. $[2]^{v6} = \{$John, Bill, Tom, Mike$\}$
b. $[4]^{v6} = \{$John, Tom$\}$
c. $[5]^{v6} = $ true if and only if $[$man$]^{v6} \subseteq [$sleeps$]^{v6}$
In other words, if and only if $[2]^{v6} \subseteq [4]^{v6}$
$[5]^{v6} = $ false because $\{$John, Bill, Tom, Mike$\}$ is not a subset of $\{$John, Tom$\}$

There is an interesting question concerning the quantifier *every* and the conjunction *or*. Let us take a look at the sentences in (76) and (77). Many people might be tempted to say that the two sentences have the same truth value, assuming that (76) is actually a shortened form of (77). This is not the case, however.

(76) Every man runs or walks.
(77) Every man runs or every man walks.

To compare the truth values of (76) and (77), let us assume the circumstance v_7, as in (78).

(78) $[$man$]^{v7} = \{$John, Bill, Tom, Mike$\}$
$[$runs$]^{v7} = \{$John, Bill$\}$
$[$walks$]^{v7} = \{$Tom, Mike$\}$

Let us first draw a tree diagram for (76), which looks like (79).

(79)

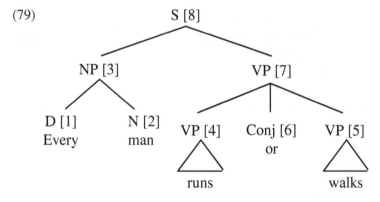

The step-by-step computation of (79) is provided in (80), where we once again omitted the denotations of [1] and [3] for the sake of avoiding redundancy.

(80) a. $[2]^{v7} = \{$John, Bill, Tom, Mike$\}$
b. $[4]^{v7} = \{$John, Bill$\}$
c. $[5]^{v7} = \{$Tom, Mike$\}$
d. $[6]^{v7} = \cup$
e. $[7]^{v7} = \{$John, Bill, Tom, Mike$\}$
f. $[8]^{v7} = $ true if and only if $[$man$]^{v7} \subseteq [$runs or walks$]^{v7}$
In other words, if and only if $[2]^{v7} \subseteq [7]^{v7}$
$[8]^{v7} = $ true because $\{$John, Bill, Tom, Mike$\} \subseteq \{$John, Bill, Tom, Mike$\}$

As illustrated in (80), (79) is true in the given circumstance v_7. What about the truth value of (77)? Let us now check the truth value of (77) under the same circumstance v_7. The tree diagram of (77) is provided in (81).

(81)

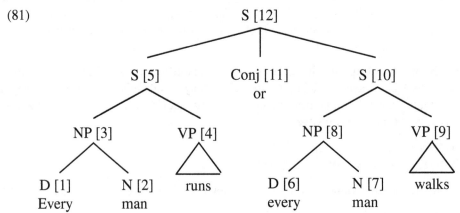

The step-by-step computation of (81) in the circumstance v_7 is provided in (82).

(82) a. $[2]^{v_7}$ = {John, Bill, Tom, Mike}
 b. $[4]^{v_7}$ = {John, Bill}
 c. $[5]^{v_7}$ = true if and only if $[2]^{v_7} \subseteq [4]^{v_7}$
    In other words, if and only if {John, Bill, Tom, Mike}$\subseteq$ {John, Bill}
    $[5]^{v_7}$ = false because {John, Bill, Tom, Mike} is not a subset of {John, Bill}
 d. $[7]^{v_7}$ = {John, Bill, Tom, Mike}
 e. $[9]^{v_7}$ = {Tom, Mike}
 f. $[10]^{v_7}$ = true if and only if $[7]^{v_7} \subseteq [9]^{v_7}$
    In other words, if and only if {John, Bill, Tom, Mike} $\subseteq$ {Tom, Mike}
   $[10]^{v_7}$ = false because {John, Bill, Tom, Mike} is not a subset of {Tom, Mike}

 g. $[11]^{v_7} = \begin{bmatrix} <T, T> \to T \\ <T, F> \to T \\ <F, T> \to T \\ <F, F> \to F \end{bmatrix}$

 h. $[12]^{v_7} = \begin{bmatrix} <T, T> \to T \\ <T, F> \to T \\ <F, T> \to T \\ <F, F> \to F \end{bmatrix}$ $(< [5]^{v_7}, [10]^{v_7} >)$

In other words,

$[12]^{v_7} = \begin{bmatrix} <T, T> \to T \\ <T, F> \to T \\ <F, T> \to T \\ <F, F> \to F \end{bmatrix}$ $(<F, F>)$

Therefore, $[12]^{v_7}$ = false.

As we saw, (77) is false, while (76) is true in the same circumstance v_7. This type of problem is often not easy to identify without recourse to a mathematical way of thinking. We have now learned that our semantic computation can provide a rigorous way of distinguishing the two seemingly identical sentences in their meanings.

7.4.2 Some

The second quantifier we will discuss is *some*. Let's look at (83). How do we know whether the proposition in (83) is true or false in a certain circumstance? If you understood the case of *every*, this should not be a difficult question to answer after some additional instruction.

(83) Some man runs.

In the case of *every*, *every* α β becomes true when the denotation of α is a subset of the denotation of β. The same type of definition can be applied to explain the meaning of (83). That is, *some* α β is true when the intersection of the denotations of α and β is not an empty set. To explain this definition, let us consider the circumstance provided in (73). We know that the denotation of *man* is the set {John, Bill, Tom, Mike} and the denotation of *runs* is {John, Tom}. Under the circumstance, and to make (83) true, at least one member of the set {John, Bill, Tom, Mike} must also be the member of the set {John, Tom}. In other words, the intersection between the two sets must not be an empty set because at least one member should overlap. To show the step-by-step semantic interpretation, the diagram for (83) is provided in (84).

(84)

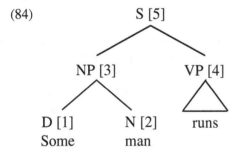

The semantic computation of (84) is then provided in (85) under the circumstance v_6. (85a) and (85b) are straightforward. (85c) seems to be a bit complicated, but this is exactly the same as the explanation provided in prose above the diagram. $[\![5]\!]^{v6}$ is true when the intersection of $[\![2]\!]^{v6}$ and $[\![4]\!]^{v6}$ is not an empty set. Under the given circumstance v_6, the intersection of the two sets is {John, Tom}, which, of course, is not an empty set. Therefore, $[\![5]\!]^{v6}$ is true.

(85) a. $[\![2]\!]^{v6}$ = {John, Bill, Tom, Mike}
　　　b. $[\![4]\!]^{v6}$ = {John, Tom}
　　　c. $[\![5]\!]^{v6}$ = true if and only if $[\![man]\!]^{v6} \cap [\![runs]\!]^{v6} \neq \varnothing$
　　　　　In other words, if and only if $[\![2]\!]^{v6} \cap [\![4]\!]^{v6} \neq \varnothing$
　　　$[\![5]\!]^{v6}$ = true because {John, Bill, Tom, Mike} $\cap$ {John, Tom} = {John, Tom}

Although the computation might look complicated, the notion itself is intuitive. If you understand the computation provided in (85), the interpretation of the quantifier *no* naturally falls out because the meaning of *no* is indeed the opposite of *some*, which is explained in the following section.

7.4.3 No

As we have discussed, *some α β* is true when the intersection of the denotations of α and β is not an empty set. When does the proposition *no α β* become true? Not surprisingly, *no α β* is true when the intersection of the denotations of α and β is an empty set. To explain the case of *no*, let us consider (86). To make (86) true, no member of the set denoted by *man* should belong to the set denoted by *runs*. If there is at least one member that belongs to the two sets, the proposition in (86) is false, which is clearly the opposite of the case of *some*.

(86) No man runs.

To provide the semantic interpretation of (86), the tree diagram for (86) is provided in (87).

(87)

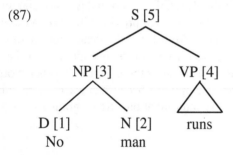

Then the step-by-step semantic computation of (87) is provided in (88), under the circumstance v_6 given in (73). Keep in mind that *no α β* becomes true in the opposite situation that makes *some α β* true. (88c) shows that $[\![5]\!]^{v_6}$ is true when the intersection of $[\![man]\!]^{v_6}$ and $[\![runs]\!]^{v_6}$ is an empty set. Because the intersection is not an empty set in the given circumstance, $[\![5]\!]^{v_6}$ is false.

(88) a. $[\![2]\!]^{v_6}$ = {John, Bill, Tom, Mike}
    b. $[\![4]\!]^{v_6}$ = {John, Tom}
    c. $[\![5]\!]^{v_6}$ = true, if and only if $[\![man]\!]^{v_6} \cap [\![runs]\!]^{v_6} = \varnothing$
        In other words, if and only if $[\![2]\!]^{v_6} \cap [\![4]\!]^{v_6} = \varnothing$
        $[\![5]\!]^{v_6}$ = false because {John, Bill, Tom, Mike} ∩ {John, Tom} = {John, Tom}

7.4.4 Most

The last quantifier we will discuss is *most*. Compared to the other three quantifiers we have already discussed, *most* is somewhat complicated. Intuitively, we know that (89) becomes true when *more than half of the men in the given situation run*.

(89) Most men run.

The question, then, is how to explain the truth condition in our system. The truth condition of *most α β* is defined in (90).

(90) $\left[\text{Most } \alpha \; \beta\right]^{v} = $ true if and only if $| \left[\alpha\right]^{v} \cap \left[\beta\right]^{v} | \times 2 > | \left[\alpha\right]^{v} |$

To understand what (90) means, we need to understand the notation | |. The | | notation returns the number of the elements in the set inside | |. For example, the result of |{a, b, c, d}| is 4, as in (91), because the number of the elements of the set {a, b, c, d} is 4.

(91) |{a, b, c, d}| = 4

Now, let us consider the circumstance v_7, where there are five men and only three of them are running. To make (89) true under the circumstance v_7, more than half of the individuals in the set represented in (92a) must belong to the set represented in (92b).

(92) a. $\left[\text{man}\right]^{v7} = $ {John, Bill, Tom, Chris, Max}
     b. $\left[\text{runs}\right]^{v7} = $ {John, Chris, Max}

The intuitive explanation can be technically accounted for like "the number of the elements in the intersection of $\left[\text{man}\right]^{v7}$ and $\left[\text{runs}\right]^{v7}$, which is multiplied by 2, is greater than the number of the elements in the set denoted by $\left[\text{man}\right]^{v7}$." This explanation sounds very complicated, but it is essentially the same as *more than half*. Based on the understanding of (90), let us provide a semantic interpretation of (89). The tree diagram for (89) is provided in (93).

(93)

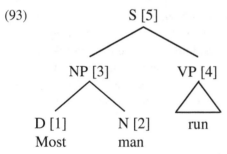

The step-by-step computation is provided in (94). Ignore some inflectional discrepancies between *man/men* and *run/runs*.

(94) a. $\left[2\right]^{v7} = $ {John, Bill, Tom, Chris, Max}
     b. $\left[4\right]^{v7} = $ {John, Chris, Max}
     c. $\left[5\right]^{v7} = $ true, if and only if $| \left[\text{man}\right]^{v7} \cap \left[\text{runs}\right]^{v7} | \times 2 > | \left[\text{man}\right]^{v7} |$
        In other words, if and only if $| \left[2\right]^{v7} \cap \left[4\right]^{v7} | \times 2 > | \left[2\right]^{v7} |$
        $\left[5\right]^{v7} = $ true because |{John, Bill, Tom, Chris, Max} $\cap$
        | {John, Chris, Max}| $\times$ 2 > | {John, Bill, Tom, Chris, Max} |
        $= | $ {John, Chris, Max}| $\times$ 2 > 5
        $= 3 \times 2 > 5$
        $= 6 > 5$

In (94c), the result of |{John, Bill, Tom, Chris, Max} $\cap$ {John, Chris, Max}| is |{John, Chris, Max}|. The result of |{John, Chris, Max}| is then 3 because the number of the elements in the set {John, Chris, Max} is 3. When 3 is multiplied by 2, it equals 6. Because the result of |{John, Bill, Tom, Chris, Max}| is 5, 6 > 5 is true, which makes the proposition *Most men run* under v_7 true.

7.5 Summary

In this chapter, we dealt with some basic formal semantic notions and we discussed the denotations of nouns and verbs. Progressing from the definitions provided in Chapter 6, we also discussed the denotations of conjunction and disjunction. We have discussed the fact that *and* and *or* have two different meanings depending on whether they combine phrases or clauses. We also discussed four quantifiers and their interpretations. This chapter might be difficult for readers who are completely new to symbolic logic and set theory. If you are not confident about the contents we discussed in this chapter, we strongly encourage you to go back to Chapter 6 and check your understanding of the basic concepts presented there. Understanding the key concepts of set theory is a very important step in understanding the semantic interpretations provided in this chapter.

7.6 Further Reading

We recommend Robert Wall's (Wall 1972) *Introduction to Mathematical Linguistics*. For readers who do not have any prior knowledge of set theory, the first four chapters serve as an informative introduction. For advanced readers, Partee, ter Meulen, and Wall (1990) is a great reference. Although the discussion in this book is somewhat dense, all the notions we discussed in this chapter are presented in great detail in this book in a readable way. Gamut's *Logic, Language, and Meaning* (Gamut 1990, Volume 1) is a great resource for readers who are willing to delve into logic.

CHAPTER 8
Meaning and Use

Thus far we have looked a good deal at the structure of language in the morphology and syntax chapters, as well as at linguistic meaning in the logic and semantics chapters. This present chapter takes a step back from there and considers language as we use it to communicate with others in particular situations, and as we communicate and imply messages above and beyond the literal meanings of the words we speak. Thus, we have looked so far at how morphemes and words are combined into sentences and at how those sentences are assigned semantic meaning. We consider now how those meaningful sentences are used in conversations. The key ideas in this chapter are conversational implicature and conventional implicature.

8.1 Sentences, Utterances, And Propositions

Before we begin discussion of the various kinds of implicatures mentioned above, it will be useful to get clear on the way we will be using terms such as *sentence*, *utterance*, and *proposition* in this chapter. We'll start with the definition for a *sentence*. A sentence is a string of words that is well-formed according to grammatical rules of a given language. For instance, (1) is a well-formed sentence of English, as defined by the grammar of English, and (2) is not a well-formed sentence.

(1) The Blue Dog Cafe will be closed until September.
(2) *Will closed Blue Dog Cafe the be September until.

This ill-formed string of words in (2) is ungrammatical, because it does not follow the syntactic rules of English. Remember from the chapters on semantics and logic, we are using the term *sentence* a little differently in this book than the normal usage. A sentence for us is an abstract entity, and it does not have a speaker or a context. It is simply a well-formed string of words that could possibly exist in a language, which can be produced by the rules of that language, like (1). The rules of English will not produce (2). This is not a sentence. It is a random string of English words.

Now, sentences are not true or false unless they are used in a context, but this does not mean that they are void of meaning. For example, imagine if you found a piece of paper on the ground with nothing other than the following sentence written on it: *The bank will be robbed at noon on Tuesday.* We know something of what this sentence means, but it doesn't describe an actual event, and we can't know what is being referred to. We don't know which bank is involved, or if the sentence was meant to describe an event that has already happened, or will happen in the future, or if it describes a fictional event, etc. All we can know here is the basic conventional, semantic meaning of the words and their syntactic combination. To know more than this, we would need to know the context in which the sentence was uttered, who uttered it, their intention in doing so, and so forth. So, a sentence is a string of words that is well-formed according to the rules of a language, but it lacks a context within which to be interpreted. Sentences are what was studied in the semantics chapter of this textbook.

An *utterance*, on the other hand, we can think of as a sentence (or sentence fragment, word, etc.) that does have a context. In other words, it has been used by a speaker in a particular situation to communicate something or accomplish something. We can think of an utterance, then, as a sentence plus a context. Speakers produce utterances in specific contexts to achieve specific results. That is, speakers produce utterances with an intention of accomplishing something, conveying some message or meaning, etc. We can call this the speaker-meaning: i.e. how the speaker intends for her words to be understood. The speaker-meaning can be the literal meaning of a sentence, but it can also be, and often is, a message that is not the same as the literal sentence-meaning. For example, a given sentence produced in a context can imply certain things; while, the same sentence produced in another context might imply a completely different set of things. If you say *I'm tired* at night, you might be implying that you are ready to go to bed. If you say *I'm tired* at 6:00 in the morning, you might be implying that you don't want to get out of bed yet. In both cases, the sentence-meaning is the same, but the speaker-meaning has changed. This latter kind of meaning falls under the purview of pragmatics and implicature, and it will be the subject of this chapter.

The last preliminary meaning to discuss is *proposition*. We have discussed propositions earlier in Chapter 6 of this book. There, we said that propositions can be judged true or false. They can also be doubted. Sentences, on the other hand, cannot be judged true or false or doubted as they do not refer to anything. They are just objects that are well-formed according to the rules of a language.

These terms all go together like this. A sentence is used in an utterance to express a proposition. Now, a given sentence can express more than just a proposition. We speak of sentences as having propositional content and non-propositional content. The propositional content is just that part of a sentence that is necessary for a truth value judgment to be made. Consider (3a-d). Each of these sentences can be used to express the same basic proposition, which is something like (3a). However, the sentences differ in other ways, such as in answering different questions, or focusing on different parts of the event in question. A good exercise for the reader here is to try and determine what the different functions or usages of (3a-d) are. See if you can come up with a question that (3a) will answer, but that (3b-d) will not.

> (3) a. John ate the pizza.
>   b. The pizza was eaten by John.
>   c. It was John that ate the pizza.
>   d. The pizza, John ate it.

In (4), we see more examples of how different sentences can be used to express the same proposition. The English sentence in (4a) and the Spanish sentence in (4b) are completely different on the surface, but they express the same proposition.

(4) a. I speak English.
b. Hablo Ingles.

This is also true in (5). If *John*, *brother*, and *jerk* are all being used to refer to the same individual, then (5a-c) would share the same truth conditions.

(5) a. Mary saw John yesterday.
b. Mary saw her brother yesterday.
c. Mary saw that jerk yesterday.

Also, the same sentence can be used to express different propositions. Consider (6). This sentence will express a different proposition every time it is uttered by a different person, or even by the same person in a different place, or at a different time. If John says it, it expresses one proposition. If Martha says it, it expresses another one. The sentence has kept the same form, but it expresses different propositions on different occasions of use.

(6) I am here now.

With this distinction in mind, we are now ready to talk a little bit more about pragmatics, implicature, and speaker-meaning. This discussion begins with H. Paul Grice, who is the grandfather of contemporary pragmatics.

8.2 H. Paul Grice And Contemporary Pragmatics

The study of how speakers convey meanings above and beyond what they literally say is commonly considered to be the subject matter of *pragmatics*, and it is a hotly-debated topic of interest among both linguists and philosophers. The most widespread approach to studying language usage of this sort comes to us from the work of the Oxford philosopher, H. Paul Grice (1913-1988), and his theory of *conversational implicature*, which was introduced in the William James Lectures he gave at Harvard University in 1967.[1] These lectures have since been recognized as some of the most important work done in contemporary semantics, pragmatics, and the philosophy of language in the twentieth century.

8.2.1 Conversational implicature

Consider the following exchange, in which Taylor invites Dakota on a date to the movies.

(7) Taylor: Would you like to go to the movies?
Dakota: I'm kinda tired right now.
Implicature: *I don't want to go to the movies.*

All that Dakota has literally said here is that she is "kinda tired"; however, in most situations Taylor should have little trouble in understanding Dakota's intended meaning, which

---

1 There have been three primary reinterpretations of Grice's program since the late 1960s. These are the Neo-Gricean programs of Horn (1984, 1989) and Levinson (2000), and Relevance Theory of Sperber and Wilson (1995). This textbook will not go into these, but will instead focus on the Gricean program as originally conceived by Grice.

is that Dakota does not wish to go to the movies. Now, Dakota didn't literally say that she doesn't want to go to the movies, but Taylor still understands this from the exchange. With Grice's Cooperative Principle and its attendant conversational maxims, we can explain how it is that Taylor comes to this understanding—i.e. how Taylor understands the implied meaning rather than the literal meaning of what Dakota has said.

8.2.2 The cooperative principle and maxims

In order to explain how conversational implicatures like that in (7) can be conveyed and understood, Grice devised what he called the "Cooperative Principle", which is a statement of the general expectations speakers have about conversational behavior:

> The Cooperative Principle
> Make your conversational contribution such as is required, at the stage at which it occurs, by the accepted purpose or direction of the talk exchange at which it occurs, by the accepted purpose or direction of the talk exchange in which you are engaged. (Grice 1989: 26)

The idea is that if parties to a conversation are adhering to the Cooperative Principle, and the relevant parties can assume that this is the case, then they will be able to understand unspoken implicatures of the kind conveyed above in (7). That is, if we can assume that speakers are being cooperative in the ways Grice outlined, then we can infer additional information that is above and beyond what a speaker has literally said.

The Cooperative Principle is Grice's bare statement regarding conversational rules; however, he elaborated on the Cooperative Principle with a more specific set of conversational maxims that he believed governed rational communication in general. These four conversational maxims he termed QUALITY, QUANTITY, RELATION, and MANNER, and they are given below in (8), following the arrangement found in Horn (2004: 7).

(8) QUALITY: Try to make your contribution one that is true.
    1. Do not say what you believe to be false.
    2. Do not say that for which you lack evidence.
    QUANTITY:
    1. Make your contribution as informative as is required (for the current purposes of the exchange).
    2. Do not make your contribution more informative than is required.
    RELATION: Be relevant.
    MANNER: Be perspicuous.
    1. Avoid obscurity of expression.
    2. Avoid ambiguity.
    3. Be brief. (Avoid unnecessary prolixity.)
    4. Be orderly.

In order for efficient communication to occur something like Grice's framework must be in place, and speakers and hearers must take for granted that it is in place. Importantly, Grice's "rules" are not prescriptive rules that are memorized or brought to a conversational setting in a conscious way; they are more like tacit knowledge of cultural norms which are acquired as one grows into a practicing member of a culture. In addition, different cultural environments might place different emphases on the various maxims. For example, in courtroom testimony, witnesses are expected to answer questions directly and concisely, without volunteering additional information. This expectation with respect to the maxim of Quantity thus varies from other, more natural, conversational settings, in which speakers might be expected to volunteer more information.

Conversational implicatures can be generated, then, by following as well as explicitly breaking (flouting) the various maxims. Let's consider how this works with some specific examples of implicatures generated by observing the maxims, as in (9). The first maxim we will consider is Quality. This maxim, which requires one to be truthful, deserves a special status apart from the other maxims. If it were not in place, then speakers and hearers would have no reason to trust or believe anything that was said. With Quality, then, we can talk about implicatures of speaker-belief, such as in (9).

(9) QUALITY
The Giants won the Pennant.
Implicature: *The speaker believes that the Giants won the Pennant, and the speaker has good evidence for believing this.*

The next maxim to consider is Quantity, which requires speakers to say not more or less but exactly enough to fit the needs of the situation. This allows speakers to convey implicatures such as in (10).

(10) QUANTITY
John has three children.
Implicature: *John has at most/only three children.*

Typically, when we hear a sentence such as (10) we take it to mean that John has only three children, or exactly three children, or something along these lines. However, (10) is also consistent with John's having more than three children; i.e. if John has five children, then it follows that he also has three children as well as two children etc. The *at most/only* reading is possible, though, if it is assumed that the speaker is adhering to the maxim of quantity, and being as informative as she can be. Thus, if she said John has three children, then she must not be able to make a stronger or more informative statement regarding the number of children John has. In other words, if the speaker knew John had more than three children, then she should have said so.

The next maxim we consider is Relation, which directs speakers to be relevant. This is exemplified in (11).

(11) RELATION
Taylor: What time is it?
Dakota: The mall's not open yet.
Implicature: *It's at least before the mall normally opens.*

Taylor expects a response that is relevant to the question she has asked; however, taken literally, Dakota's response does not appear to be directly relevant to Taylor's question. Taylor is faced with a choice, then: a) assume that Dakota's answer is not responsive; or, b) trust that Dakota's response must somehow be relevant. Since Taylor has no reason to believe that Dakota is deliberately ignoring the Gricean maxims, she must search for a way to make Dakota's response relevant to her question. Such reasoning would allow her to arrive at an implicature similar to the one in (11), which implies (but does not literally say) that the time is at least before the mall opens. In order for this response to ultimately be successful, then, Dakota must assume that Taylor knows at what time the mall normally opens.

The final maxim to consider is Manner, which directs the speaker to be brief, clear, and orderly, and which is illustrated in (12a).

(12) MANNER
      a. Taylor showered and went to bed.
          Implicature: *Taylor showered and THEN went to bed.*
      b. Taylor went to bed and showered.

Example (12a) shows the description of two events, which are conjoined by *and*. Taken literally, the meaning of *and* is essentially that of logical conjunction (discussed above in Chapter 6). There is no actual comment on the order or time relation in which the two events occurred, and evaluating the truth of the statement does not require an ordered relation. As long as Taylor both went to bed and showered, the statement can be true. It does not matter to the truth conditions in which order these two events occurred. Thus (12a) and (12b) have the same truth conditions. However, if we assume that the speaker is adhering to the maxim of Manner (i.e. is relating events in the order in which they occurred), we can infer that the events occurred in the order in which Taylor relates them, and this gives us the most natural reading of (12a), which is that Taylor showered and went to bed, in the given order.

The result so far is that speakers and hearers can be seen to rely on the Cooperative Principle and relevant assumptions in order to convey more than they actually say. This works in two different ways. Speakers can convey implicatures by adhering to the maxims, as in (12), but they can also convey implicatures by flouting (explicitly and obviously breaking) or exploiting the maxims as well. Let's look at how this works with two examples in which the maxim of Quantity is flouted. Example (13) is taken directly from Grice (1989: 33).

(13) A is writing a testimonial about a pupil who is a candidate for a philosophy job, and
      his letter reads as follows: '*Dear Sir, Mr. X's command of English is excellent, and
      his attendance at tutorials has been regular. Yours, etc.*'

The maxim of Quantity imparts us to be as informative as we can. In a letter of recommendation, the author of the letter is expected to comment on the candidate's ability to do the job for which she is applying. Now, command of English and tutorial attendance are not directly relevant to one's ability to do philosophy; thus, A's letter of recommendation is not informative. The reader of the letter can then draw the inference that there is something the author is reluctant to write down and that it is likely the case that the candidate is not good at the job for which she is an applicant. So, by flouting the Quantity maxim the speaker can convey the further, unspoken implicature.

Importantly, it is necessary for the hearer to be aware of the speaker's exploitation of the maxim if the intended implicature is to be understood. For instance, consider cases of irony, in which a speaker says something which she intends to be interpreted in a nonstandard way. The hearer has to recognize that the speaker's intention runs counter to what has actually been said, or else the ironic speech might receive a literal interpretation and so fall flat. Grice (1989: 34) provides the following example in (14), in which the maxim of Quality is flouted.

(14) X, with whom A has been on close terms until now, has betrayed a secret of A's to a business rival. A and his audience both know this. A says: 'X is a fine friend'.

In this case, the speaker has overtly violated the maxim of Quality, which instructs speakers to say only what they believe to be true. The hearer, recognizing that the speaker has intentionally and obviously said something that the speaker does not believe to be true, can then calculate what the speaker's actual, unspoken intention was: namely, that X was not a fine friend. Thus, implicatures can be conveyed by flouting the maxims as well as by adhering to them.

8.2.3 Opting out of the maxims

In addition to flouting and adhering to maxims, speakers can also opt out of them, or signal to their hearer that they are not adhering to a maxim in what they are about to say. As an aside, this provides strong evidence for the existence of the maxims in the first place. That is, if you can opt out of something, then that something must exist! The exception proves the rule. Consider the way that speakers commonly "hedge" their statements. There are a few examples in (15), in which the speaker opts out of the maxim of Quality.

(15) All I know is that X.
      They say that X.
      X is the case. Ish.

Quality tells speakers to say only what they believe to be true. The constructions in (15), however, are used to both make claims and to alert hearers that the speaker might not be committed to the truth of the claims. In other words, speakers can use hedge constructions to opt out of the maxim of Quality. It is similarly possible to opt out of the other maxims; a good exercise for the reader here is to come up with means of opting out of the remaining maxims.

8.2.4 Empirical properties of conversational implicature

So far we have considered conversational implicature from a theoretical perspective, as they were originally defined and described by Grice. There are also several empirical properties of conversational implicatures that allow us to identify them. Thus, linguists and philosophers are concerned with several different dimensions of meaning. The way these dimensions of meaning are differentiated from one another is through their various empirical properties, which can be seen to differ across levels of meaning. For example, conversational implicatures are generally considered to be *calculable*, *cancelable*, *non-detachable*, and *reinforceable*. In the rest of this section, we will illustrate how these properties can be used to identify conversational implicature content. Let's look first at *calculability*.

Consider example (13) again, from above. In this example the conversational implicature *Mr. X is no good at philosophy* is conveyed by the author's flouting of the maxim of Quantity. The conversational implicature itself is not directly (conventionally) associated with the meanings of the words used by the author; rather, the conversational implicature is conveyed as a result of the author being less informative than he could have been, and of the hearer's recognition of this fact. So, the conversational implicature is not conventionally associated with the meanings of the words the author uses. Thus, in (13), the author of the letter writes only what we have labeled below as "Actual text". Yet, the author conveys the conversational implicature, which is very different from the actual text.

> Actual text: Mr. X's command of English is excellent, and his attendance at tutorials has been regular.
> Implicature: *Mr. X is no good at philosophy.*

There is no manner in which the meanings of the words of the actual text (along with their syntactic combination) can add up to the implicature that they are used to convey. The implicature meaning is thus not part of the *conventional* meaning of the words used. If the meaning of a given word is conventional, then it should be present in every usage of that given word. But, we can easily imagine contexts in which the actual text above does not convey the implicature that Mr. X is no good at philosophy. Consider, for example, if the actual text were used in a letter of recommendation for a job as a secretary or office administrator. That is, the job description was for an office administrator, and Mr. X had letters written in support of his application for the office administrator job. Then, the line of actual text would be positive, and it would be a good for his application. The reason for this is that the author of that letter would not be flouting the maxim of Quantity in this case. The author of the letter would be being informative, and the actual text would not be used to convey the implicature that Mr. X is no good at philosophy. As such, we can see that the implicature conveyed is not present in every context. It is not conventional. The question is, how does one get from the actual text to the implicature? How does a hearer infer the implicature from the use of the actual text. Essentially, the hearer goes through a reasoning or calculating process based on what she knows about the context and the speaker's intentions in saying what he has said. This reasoning process is known as *calculation*, and for (13), the calculation process goes something like what we see here:

> [the author of the letter] cannot be opting out, since if he wished to be uncooperative, why write at all? He cannot be unable, through ignorance, to say more, since the man is his pupil; moreover, he knows that more information than this is wanted. He must, therefore, be wishing to impart information that he is reluctant to write down. This supposition is tenable only if he thinks Mr. X is no good at philosophy. This, then, is what he is implicating.

So, to understand a conversational implicature, hearers must go through a calculation process such as the one above. By contrast, such a calculation process is not necessary to understand the literal meanings of words. The actual text in (13) has a literal meaning, which is just that Mr. X's command of English is excellent and that he is punctual in attendance. No calculation is required to understand this. This literal (conventional) meaning, then, is not calculable, while conversational implicature meaning is calculable and is not conventional.

The next property to consider is *cancelability*. Since conversational implicatures are not conventional meaning, they are cancelable. Essentially, a conversational implicature is a guess—albeit an educated one—as to what the speaker intends to convey by saying what she chooses to say in a particular situation. As such, a conversational implicature isn't something that is spoken or that the speaker is on record as being committed to. As a result of this implicatures can be canceled without contradiction. The same is not true of conventional meaning. Consider again the conversational implicature conveyed in (13): i.e. that Mr. X is no good at philosophy. This was strictly an implicature, and so the speaker is not on record as being committed to it. As a result, the speaker could speak additional words that would effectively cancel the implicature. Consider (16), which is an adapted version of (13).

(16) Actual text: Mr. X's command of English is excellent, and his attendance at tutorials has been regular. He is also an excellent philosopher.

If the letter of recommendation of (13) had been worded as in (16), the implicature that Mr. X is no good at philosophy would no longer go through. It would be canceled by the actual speech that conflicted with it. This is an important characteristic of conversational implicatures, but it does not hold for literal, conventional meaning. For example, if we try to cancel parts of the actual text above, it winds up sounding as if the author is contradicting himself. Consider (17), where we apply the same cancelation technique, and the result sounds contradictory. The infelicitous nature of the example is indicated with #.

(17) Mr. X's command of English is excellent. #He also has a poor command of English.

In this version of the letter, the author has gone on record stating that Mr. X has an excellent command of English. Then, when the author tries to explicitly cancel that meaning, as in (17), he cannot do so without contradicting himself. However, as we saw in (16), this is not the case with conversational implicature. In this latter case, the speaker has not gone on record and so can cancel the implicature without seeming contradictory. Thus, we say that conversational implicatures are *cancelable*; and this is perhaps the most important characteristic of this class of meaning. If a type of meaning can be canceled without contradiction, then this is a strong argument that it is a conversational implicature. It is not a conclusive argument on its own, though, as many kinds of presuppositions are also seen to be cancelable. This will be discussed in more detail in Chapter 9 below.

The next property we will consider is *non-detachability*. This one is a bit more complicated to understand. The idea is that conversational implicatures are generated based on a statement made against a given context. According to Grice, this generation is due to the relation between the semantic content of what is said in the statement, rather than to the forms of individual words that have been said. What this means is that if we paraphrase what is said, keeping the context the same, then the same conversational implicatures should be generated. Consider (18), which is yet another adaptation of example (13) from above.

(18) A is writing a testimonial about a pupil who is a candidate for a philosophy job, and his letter reads as follows: '*Dear Sir, Mr. X's ability to use English is wonderful, and his presence at tutorials has been consistent. Yours, etc.*'

This italicized sentence is a paraphrase of the relevant sentence in (13). It differs in choice of words, but it maintains the same truth conditions as that in (13). That is, if the sentence in (13) is true, then the sentence above in (18) is also true. Likewise, if one of the sentences is false, then the other will also be false. Importantly, the same conversational implicature is also present in both examples: i.e. that Mr. X is no good at philosophy. So, we say that the implicature then cannot be detached from the semantic content of the statement and the context. We can show this by paraphrasing the relevant statement in (13) (while maintaining the same truth conditions) and then observing whether or not the relevant conversational implicature is still present. In a case like (13) and (18), the implicature does survive. It is thus non-detachable, and this is an important property of conversational implicatures. What it really means is that the implicature is not associated with the form of a word or sentence, but rather with the semantic/truth conditional dimension of the sentence in a given context. Conversely, *conventional* implicatures, which will be discussed below in 8.4, are detachable.

A final diagnostic property to consider is *reinforcability*. For this property, it is useful to consider another kind of example. Consider (19a). If a speaker says (19a), she will generally implicate that she believes that (19b) is the case. (This is an example of a scalar conversational implicature, which will be discussed in detail below in 8.3.1.)

(19) a. Some of John's kids were at the party.
b. Not all of John's kids were at the party.
c. Some of John's kids were at the party; in fact, they all were.
d. Some of John's kids were at the party; #in fact, none of them were.

Example (19b) is only implied though; it can be canceled in much the same way that we discussed with (13), above. This cancelation is shown in (19c), where the implied *not all X* is canceled by the following *in fact, all X*. In (19d) we see what happens if we attempt to cancel non-implied content. The result is contradictory in the same way that we saw above in (17). The first clause in (19d) entails that at least one of John's kids is at the party. The speaker is committed to this. Thus, when the second, canceling clause is conjoined to it in (19d), the result is contradictory. So, what we need to do is show how the conversational implicature of (19b) can be reinforced. This is done in (20).

(20) Some of John's kids were at the party; but not all of them were.

What we do to test reinforceability is conjoin a statement to the original one that basically states the content of the conversational implicature in question. The implicature in question is (19b), so we need to conjoin that to the original and see if the conjunction is felicitous. In this case, in (20), it is perfectly fine. Thus, the conversational implicature is reinforceable. Now, if we try to reinforce non-implied content, the result is redundancy, as in (21).

(21) Some of John's kids were at the party; #in fact, some of them were.

What has happened in (21) is that the second clause attempts to reinforce the non-implied content of the first clause, and this is redundant. Whereas above in (20), reinforcement of conversational implicature content is perfectly felicitous.

These properties of conversational implicatures—i.e. calculability, cancelability, non-detachability, and reinforceability—can thus be used as diagnostic tools to identify suspected conversational implicatures. This is similar to the other kinds of linguistic diagnostics that we saw earlier in the textbook. For example, recall the syntactic case studies described in the beginning of Chapter 4. The first case study has us arguing for the subject of an imperative sentence. We used linguistic tests, such as the reflexive test, to argue that the subject of an imperative sentence is *you*. The properties we have just considered for conversational implicature should be used in the same way.

8.3 Generalized And Particularized Conversational Implicature

So far we have been treating conversational implicature as a unified phenomenon. In reality, though, there are sub-types of conversational implicatures that need to be considered. We can make a rough division of this class of meaning into *generalized* and *particularized* conversational implicatures. The former, generalized implicature, occurs in a general fashion across a wide range of contexts; the latter, particularized implicature, occurs only in specific contexts. We'll look at a range of generalized implicatures first.

8.3.1 Generalized conversational implicature

There have been several kinds of generalized implicatures identified since the late 1960s when Grice first described the category. We'll consider many of these; but, we should begin with Grice's (1989: 37) own examples on the subject.

> Anyone who uses a sentence of the form *X is meeting a woman this evening* would normally implicate that the person to be met was someone other than X's wife, mother, sister, or perhaps close platonic friend. Similarly, if I were to say *X went into a house yesterday and found a tortoise inside the front door*, my hearer would normally be surprised if some time later I revealed that the house was X's own. I could produce similar linguistic phenomena involving the expressions *a garden, a car, a college,* and so on. Sometimes, however, there would normally be no such implicature ("I have been sitting in a car all morning"), and sometimes a reverse implicature ("I broke a finger yesterday").

The idea here is that the use of the indefinite article *a/an* commonly results in a certain kind of conversational implicature. Let's look at Grice's first example, which is provided below as (22). Consider what such an utterance literally means, and what it might be used to actually convey. They are different messages.

(22) X is meeting a woman tonight.

The first message here (i.e. the literal, conventional meaning) is just that X is meeting a woman that evening. Basically, X is meeting a person who is adult and female, and there is no comment on the identity of that adult female person. But, this sentence with the indefinite article would generally be used to convey something more than that with respect to the identity of the woman: namely, that the speaker does not believe X to be in a close relationship with the woman. However, this is not part of the conventional meaning of the sentence; it is only implied. If, for example, X was meeting his wife that evening, this would be truth condition-ally consistent with X's meeting a woman, if his wife is in fact a woman. The relationship business is an implicature, and we can see that this is so by applying the basic implicature diagnostics given above in 8.2.3. In (23), we have shown how the relationship implicature can be canceled. (23b) is a generalized implicature of a normal use of (23a). Finally, (23c) shows a use of (23a) in which the implicature of (23b) is canceled.

(23) a. X is meeting a woman tonight.
    b. The woman is not X's wife.
    c. X is meeting a woman tonight; in fact, the woman is X's wife.

We will leave it to the reader to apply other conversational implicature diagnostics of 8.2.3—i.e. calculation, reinforceability, etc.—to this example.

The basic idea here comes from the way speakers expect indefinite articles *a/an* to nor-mally be used. Indefinite articles are normally used to introduce new referents into a discourse, or to introduce referents that the speaker does not believe to be identifiable to the hearer. Now, if the woman in question in (22) was in a close relationship with X, she could be identifiable to the hearer based on that relationship. It is straightforward for us to identify people based on their relationship to those we know. Consider a case where you don't know a particular woman personally, but you do know that she is married to an acquaintance of yours named John. It is straightforward to identify her as *John's wife*.

Thus, in (22), when the speaker uses the indefinite noun phrase *a woman*, it is natural for the hearer to assume that no further identifying information can be provided. This assumption follows directly from hearers' expectations that speakers will be as informative as they can be: i.e. from hearers' expectations that speakers will adhere to Grice's maxim of Quantity. And, as we saw in (23c), the implied content is cancelable; it is in fact an implicature. What's more, this kind of implicature happens generally in most cases when indefinite articles are used. As such, we call it a generalized conversational implicature; it is less dependent on spe-cific contexts than is the case with particularized conversational implicatures, which we will return to briefly in 8.3.2. below. For now, we want to consider additional means of conveying generalized conversational implicatures.

Probably the most discussed of the generalized conversational implicatures are what Horn (1972, 2005) terms "scalar implicatures". These are implicatures that are generated based on speakers' and hearers' understandings of the nature of scalar terms in conversation. Consider the following linguistic scales in (24), which come from Horn (1972) and Levinson (1983). The scales are formulated with the "strongest" term on the far left, with the terms weakening progressively as the scale moves to the right. For example, in the first scale *all* is used to make a stronger or more inclusive statement than *most*, and *most* is used to make a stronger or more informative statement than *many*, etc. So, *All of John's kids are here* is a stronger statement than *Some of John's kids are here*.

(24)   <all, most, many, some, few>
      <and, or>
      <excellent, good>
      <hot, warm>
      <always, often, sometimes>
      <succeed in Ving, try to V, want to V>
      <necessarily p, p, possibly p >
      <certain that p, probable that p, possible that p >
      <must, should, may>
      <cold, cool>
      <love, like>

The scales given in (24) are only a handful of the many scalar terms that can be found in English, and a good exercise for the reader is to try and identify other such linguistic scales. Let's look now at the way that the scalar implicature process works in (25).

(25)   a. *Some* of John's kids are here.
     b. Not all of John's kids are here.

Normal use of a sentence such as (25a) will convey the conversational implicature shown in (25b). Note that in the scale in (24), above, *some* is lower on the scale than, or to the right of, *all*. And, use of the weaker *some* generally implies that the stronger term *all* does not hold; or, the use of the weaker term at least implies that the speaker was not in a position to use the stronger term. That is, in (25a), if the speaker knew that *all* of John's kids were there, then the speaker should have said that. The fact that she chooses to say *some* instead of *all* conveys to the hearer the implicature that the speaker didn't know for sure whether *all* would have held. This is the basic mechanism: use of a weaker term implies that the stronger term is not appropriate. Importantly, though, this is only an implicature, and as such it has the same implicature diagnostics and empirical properties as the implicatures described above in 8.2.3: i.e. calculability, cancelability, non-detachability, and reinforceability. We can see that this is so by testing an example such as (25) against these diagnostics.

Before we do this, though, we want to remind the reader that the truth of *some X* is consistent with the truth of *all X*. Thus, if we say *Some of John's kids are here*, then it could also be true that *All of John's kids are here*. However, it is implied that this is not the case, or that the speaker doesn't know if it is the case. For comparison, if John has three kids, then he also has two kids, and one kid, etc. In the same way, if *all* of John's kids are here, then it is also true that *some* of John's kids are here.

Now, the first diagnostic to consider is calculability. This property was discussed above with respect to example (13), and it is an important one with scalar implicatures. Levinson (1983: 134) provides a formalization of how calculability is seen to occur with scalar implicatures. This is given below in (26); and importantly, all of the scales in (24) have a basic form like that of (26).

(26) $< e_1, e_2, e_3, ..., e_n >$
The speaker S has said $A(e_2)$; if S was in a position to state that a stronger item on the scale holds—i.e. to assert $A(e_1)$—then he would be in breach of the first maxim of Quantity if he asserted $A(e_2)$. Since I, the addressee, assume that S is cooperating, and therefore will not violate the maxim of Quantity without warning, I take it that S wishes to convey that he is *not* in a position to state that the stronger item e_1 on the scale holds, and indeed knows that it does not hold.

The idea is that a hearer's reasoning process runs something like that in (26). When a speaker hears *some X*, she assumes that the speaker didn't possess the knowledge of the situation that would have been required to have said *all X*. The hearer thus infers that *all X* doesn't hold, or that the speaker doesn't know if it holds. A similar calculation process occurs with all such scalar terms.

There are three other diagnostics to consider; however, two of them—i.e. cancelability and reinforceability—have been illustrated above in (19) for scalar implicature. This leaves non-detachability, which is itself an important diagnostic. According to Grice "it is not possible to find another way of saying the same thing, which simply lacks the implicature in question" (1989: 43). In other words, we cannot detach the implicature from a different, but truth-conditionally equivalent, statement occurring in the same context. The most straightforward test for this involves paraphrasing the statement in question, while keeping it truth-conditionally equivalent, and then observing if the same implicature holds. We saw this illustrated above in (18) for non-scalar implicatures. Granted, it can be hard to find close paraphrases of some of the scalar terms in (24); but it is straightforward to show that approximations to the scalar terms can be used to convey similar implicatures. Thus, consider (27), which is a paraphrase and adaptation of (25). Here, we have paraphrased the indefinite *some X* with a similarly indefinite *a number of X*.

(27) a. *A number* of John's kids are here.
      b. Not all of John's kids are here.

It seems reasonable to assume that (27b) can survive as a conversational implicature of (27a). And, the reason for the presence of the implicature is the same as what is described above in (26). Essentially, if the speaker could have used the stronger term *all*, then she should have done so. The fact that she did not suggests that she wasn't in a position to do so in the first place.

There are of course other questions at work here in the paraphrase from (26a) to (27a) as well. Anytime that any aspect of a sentence—from syntax to word choice to pronunciation—is changed, then some aspect of the sentence's meaning or usage restrictions will also change. Thus, while *a number of X* and *some X* are very similar, there are minor differences that native speakers might feel intuitively. This is a good place for the reader to pause and ask what exactly the differences are between these two terms? When might you use one and not the other? This is similar to the claim that there are no true synonyms: all synonym pairs, no matter how similar, will vary in some way, no matter how slight the nuance might be. What do you make of this claim? Can you find synonym pairs which are truly synonymous? Answering this question takes us further afield than we need to be right now; but, it is an interesting thought question for the reader who is interested in semantics and pragmatics.

In any case, use of a scalar term generally conveys the conversational implicature that the terms that are higher on the scale (to the left) do not hold. At the same time, scalar terms generally entail the weaker terms (to the right) of them on the scale. We have alluded to this latter part regarding rightward entailment above in the discussion of *all* and *some* in discussion of (26). Let's look briefly at this relationship in another real-life example, taken from courtroom testimony from President Bill Clinton. In (28) below, President Clinton was being questioned under oath about his relationship with Monica Lewinsky, a young woman with whom Clinton had been accused of having an improper relationship. The questioner was trying to determine whether President Clinton had been alone with Ms. Lewinsky in the Oval Office, where much of the improper relationship had allegedly occurred.

(28) QUESTION: So I understand, your testimony is that it was *possible*, then, that you were alone with her, but you have no specific recollection of that ever happening?
CLINTON: Yes, that's correct. It's *possible* that she, in, while she was working there, brought something to me and that at the time she brought it to me, she was the only person there. That's *possible*.

Now, it turns out that Clinton actually had been alone with Lewinsky in the Oval Office on many occasions. But, that is not what he said. Instead, he said that it was *possible* that he had been alone with her. Thus his statement here was weaker than it could have been. He wasn't being cooperative, and he was violating the maxim of Quantity. What Clinton did not do, though, was to say something that was literally false. In order for something to happen, it has to be possible for that something to happen, or else it couldn't happen in the first place! If Clinton was alone with Lewinsky, then it also had to be *possible* for Clinton to be alone with Lewinsky.

Even if what Clinton literally said was true, he certainly implied something that was false. And, he did so with a skillful use of a scalar implicature. The scale he was using is something like that in (29), which we saw above in (24).

(29) < certain that *p*, probable that *p*, possible that *p* >

So when Clinton said "That's *possible*" that he was alone with Lewinsky, he implied that it was not *probable* and not *certain* that he was; however, what he said didn't *entail* that.[2] Thus, Clinton was playing off of the way people normally interpret scalar terms in order to imply something false by saying something that was literally true.

In sum, scalar implicatures are a kind of generalized conversational implicature, which means that the implicatures occur in many contexts as opposed to only limited specific

---

2 The United States House of Representatives, where the case was being considered, called Clinton's statement a "verbose lie" because they claimed it was clear that Clinton knew the intention of the question. So even though his statement was literally true, it wasn't true to the intentions. For a much more detailed version of this story, see Solan and Tiersma (2008: Chp. 11).

contexts. This happens because speakers and hearers tacitly assume a mutual scalar reasoning process like that in (26) and of the Cooperative Principle as described above in 8.2.1.

There are many kinds of generalized implicatures; however, particularized, or one-off conversational implicatures are far more common. These are implicatures which depend on a statement that has been made against a specific background context. If the background context is changed (and the statement left the same) the particularized implicature might cease to be present. For example, consider again (13) from above. Against the background of the philosophy job, the implicature is conveyed that Mr. X is no good at philosophy. But, when the background context is changed to the secretary job, the original implicature is no longer present.

Speakers and hearers must keep track of many kinds of background contexts as a conversation progresses, and statements that are made in the conversation are evaluated against these contexts and against what the hearer believes the speaker's intention to be. In the process, hearers are able to guess (infer) what speakers are implying above and beyond what they have literally said. Contexts are unique, in that they involve specific times, places, people, world knowledge, etc. It is no surprise, then, that the many implicatures depending on these contexts are unique (i.e. particular) as well.

Further, most of the implicatures that depend on flouting the maxims are also particularized. This is not hard to see either, as the requirements of the various maxims are themselves context-dependent. Thus, the maxim of Quantity tells us to say just enough; but, "just enough" depends on the situation and what is expected within it. And if one says too little and thus generates a Quantity implicature, it is because too little has been said in that given context. (In a different context, what was said might have been "just enough" or maybe too much.) It is also easy to see how implicatures depending on the maxim of Relation, as in (11), are particularized as well, as being relevant depends on a particular context: i.e. relevance is at least a two-part relation.

We see, then, that the class of *conversational* implicatures can be divided into roughly two subsets, depending on whether they are general or particular, with the two groups sharing the same empirical, diagnostic properties. However, Grice (1989) also identified a third kind of implicature, which has its own set of empirical properties. This third type he termed *conventional* implicature, and it is to this that we now turn.

8.4 Conventional Implicature

Recall again the discussion of conventional meaning at the beginning of 8.2.3. There, we saw how conversational implicatures are not conventionally associated with the meaning of a word or a sentence; rather, conversational implicatures are above and beyond the conventional, literal meaning of a word. In contrast, conventional implicatures are part of the conventional meanings of various words and sentence types. In this section we will consider the empirical properties of conventional implicatures as well as the way they contrast with conversational implicatures.

8.4.1 Empirical properties of conventional implicature

Grice's primary description of conventional implicature occurs in a brief paragraph in "Logic and Conversation" (1989). It was not a class of meaning which much interested Grice, and it was introduced primarily to clear the way for his discussion of *conversational* implicature, in which he was directly interested. Here are Grice's words:

> In some cases the conventional meaning of the words used will determine what is implicated, besides helping to determine what is said. If I say (smugly), *He is an Englishman; he is, therefore, brave,* I have certainly committed myself, by virtue of the meaning of my words, to its being the case that his being brave is a consequence of (follows from) his being an Englishman. But while I have said that he is an Englishman, and said that he is brave, I do not want to say that I have *said* (in the favored sense) that it follows from his being an Englishman that he is brave, though I have certainly indicated, and so implicated, that this is so. I do not want to say that my utterance of this sentence would be, *strictly speaking*, false should the consequence in question fail to hold. So *some* implicatures are conventional, unlike the one with which I introduced this discussion of implicature (1989: 25-26).

The conventional implicature, then, is part of the conventional meaning of a lexical item. It is not truth conditional, nor is it derivable as a conversational inference. We can translate Grice's words here into the diagnostic properties we have been discussing so far for conversational implicature, and we can see quite clearly that the conventional implicatures fare differently in the diagnostics than do their conversational counterparts. We saw that conversational implicatures were: calculable, cancelable, and non-detachable. On the other hand, conventional implicatures are: non-calculable, non-cancelable, and detachable. Thus, we can begin to see how a small number of linguistic tests can be used to sort out the differing dimensions of linguistic meaning. We can thus apply a manner of argumentation that is very similar to the way we made claims and arguments in the earlier chapters on syntax.

Let's take a closer look now at a Gricean conventional implicature in (30). The most commonly cited example of a Gricean conventional implicature is the conjunction *but*, as in (30a), which entails logical conjunction (see Chapter 6) and in addition carries the conventional implicature of contrast between the two conjuncts: i.e. *poor* and *honest*.

(30) a. He is poor but honest.
CI: *there is some contrast between being poor and being honest.*
b. He is poor and honest.
c. He is poor but honest-- #not that there is any contrast between being poor and honest.

Basically, *but* carries the truth conditional meaning of *and*. It also carries the non-truth conditional meaning of contrast. What this means is that the contrast component of *but*'s meaning doesn't have an effect on whether a *but*-sentence is true or false. Only the *and*-component of *but*'s meaning affects the truth of the sentence. So in this sense, the meaning of *but* is more complex than the meaning of *and*, and this is represented in a very basic way in (31).

(31) *but* = *and* + contrast

Grice provided only a couple of examples of conventional implicatures; but, they can be found all over the English language and other languages. Here is a partial list of linguistic data that have been analyzed as conventional implicature over the past three decades: connectives such as *therefore*, *but*, *however*, *moreover*, adverbs *even* and *just*, sentence adverbs and other utterance modifiers, factive verbs, iterative verbs, rise-fall-rise intonation, parentheticals, epithets, honorifics, definite articles, personal datives, negative concord, information structure word orders, passives, cleft constructions, *tu-vous* pronouns, and many more. Essentially, if a word or sentence structure carries a meaning that is conventional, but that is not truth conditional, then a strong argument can be made that that particular component of the meaning is a conventional implicature. Let's look now a little closer at the empirical properties of a couple of these conventional implicature devices.

Consider (30) again. The component of meaning in question is the contrast part of *but*. It is straightforward to see that this meaning is not calculable, as conversational implicatures are. The contrast meaning is tied specifically to the conventional meaning of *but*. Similarly, in (30c), we have attempted to cancel the contrast meaning with a continuing clause. The result here is very awkward and contradictory. This contrasts with conversational implicatures, which we can cancel very straightforwardly. Lastly, there is detachability. We have shown throughout that detachability is best tested by paraphrasing the sentence in question, while maintaining the same truth conditions, and then seeing if the implicature survives. This has been attempted in (30b), in which *but* has been replaced with *and*. These two conjunctions offer the same truth conditional content, so (30a) and (30b) are truth conditionally equivalent. That is, they are true in all the same situations and false in all the same situations. (To test this latter claim, the reader should try to imagine a scenario where (30a) is true and (30b) is false, or vice versa.) Importantly, we see that the conventional implicature component of meaning (i.e. contrast) is absent in (30b). With the removal of the specific word *but*, the conventional implicature has been removed as well. Recall the discussion of detachability for conversational implicatures above in (18) and (27). There we saw that the implicature could not be detached via paraphrase. With conventional implicature, though, the implicature is detachable. So, the two species of implicature differ along these lines.

In (32), we see one more example of a conventional implicature: this time with French second person pronouns. Anyone who has studied a Romance language such as Spanish, Portuguese, or French knows the importance of using the correct form of address for one's conversational partner. If the relationship is on a friendly or familiar level, one might use (32a). If the relationship is more formal, than (32b) might be more appropriate.

(32) a. Tu es le professeur.
     b. Vous êtes le professeur.
        'You are the teacher'.

Importantly, though, (32a) and (32b) have exactly the same truth conditional meaning. If the speaker misjudges the relationship and uses *tu* instead of *vous*, it doesn't make the sentence false. It might be awkward, and it might upset the addressee, but it doesn't change the truth or falseness of the sentence.

8.5 Dimensions Of Meaning

We have arrived now at a place where we can represent schematically the different dimensions of meaning we have been discussing so far. Following Levinson (1983: 131) and Huang (2007: 57), this can be done as in (33).

(33)
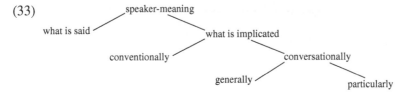

This schema represents the primary dimensions of meaning contained in the Gricean paradigm. We will see in the next chapter, though, on *presupposition* that linguistic meaning can be carved up along still other dimensions as well.

8.6 Summary

This chapter has taken a close look at the traditional Gricean paradigm of linguistic meaning. Grice's program has been immensely influential in linguistics and philosophy; but, it is not the only attempt to deal with these kinds of issues. (See Horn 2004 for a review of other such attempts.) In addition, Grice's program has been reinterpreted by others through the years, most significantly by Horn (1972, 1984, 2004), Levinson (1983, 2000), and Sperber and Wilson (1995). What we have seen in this present chapter is the way these concepts were originally assembled by Grice. This is still a very important set of concepts to master in linguistics; and anyone who wishes to grapple with pragmatic issues must have an understanding of it.

8.7 Further Reading

An excellent resource for further reading on implicature is H. Paul Grice's 1989 book *Studies in the Way of Words*, especially chapters 2 and 3. These are the primary sources of Grice's thought on implicature, and readers will almost certainly enjoy Grice's informal style of writing. Very informative states of the art of implicature can be found in Horn (2004) and Huang (2007). Both of these sources also discuss reinterpretations of Grice's work and provide reference information for further sources on those matters.

CHAPTER 9
Presupposition

So far in this course we have considered different dimensions of meaning based on whether they are conventional or non-conventional, based on words or proposi- tions, and whether or not they are truth-conditional. This chapter considers yet another relation of meaning, which has to do roughly with whether certain infor- mation is "at issue" or whether it is "taken for granted" in a conversation, and how this is represented in the structure of a sentence. That is, speakers and hearers do not enter a conversation as tabulae rasae. *They bring many kinds of knowledge to that conversation, such as encyclopedic world knowledge, knowledge of their environment, knowledge of their interlocutors, their interlocutors' backgrounds, as well as a general idea at least of the knowledge that their interlocutors themselves are bringing to the conversation. Further, speakers keep track of the information that has been added to the common ground of knowledge as a conversation unfolds. As a result, much of this information is assumed, or taken for granted. However, an important objective of a conversation is to share information that is new and which is not taken for granted. Speakers generally do this by building upon given information in order to share new or "at issue" information. This is where the linguistic concept of presupposition comes in. Speakers need a way of indicating which information is at issue in an utterance and which information is presupposed, or is to be taken for granted, backgrounded, etc. How speakers manage these relationships between pieces of information, and how this is reflected in the grammar, is the subject of this chapter.*

9.1 Introduction

Consider example (1). There is a statement about where the governor of Minnesota lives: i.e. St. Paul, Minnesota. This is what appears to be asserted in the sentence; however, parts of the sentence contain information that must be taken for granted before anything can be asserted at all. For example, we normally take for granted that the referent of a definite noun phrase exists. In this case, we presuppose that the person who is governor of Minnesota exists. It doesn't make sense to assert that the governor lives in St. Paul if the governor doesn't exist. So, the existence of that referent must be presupposed.

(1) **The governor of Minnesota** lives in St. Paul.

The same kind of existence presuppositions are also said to occur with possessives and proper names. Thus, use of a possessive form such as *my dog*, or of a proper name like Bill or George or Sue, would also presuppose the existence of the relevant referents.

In (2), the concern is with the factive verb *regret*. In this case, the complement of that verb—i.e. buying that car—is what is taken for granted.

(2) John **regrets** buying that car.

In uttering (2), the speaker likely takes for granted that the hearer already knows that John has bought the car. And, John's buying the car is not the central point of the utterance; rather, the speaker wants to communicate that John *regrets* having bought the car. This is what the speaker is said to have asserted: it is the at-issue information. So, the sentence is primarily about regret, with the part about buying the car in the background as presupposed information. One way of visualizing this relationship is as in (3).

(3) John **regrets** buying that car.
   a. John bought that car = X
   b. X = taken for granted by the speaker
   c. John regrets X = at issue for the speaker

So, when the speaker asserts *John regrets X*, she presupposes that the hearer already takes X for granted, or at least won't find X controversial. Of course, if the hearer doesn't already take X for granted, she might feel compelled to stop the conversation and clarify facts, as in (4).

(4) Hey, wait a minute! I didn't know John had bought that car!

This intuition can be felt more strongly with a change of state verb, such as *stopped*, as in (5). Similar to (2), we say that the complement of the verb is presupposed by the speaker. So, in (5), the speaker would most likely be presupposing that John previously did drink. The speaker would also probably assume that the hearer knew this information, or at least that the hearer wouldn't find it controversial.

(5) John **stopped** drinking.

However, if the hearer was not already aware of John's drinking, she might stop the conversation and take issue with the presupposed content. What she is really doing here is telling the speaker that the way the speaker has imagined the common ground of information between them is not accurate.

(6) Hey, wait a minute! I didn't know John DID drink!?

Thus, in order to speak to an audience, the speaker needs to have a pretty good idea of what information the audience already possesses and what information they will take for granted. This shared body of knowledge is often referred to as the *common ground*, and it has a serious impact on how we structure our utterances: from the words we choose, to the syntactic structure of sentences, to the way we pronounce words, and more. We will see as the chapter unfolds that it is crucial for speakers to correctly assess the state of the common ground in order for effective communication to occur. If a speaker constructs the common ground incorrectly, it can lead to incorrect assumptions about what is presupposed, and result in interruptions such as (4) and (6).

9.2 Presuppositions And Grammatical Forms

Presuppositions are said to be "triggered" by many kinds of grammatical forms, including individual words, word orders, pronunciations of words, and so forth. What this means is that speakers use these various grammatical forms to signal how they are viewing certain pieces of information in relation to other pieces of information and in relation to the common ground. For example, in (5), there are two major parts of the utterance: (i) that John drank in the past, and (ii) that John no longer drinks. Part (i) is taken for granted, and part (ii) is asserted as new information. With the use of the verb *stopped*, the speaker relates these two pieces of information together in the relevant way, presupposing the piece of information communicated in (i), with (ii) being what is at issue in the sentence.

We've looked thus far at definite descriptions in (1), factive verbs in (2) and (3), and change of state verbs in (5) as presupposition triggers. In this section we will look briefly at a range of additional triggers that speakers use to convey many different kinds of presuppositions. The following list in (7) is inspired by Levinson (1983: 181–183) and Grundy (2008: 52–53). Each example includes a grammatical name for the various phenomenon, a sentence exemplifying the phenomenon (with the trigger in bold), and then a presupposition (in italics) that likely is conveyed by use of that example sentence. Importantly, it isn't necessary for the given presuppositions to be conveyed in every instance in which the sentence is used (we'll talk about this below in terms of cancelation and defeasibility). Also, each example sentence below can be used to convey additional presuppositions that are not listed here, as there can be multiple presupposition triggers in a single sentence. Finally, this is not an exhaustive list of presupposition triggers; there are many more to be found across English and the other languages of the world.

(7) a. Iteratives
    John drank **another** glass of sherry.
    John had already had at least one glass of sherry.
  b. Temporal clauses
    He thought he was lucky **until/before/after** he met you.
    He met you.
  c. Clefts
    It was John that ate the pizza.
    Someone had eaten the pizza.
  d. Pseudo-clefts
    What John ate was the pizza.
    John ate something.
  e. Counterfactual conditionals
    If John had eaten the pizza, **then** he wouldn't be hungry now.
    John didn't eat the pizza.
  f. Stress
    Tide removes stains **AND** odors.
    Other detergents don't remove both stains and odors.

g. Implicative verbs (e.g. *remember, forget, manage, happen, improve*)
John's game has **improved** quite a bit.
John's game wasn't very good before.

h. Wh-questions
When will John arrive here**?**
John is expected to arrive.

i. Factive predicates
The fact that John ate the pizza is upsetting.
John ate the pizza.

We see then that the language and the grammar give us many ways of dividing information into presupposed (taken for granted) and non-presupposed. And, this has an effect on the structure of the sentences we use in our everyday lives. In normal language usage, we have continually differing expectations about the level and kind of background knowledge that our interlocutors bring to a conversational setting, and this has an effect on the form of a sentence that we choose to use. For example, (8a–c) are truth-conditionally equal; yet, they are used in different situations, depending on what the speaker believes the hearer's background knowledge to be and what the purpose of the conversation is.

(8) a. It was John that ate the pizza.
b. John ate the pizza.
c. What John ate was the pizza.

If the speaker believes the hearer already knows that the pizza was eaten by somebody, but that the hearer might not know who it was that actually ate the pizza, then the speaker can use (8a). On the other hand, if the hearer doesn't know that the pizza has been eaten, it might be better to use something like (8b), which doesn't carry the same presupposition. The pseudo-cleft in (8c) is used to convey yet another presupposition, which assumes that John ate something, but then asserts that that something, was the pizza. The sentences in (8) are all equivalent in terms of truth conditions. That is, if (8a) is true, then so are (8b–c), and if (8a) is false, so are (8b–c). (Take a moment here and test your intuitions on this. Can you think of a situation in which (8a) is true, but one of the others is false?) So, the sentences share the same truth conditions, but they differ in that they can be used to answer different questions. Let's look at some examples of this in (9–10). Here, we see that the pseudo-cleft in (9b) is not a felicitous response to the question in (9a); however, the cleft in (10b) is felicitous in response to this same question, even though (9b) and (10b) share the same truth conditions.

(9) a. Who ate the pizza?
b. #What John ate was the pizza.
(10) a. Who ate the pizza?
b. It was John that ate the pizza.

So, the sentences can share the same truth conditions with respect to the events they can describe; however, they offer different points of view on that event. And, this is a useful way of understanding what presuppositions are good for. Speakers can use them to relate new or at-issue information to information that the speaker believes is already taken for granted by the hearer. This is extremely useful, as we communicate by adding new information to information that the hearer already possesses. Presupposition triggers then can be a way of signaling to the hearer where in their old information store they should add the new information. Thus, information that you already know is stored and organized in your mind in a certain way. When new information comes in, it must be processed and entered into this storage system in the appropriate place somehow. One metaphor that has been used compares the mind's information storage system to that of a file-card system, where each file contains cards with all the information that the person knows about a given topic. Then, when the person learns new information, it is added to the appropriate file card, which already contains the old information that the person knows. Some kinds of presupposition triggers can be thought of as aids or tags in directing this flow of information.

Thus, with the cleft in (10b), the speaker assumes it is already taken for granted by the hearer that somebody ate the pizza; i.e. there is a file card in the hearer's mind that contains this information. The hearer might not know that it was John that ate the pizza, but they do know that somebody did. With the cleft sentence, then, the speaker directs the new information that it was John who has eaten the pizza to the appropriate file card in the hearer's information storage system.

This is a rough description of the kinds of work that speakers do with presuppositions. There is of course much more to the story; but, this should give you a general idea to work with. In the next section, we turn to look at some empirical properties that have been observed of presuppositions in the last four decades.

9.3 Empirical Properties Of Presupposition

Thus far in this course, all of the linguistic phenomena we have considered have been identifiable based on empirical properties that we know are associated with them. For example, consider the ways we have defined what it means to be a noun, a verb, etc. Each of these categories has identifiable empirical properties, which allow us to argue that specific pieces of language either do or do not fit into a given category. The same was true in the previous chapter where we discussed diagnostics for conversational and conventional implicatures. Presupposition is no exception. It too has a range of identifiable empirical properties, which we can use as diagnostics and as a means of grouping related phenomena together into a class and subclasses. This section looks at some of the more important properties of presupposition, such as the fact that they remain constant under negation, constant in conditionals, and constant in questions, their being taken for granted, and the fact that they are generally defeasible. We'll begin here by looking at presuppositional content under negation, conditionals, and questions, in a set of diagnostics that have come to be known in the presupposition literature as the "family of sentences" tests. These environments have also been referred to as "presupposition holes", for reasons that will become clear in the following two sections.

9.3.1 Family of sentences

Consider again how we have described presuppositional content thus far; it is content in a sentence that is somehow backgrounded or taken for granted compared to another part of the sentence in which it appears. The family of sentences is a collection of sentence types that is basically used to test for exactly this. Essentially, the family consists of a negated sentence, a question, and a conditional. The idea is that if we put a presupposition trigger in these environments, the trigger will still mark the relevant content as presupposed. Let's look briefly at how this works, using a negative test sentence. Consider (5) again, which is given below as (11a). Use of this sentence, with the change of state verb *stopped*, which is a presupposition trigger, would normally presuppose something like in (11b).

(11) a. John **stopped** drinking.
     b. John drank in the past.

Now consider what happens when the presupposition trigger is located under (i.e. in the syntactic scope of) negation, as in (12).

(12) John did*n't* stop drinking.

Use of this sentence would still seem to presuppose something like (11b). So, even though the presupposition trigger is located within the scope of negation, the presupposition itself remains constant. It is not negated. The at-issue part of the sentence—i.e. that John *stopped* drinking—is negated, but the presupposed part, that John drank in the past, is not negated.

For comparison, let's look at how negation works in a pair of non-presuppositional sentences like (13a) and (13b). In (13b), we see that negation reverses the claim that is at issue in (13a). In the first sentence, John smiles; in the second sentence, he does not. Negation seems to target precisely that part of the sentence that is at issue.

(13) a. John smiled.
     b. John did*n't* smile.

Conversely, presupposed content is generally not at issue in a sentence; it is taken for granted. As such, negation doesn't target it. Let's look at one more way of illustrating this, in (14), in which a simple negation is used in response to an immediately preceding statement. This time, we'll reuse example (1), which has a definite noun phrase as presupposition trigger.

(14) Mark: **The governor of Minnesota** lives in St. Paul.
     Jesse: No.

Recall we said that use of a definite noun phrase generally presupposes that the referent of that noun phrase exists; i.e. it carries an existence presupposition. In (14) Mark asserts that the governor of Minnesota lives in St. Paul. This is what is at issue in that sentence. Now, in uttering this sentence Mark also presupposes that the governor of Minnesota exists. This is not at issue, though; it is taken for granted. Thus, when Jesse responds with a simple negation, he appears to be targeting the at-issue part of Mark's assertion, which is that the governor lives in St. Paul. He is not denying the existence presupposition, or the fact that the governor exists. Once again, then, we see the negation targeting the at-issue component of a sentence and not the presupposed content. Another way of saying this is that the presupposition remains constant under negation.

Let's return now to the family of sentences, in which presupposed content is seen to remain constant in a variety of sentence types. We can formalize this set of diagnostics as in (15), where "S" stands for "sentence".

(15) a. S.
   b. It is not the case that S.
   c. Is it the case that S?
   d. If S, then S'.

Essentially, the idea is that presuppositions of a sentence S will survive when S is negated, questioned, and placed in the protasis of a conditional. So, let's take an example presupposition sentence and run it through the diagnostics to see how it works. We can use an example of an iterative such as the one we saw above in (7a). This is repeated below in (16).

(16) Iteratives
   John drank **another** glass of sherry.
   Presupposition: *John had already had at least one glass of sherry.*

What is needed here is to take (16) as "S" in the family of sentence diagnostics, and then observe whether the presuppositions of (16) are seen to survive in the various environments. This has been done below in (17b–d). In (17b), we see the iterative presupposition trigger *another* under negation. This sentence clearly still carries the presupposition that John had already had at least one glass of sherry. In (17c) we see *another* embedded in a question, and the relevant presupposition is still present. For that matter, consider how hard it is to respond to a question whose presuppositions you disagree with. A famous example of this is found in this question: *Have you stopped beating your wife?* Whether you answer *yes* or *no*, you have unfortunately agreed that you at least "used to" beat your wife! Returning to the family of sentences, we see that in (17d), in which *another* is located in the protasis (the *if*-clause) of a conditional sentence, the presupposed content is still present. (See Chapter 6 above for more on the logical properties of conditionals in general.)

(17) a. John drank **another** glass of sherry.
   b. John didn't drink another glass of sherry.
   c. Did John drink another glass of sherry?
   d. If John drank another glass of sherry, then he is probably drunk by now.

So, the presuppositional content of *another* seems to survive in these diagnostic environments. This is a good argument that that content is in fact presuppositional. A good exercise here for the reader is to test the other triggers mentioned above in (7) in this same way, using the family of sentences as diagnostics.

9.3.2 Presuppositions are taken for granted

The property of being "taken for granted" is a little bit different than those we have discussed so far. This one is more of a basic intuition about the presupposed content. Kadmon (2001: 14) describes the effect this way:

> [O]ur intuitions regarding 'being taken for granted' remain an important and indispensable criterion for identifying presuppositions. There is no better proof that a sentence S presupposes a proposition B than our intuition that B is 'taken for granted' and is a precondition for felicitous use of S.

We discussed what it means to be taken for granted above in the discussion surrounding (8)-(10). It will also be helpful here to unpack Kadmon's description of a presupposition as being "a precondition for felicitous use" of a sentence. We can think of "felicitous" as meaning something like "appropriate". If a sentence is used felicitously in a context, then it has been used appropriately. To understand this better, consider example (5) and (6) again, repeated here for convenience.

(5) John **stopped** drinking.
(6) Hey, wait a minute! I didn't know John DID drink!?

A sentence like (5) is appropriate when uttered in a context where the hearer already knows that John used to drink. This would mean that a proposition such as (17) would already need to be part of that common ground.

(17) John drank in the past.

In a different context, though, in which (17) is not part of the common ground, (5) would not be appropriate, since an utterance of (5) would normally presuppose that something like (17) is taken for granted. In this latter scenario, where (17) is not taken for granted, (5) would not be felicitous, and the hearer may very well interject with something like (6). What this means is that presuppositions act as kinds of constraints on the kind of discourse that can occur, and on the kinds of things that a speaker can say in a given discourse; however, there is more to the story. Sometimes speakers do say things that presuppose information that is not part of the common ground. And, sometimes this doesn't disrupt the discourse like the examples we see in (5) and (6). In this case, a process called *accommodation* is seen to occur.

Accommodation is a process in which speakers and hearers pretend that presuppositions are already a part of the common ground, even if they are not part of the common ground at the time. Consider an iterative, similar to (7a), above. There, we used *another*. Let's use *some more* (pronounced *sm'more*) this time, as in (18a). Suppose you are at a party, and the hostess comes by where you are sitting and says (18a) to you. This would most likely carry the presupposition that (18b).

(18) a. Would you like **some more** beer?
     b. You have had some beer already.

Now suppose you haven't had any beer yet at the party. You are faced with a choice of how to respond to the hostess, and you can say something like that of (19a–c).

(19) a. I haven't had any beer yet.
    b. No thanks.
    c. Sure.

More than likely, you would just say (19b) or (19c), either of which would go along with the presupposition that you have already had some beer. By doing this, you would have allowed the presupposition (18b) to be entered into the common ground of knowledge between you and the hostess. You have accommodated her presupposition use. This is a kind of obvious case of accommodation; however, we actually do this all the time in conversation without noticing.

Suppose your coworker is late to a meeting. When she arrives, she says to the people in the meeting, breathlessly, (20).

(20) I'm sorry I'm late! **My car** broke down!

Your coworker's use of the possessive *my car* presupposes that her car exists, and that she and her audience take this for granted. Now, you might not have ever known that she had a car, but this doesn't stop her utterance from being felicitous. Chances are slim that someone in the meeting would respond to her *Hey, wait a minute! I didn't know you had a car!* This is because in many situations it is easier to "pretend" that the information is part of the common ground than it is to interrupt the conversation for clarification. The fact that the coworker has a car isn't central to discourse at that time, so the audience lets it go without questioning it.

Sometimes, though, there are situations where the information is too controversial for us to simply accommodate. In the same scenario as (20), imagine that your coworker had come late to the meeting and said (21).

(21) I'm sorry I'm late! **My fire truck** broke down!

In this case, somebody would probably interrupt her with *Hey, wait a minute! You have a fire truck?* In this case, the coworker would be asking her audience to accommodate a presupposition that is controversial, and the audience would most likely be unwilling to do so. (Unless, of course, your coworker was a fire fighter, and then it would be uncontroversial that she drove a fire truck to work.) Or, a statement like (20) might actually be controversial in other contexts. Consider, for example, how the audience might react if the speaker of (20) was only a child and so too young to drive. We would probably be less willing to accommodate the existence presupposition of (20) in such a context.

The phenomenon of accommodation was first described by David Lewis in 1979, and he described it like this:

> if at time *t* something is said that requires presupposition *p* to be acceptable, and if *p* is not presupposed just before *t* then—ceteris paribus—presupposition *p* comes into existence.

And, it is clear that accommodation is a very useful notion in considering common ground and how it is constructed, understood, and used in communication.

In terms of presupposition being 'taken for granted', then, we need to adjust our view slightly here for those times when presuppositions are not taken for granted, but are also not controversial enough for hearers to object to them. In these latter cases, presuppositions are allowed to enter the common ground through the process of accommodation. This means that a further kind of information a speaker needs to know about the hearer is how far the hearer will be willing to go with respect to presupposition accommodation. That is, a speaker would need to be able to predict which hearers will accommodate the presuppositions of something like (20), and how controversial a putative presupposition is likely to be to the hearer.

9.3.3 Presuppositions are cancelable

Like we saw in Chapter 7 with respect to conversational implicatures, many kinds of presuppositions are cancelable. What this means is that in the right circumstances, presupposition triggers can fail to trigger presuppositions. In cases like this we say that the presupposition has been *canceled*. Huang (2007: 68) spells out this observation quite succinctly:

> [...] unlike semantic entailments, presuppositions are cancelable. They are nullified if they are inconsistent with (i) background assumptions, (ii) conversational implicatures, and (iii) certain discourse contexts. Furthermore, they can also drop out in certain intrasentential contexts, some of which give rise to the projection problem of presupposition. [Cancelability] has in general been taken as the second most important property of presupposition.

So, in the kinds of contexts Huang describes, we can often expect presuppositions to be canceled, and this is an empirical property of the class of meaning. There is much disagreement about the extent to which presuppositions are cancelable, but in general it is a well known property of presuppositions. Let's look at how this works in (22a–c). Here, the complement of *before* is said to be presupposed—i.e. it is presupposed that John finished his exam. We can test this claim quickly by seeing that this information survives under the negated instance of the example in (22b). A natural reading of the negative (22b) still involves John having finished his exam.

(22) a. John cried **before** he finished his exam.
      b. John didn't cry before he finished his exam.
      c. John died before he finished his exam.

Now look at (22c) in which the presupposed content appears against conflicting background assumptions. That is, we assume that when someone dies, they do not go on to finish their exam. Thus, the presupposition is canceled. Let's look now at another means of canceling presuppositions: this one sets the presupposition against conflicting conversational implicatures.

(23) If Tony has wrecked the car, then he will regret it.

We saw above in (2) that the factive verb *regret* normally presupposes its complement. In this example, then, *it* which stands for Tony's wrecking the car, should be presupposed. However, this example is more complicated than that, because the *if... then* conditional would generally be used to convey the conversational implicature that the speaker isn't sure whether Tony wrecked the car or not. This implicature of uncertainty conflicts with the presupposition that Tony has in fact wrecked the car. And, as a result, the presupposition is canceled.

Presuppositions can be also canceled when they conflict with the surrounding discourse context. Consider (24), which has a definite noun phrase *the president of Minnesota*. By now you should know that the use of a definite noun phrase generally presupposes the existence of its referent. This does not seem to happen in (24), though, because the immediately surrounding discourse has denied the existence of that referent. As such, the existence presupposition has been canceled.

(24)   There is no president of Minnesota; therefore, **the president of Minnesota** doesn't live in St. Paul.

Another much-discussed example of presupposition cancelation can be seen in cleft sentences, as in (7c), above. Consider (25a–b), which are taken from Levinson (1983: 189). It is generally expected that a use of (25a) would presuppose something like (25b); however, in certain kinds of contexts, this presupposition can be defeated.

(25)   a. **It** isn't Luke who will betray you.
       b. Someone will betray you.

Thus, in a context where possibilities are being eliminated, as in (26), the presupposition does not persist. Each of the cleft sentences in (26) (there are four) should presuppose that somebody is going to betray the hearer. However, the main point of (26) from the speaker's perspective is to convince the hearer that no one will betray him. As a result of this special context with this special intention, the expected presuppositions of the cleft sentences do not come through; they are canceled.

(26)   You say that someone in this room will betray you. Well maybe so. But it won't be Luke who will betray you, it won't be Paul, it won't be Matthew, and it certainly won't be John. Therefore no one in this room is actually going to betray you.

In summary, we have seen that many kinds of presuppositions are cancelable in contexts where there are beliefs that conflict with the presuppositions. Some researchers have gone so far as to say that every kind of presupposition is cancelable. For example, Kadmon (2001) takes this position and defends it very strongly. Other researchers are less sure about this idea and maintain that some kinds of presuppositions are not cancelable. It is an interesting and important question, but we will not pursue it further here. However, in spite of this differing of beliefs, it is generally accepted that cancelation is one of the most important identifiable properties of presuppositions.

9.3.4 Presuppositions are suspendable

This brief section is closely related to the previous section on presupposition cancelation. It basically illustrates the claim that presupposed material can be suspended with certain grammatical devices. Consider (27). We have seen in this chapter thus far that possessive noun phrases generally trigger an existence presupposition similar to that of a definite NP. Thus, in (27) we would expect a presupposition that Tony has a car, or that Tony's car exists, etc.

(27)   **Tony's car** is expensive; if, in fact, Tony has a car.

This doesn't have to be the case in (27), though. With the *if* clause, the existence presupposition is suspended. The natural reading of (27) with the *if* clause is more a comment about the way Tony is in general than it is about Tony's car. For example, the speaker might know that Tony likes to buy expensive things. So, we might paraphrase (27) like this: *I don't know if Tony has a car, but if he does, it's an expensive one.* The point is that there does not seem to be a presupposition of the car's existence in (27). It has been suspended with the *if* clause. A good exercise for the reader here is to try and perform similar suspensions with the numerous other presupposition triggers we have seen in this chapter.

9.3.5 Summary of empirical properties

Thus far in 9.2 and 9.3 we have seen two important but seemingly conflicting aspects of presuppositions. The first, which we saw in 9.2, has presuppositions being triggered by various words and grammatical devices, such as those in (7). This would suggest that the presupposition is a part of the conventional meaning of those words and pieces of grammar. By "conventional" here, I mean part of the lexical entry of a lexical item: i.e. part of the information that is stored in the language user's mental dictionary, including but not limited to how the word is pronounced, what kinds of affixes it can take, what other words it combines with in phrases and sentences, and what it means as well. Essentially, the lexical entry of a word tells the language user everything they need to know in order to use the word correctly. When meaning is lexical, or conventionally associated with a word, we tend to think of that meaning as arising in every situation in which that word is used. In the terms we have been using so far in this chapter, we tend to think of conventional/lexical meaning as *non-cancelable*. Recall the discussion above in Chapter 8 regarding conversational implicature. Those meanings were non-conventional, and we saw how they could very readily be canceled. Conversely, we saw that the meaning conveyed as a conventional implicature could not be canceled.

The problem here with presupposition is that since it seems to be triggered by specific words, we want to say that it is a conventional meaning, that it is conventionally associated with the specific words that trigger it. However, as we have seen in 9.3, this is not the case: presuppositions can be canceled quite straightforwardly. This suggests that perhaps the presupposition meaning is not in fact conventional, because if it were, we wouldn't expect to be able to cancel it. Therein lies the problem: it seems like it should not be cancelable, but in fact it is cancelable. This suggests that problem of presupposition has a solution that is not purely semantic and not purely pragmatic, but is rather a bit of both. We will take up this problem in more detail in the following section in discussion of The Projection Problem.

9.4 The Projection Problem

The kinds of examples in the preceding discussions of cancelation and suspension of presuppositions gave rise to what early researchers called The Projection Problem. Conceptually, this problem is a very simple one; but, the details are incredibly complex! Consider what we have done so far in this course in the syntax and semantics chapters. (See especially the discussion on compositionality in 7.1.2 in Chapter 7 Semantics.) There, we have been working toward an understanding of the way sentences are structured or put together. Here is a quote from the chapter on Semantics.

[E]ach lexical item (word) has its own meaning [...]. When lexical items are combined, they form a phrase. The meaning of the phrase is coming from the combination of each lexical item. When you combine phrases, you will get a sentence, whose meaning is again obtained by combining the meanings of phrases.

The idea is that in structuring a sentence, we combine words and their meanings into phrases, then combine those phrases into sentences. This is the linguistic process known as *compositionality*. The projection problem is concerned with how and where or if presuppositions should fit into this process. For example, if a presupposition is associated with the meaning of a given word (such as those above in (7)) then the presupposition should also participate in the composition process. When a presupposition trigger word combines with other words to form a phrase, then the presupposition should also become a part of that phrase. Likewise, when a phrase with a presupposition trigger word combines with other phrases to form a sentence, then the sentence should also carry that presupposition. This seems simple enough on the face of it, and this is what we would hope for: that we could treat presupposition meaning as just another kind of word meaning to undergo the composition process. However, this view of things becomes problematic due to the fact that presuppositions can be canceled and suspended. Further, we also find cases where a presupposition that is present in a simple sentence disappears when that simple sentence is embedded into a more complex sentence. (Similar syntactic embedding was discussed above in the Syntax I chapter.) This is especially true when the embedding occurs under a verb of saying or a propositional attitude verb: environments that have been referred to as "presupposition plugs" in the literature. Let's look at an example of this in (28).

We expect a use of (28a) to presuppose (28b). The question is, what happens when (28a) is embedded into a still larger sentence, such as (28c)? Is the presupposed (28b) still present in (28c)?

(28) a. John **regrets** buying that car.
    b. John bought that car.
    c. [Mary said [that John regrets buying that car]].

The answer to the question is that the presupposition doesn't have to be there anymore. There is a perfectly natural reading of (28c) in which John didn't buy the car. This could, for example, be a reading where Mary has her facts wrong, perhaps as in (28d), below.

    d. Mary said that John regrets buying that car; but, she doesn't know that John never actually bought it.

In (28c–d), then, the presupposition does not become part of the larger sentence. Another way of saying this is that the presupposition of the embedded sentence does not *project* up to the main (embedding) sentence. The presupposition has been suppressed (plugged) by the verb of saying. We see similar behavior under propositional attitude verbs such as *think*, *believe*, etc. Test your presupposition projection intuitions on (29). Does the iterative pre-supposition of *again* in the embedded sentence necessarily project up to the main sentence in (29b)?

(29) a. John is drinking **again**.
   b. [Mary believes [that John is drinking again]].

No, it does not. It is straightforward to come up with scenarios for (29b) in which the speaker consciously reports on Mary's false belief. That is, in which the speaker does not believe that John had previously been drinking, even if Mary holds that belief, as in (30). It is useful to introduce another speaker (in this case, Tony) to make the relevant perspective more obvious.

(30) Tony: Mary believes that John is drinking **again**. That's silly, though, because John has never had a drink in his life.

There has been a lot of research done on the projection problem since the 1970s, and much of it is very technical and beyond our current interests here. It is perhaps best to leave the question here with the idea that presuppositions can be triggered conventionally, but that they depend on the intentions of the speaker in order to surface as a presupposition in actual use. Another way to think of this is to think of all the different presupposition triggers in (7) as carrying "potential" presuppositions, which only become "actual" presuppositions when used in sufficient contexts to support this.

Consider the discussion above regarding speaker-hearer common ground, or their shared state of information. As a conversation unfolds, information is constantly being added to the common ground, and this information can be taken for granted: i.e. presupposed. This is part of what a presupposition trigger actually signals: that the information content in question is part of the common ground and that it can be taken for granted. Thus, when a speaker uses a presupposition trigger in a context in which the relevant information is presupposed, the presupposition goes through in a felicitous way. On the other hand, when a speaker uses a presupposition trigger in an insufficient context, the presupposition is either accommodated (if it is not too controversial) or canceled. So, presuppositions can be thought of as being highly dependent on the context in which they appear: if the context is sufficient for use of the presupposition trigger, then the presupposition goes through. If the context is insufficient for use of the given trigger, then the presupposition is either accommodated or canceled. The state of the common ground, what information it includes, etc., is something that speakers must keep track of as the conversation progresses, and they must use their presupposition triggers accordingly, or risk inefficient communication and possible interruption of the conversation.

We can compare the entire process here to what speakers do with pronouns such as *he, she, it,* etc. We use many pronouns in any given discussion; but, in order to use a pronoun in a felicitous way, the speaker must keep track of how the common ground is configured at that time. You cannot use *he*, for instance, if it is not clear to the hearer to which individual *he* is being used to refer. If a speaker says (31) against an insufficient context, interpretational problems can arise. Imagine if you said (31) to someone out of the blue. They would probably not know whom you were talking about, and communication would break down: *Hey, wait a minute! WHO ate the pizza?*

(31) He ate the pizza.

Presuppositions work in a similar way. With use of a pronoun, speakers are signaling that a referent is familiar or identifiable to a hearer; with presupposition triggers, speakers are signaling that a piece of information should be considered as non-controversial or taken for granted. Importantly, here, just as referring is something that speakers use nouns to do, presupposing is also something that speakers do with words in contexts, rather than being simply a property of the words themselves. So, words don't presuppose things: speakers do. Thus, presupposition triggers seem to offer a conventional *potential* to presuppose, but it depends on the state of the common ground at the relevant moment as to whether the potential is realized or not. Another way of saying this is that the presupposition is "licensed" pragmatically.

We have been talking thus far about empirical properties of presupposition in English. However, presuppositions are not just a phenomenon of English; they exist across languages. Interestingly, there is no reason that presuppositions in other languages should work the same as they do in English, and researchers have argued that in fact they can be radically different in other languages. Let's look briefly in the following section at presupposition in St'át'imcets, which is also known as Lillooet, and which is a Northern Interior Salish language with a few hundred speakers in British Columbia on the west coast of Canada.

9.5 Presupposition In St'át'imcets

As we have seen thus far, many presuppositions in English seem to place a constraint on the common ground. That is, the common ground has to be configured in certain ways if certain kinds of presuppositions are to be felicitous. Matthewson (2006) argues that these kinds of presuppositions do not exist in St'át'imcets. Let's consider an English example of the iterative *again* to get us started, in (32) [Matthewson's (1)].

(32) A_1: Mark phoned **again**.
     B_1: Mark? Which Mark?
     A_2: Portland Mark.
     B_2: Again? I didn't know he phoned in the first place!

The reaction in B_2 to A_1 should be familiar to you by now. It is a standard presupposition failure: i.e. a presupposition trigger used against an insufficient common ground, with the result that B_2 feels compelled to disrupt the flow of conversation in order to clarify information. (B_2 could just have easily gone the *Hey! Wait a minute!* route we saw above in similar presupposition failure scenarios.) Let's look now at what happens in similar situations in St'át'imcets. Consider (33) [Matthewson's (2)]. She describes the scenario like this:

At the time of A's utterance, B had just walked into A's house and there had been no prior conversation apart from greetings. In spite of this, B did not challenge A's use of *hu7* 'more'.[1]

(33) A: wá7-lhkacw   ha   xát'-min'   ku   **hu7**   ku   tih
          IMPF-2SG.SUBJ   YNQ   want-APPL   DET   **more**   DET   tea
          'Would you like some more tea?'
      B: iy
          'Yes.'

Speaker A thus asks B if she would like some more tea. B doesn't have any tea at the moment, but nonetheless affirms that she would like some tea. You should take a moment and consider how an English speaker would probably react if she were in B's position. Quite likely, the English speaker would let A know that she hadn't had any tea yet, or otherwise challenge the question, similar to the scenario we saw in (18) above.

Let's consider another of Matthewson's examples, in (34) [Matthewson's (9)] with *múta7* 'again'. The idea here is that B knows that Henry is not a millionaire. And, B doesn't know whether Henry had previously won the lottery. As a result, what A has said can be regarded as particularly controversial. An English speaker would probably take issue with this presupposition and interrupt the conversation.

(34) Context: Interlocutors all know that Henry is not a millionaire.
      A: t'cum   **múta7**   k   Henry   l-ta   lottery-ha
          win(INTR)   **again**   DET   Henry   in-DET   lottery-DET
          'Henry won the lottery again.'
      B: o, áma
          'Oh good.'

We see something similar in (35) with *t'it* 'also'. Lisa (the author of the St'át'imcets research being discussed here) is known to the St'át'imcets speakers; and, they know that she is not particularly prone to illegal activity. Thus, when the St'át'imcets speaker is told that Lisa is also in jail, we would again expect a question or surprised response. This is not what happens with the St'át'imcets, though.

(35) Context: No prior discussion of anyone being in jail
      A: wá7   **t'it**   l-ti   gélgel-a   tsitcw   k   Lisa
          be   **also**   in-DET   strong-DET   house   DET   Lisa
          'Lisa is also in jail.'
      B: stam' ku s-záyten-s
          what DET NOM-business-3POSS
          'What did she do?'

---

1 Matthewson uses Jan van Eijk's grammatical abbreviations, where APPL = applicative, CAU = causative, CONJ = conjunction, DEIC = deictic, DET = determiner, DIR = directive transitivizer, FUT = future, HYP = hypothetical, INTR = intransitive, NEG = negative, NOM = nominalizer, OB = object, OOC = out of control, POSS = possessive, SG = singular, SUBJ = subject, YNQ = yes-no question.

The responses in (33–35) would be unexpected on an English understanding of the role of presupposition in conversation. Thus, Matthewson argues that presuppositions are of a rather different nature in St'át'imcets. In St'át'imcets (unlike in English) a speaker who is presupposing something is not necessarily making an assumption about the beliefs of the addressee. Instead, the St'át'imcets speaker in presupposing is only commenting on her own beliefs. Speakers of St'át'imcets are of course aware of this, and as a result, there is no need to object when their interlocutor presupposes something that is not already taken for granted as part of the common ground, like we saw in the English (32). Their intuition is that the presupposition comments only on the information state of the speaker. As a result, presuppositions can straightforwardly convey new information in St'át'imcets.

This of course raises the question of exactly what a presupposition does in St'át'imcets. If it is not information that is expected to be taken for granted, then what is it for? According to Matthewson, the presupposition in St'át'imcets is more akin to a kind of backgrounded or secondary assertion. That is, an uttered sentence can have a primary point to convey, but can also convey secondary, perhaps less important, information as well. This secondary information can be new to the hearer just like the primary information, and the hearer can object to it if they disagree. This much is similar to English. The big difference, though, is that the hearer doesn't feel as if they are expected to know the secondary information, as is the case in English presuppositions. As a result, there is no need to challenge the secondary information on these grounds.

We see, then, two quite different kinds of presuppositions across languages. And, as we mentioned above, there is no reason to expect that presuppositions should be uniform or universal across languages. If you are a native speaker of a language other than English, it will be interesting for you to consider similar such scenarios in that language and see how they compare to English and St'át'imcets.

9.6 Presuppositions In Courtroom Testimony

As we've been discussing throughout this chapter, presupposition is usually considered to consist of backgrounded information that is part of a larger assertion—that is, presuppositions are generally not the primary points of an utterance, but rather are supporting information for an at-issue or primary point. We've also seen how direct responses to questions and assertions seem to respond not to the presupposed content, but to the at-issue content of the utterance in question. For example, consider (36). The point of John's question is to ask where the president of Minnesota resides. John's use of the definite NP presupposes the existence of the president of Minnesota.

(36) John: Does **the president of Minnesota** live in St. Paul?
Jane: No.

Jane's simple response to the question seems to respond only to the main point of John's question, not to the presupposed content. Her negation doesn't negate the presupposed existence of the president of Minnesota. This presupposition, if left unchecked, will likely enter the common ground of knowledge shared by John and Jane, and it will appear as if Jane too presupposes the existence of a president of Minnesota, even though there is no president of Minnesota. With this kind of example in mind, then, we can raise the question of presupposition issues in a courtroom environment. Especially of interest here is the extent to which it is possible for a witness on the stand to assent to unwanted presuppositions in the process of answering a different question. Thus, if (36) were courtroom testimony, Jane would be on record as accepting the existence of the president of Minnesota, even if she didn't believe that there was a president of Minnesota in existence.

At the same time, it can be difficult to object to unwanted presuppositions in conversation, because it can seem as if the person objecting is not being responsive to the main point of her interlocutor's utterance: i.e. it can feel as if the person objecting is changing the topic of conversation. We can get a feel for this kind of communicational mismatch in the constructed example (36), in which Martha believes that the main point of her utterance was that John was crying, and it seems to her that Bob is not responding to her main point.

(36)   Martha: John started crying before he finished the test.
　　　　Bob: Uhh, John didn't finish the test.
　　　　Martha: That's not the point.

As we saw above in (7b), the complement of *before* is commonly considered to be presupposed, or backgrounded. Thus, when Bob takes issue with the backgrounded information, it is frustrating to Martha, and it seems like he is not responding to her assertion. It might very well be the case that John didn't finish the test, and so Bob's objection is technically correct; however, Martha still feels as if Bob is not responding to the main point of her utterance, which is that John was crying.

As tricky as this can be in natural speech, it can be even more complicated in some courtroom discourse, where the type and nature of responses that are allowed can be highly restricted. In some kinds of court discourse, there are strict procedural rules for how witnesses can respond to questions, and judges can require witnesses to answer only *yes* or *no* to a lawyer's question. This can be problematic, though, because if a witness is required to answer only *yes* or *no* to a question, then she has no room left to respond to what she perceives as false presuppositions in the question. As a result, it is possible for false presuppositions to go down in the court record, simply because a witness was not allowed or not able to respond to them to set the record straight. For instance, imagine if you were required to give only a *yes* or *no* answer to the question: *Have you stopped beating your wife?* Regardless of what you chose here, you would be allowing the presupposition that you had beaten your wife in the past to go on record. So, this kind of problem has real-life implications in courtroom testimony.

Let's look now at a couple of examples of testimony from an actual courtroom inquiry. The examples come from a 2006 article by Ehrlich and Sidnell. The inquiry in question considered "the deaths of seven people as a result of water contamination in a small Ontario town, Walkerton, and, specifically, from the testimony of the then premier of Ontario, Michael Harris" (657). As the authors go on to describe, Harris felt compelled to take issue with several backgrounded presuppositions put forth by the questioning attorneys, which suggested that he was in some way culpable for the incident: i.e. in the course of asking "fact-finding" questions, the questioning attorneys had presupposed information with which Harris disagreed. To Harris, these presuppositions would be damaging if he let them go unanswered.

The first example we'll consider contains the factive predicate *regret*. As we saw above in examples (2) and (3), the complement of *regret* tends to be presupposed. Here is (2) again:

(2) John regrets buying that car.

As we said above, in uttering (2), the speaker likely takes for granted that the hearer already knows that John has bought the car. We also saw above in §9.3.1 that presuppositions survive in questions. So, if we turn (2) into a question, as in (37), the presupposition is still present.

(37) Does John regret buying that car?

Both (2) and (37) presuppose that John bought the car in question. Further, a simple *yes* or *no* answer to (37) would likely be a tacit acceptance of that same presupposition. Thus, it is very important that testimony in courtroom inquiries and cross-examination proceed with care in this area. Now consider (38), which is actual courtroom testimony taken from Ehrlich and Sidnell (2006).

(38) Attorney: Do you have any **regret** in not intervening in the business plan process and saying 'you're going too far'?
Harris: Well, you assumed that I didn't intervene in the business process and I think that's—that's not an assumption you ought to make.

What is happening in (38) is that the questioning attorney has presupposed that Mr. Harris did not intervene in the situation, which resulted in the contaminated water and so the deaths of seven people. As a result, she suggests that Mr. Harris should bear some of the blame for the situation. Notice that the attorney's question in (38) is phrased as a *yes/no* question, and that if Mr. Harris answered either *yes* or *no*, he would be assenting to the presupposition that he didn't intervene in the process. What Harris chooses to do is ignore the primary question and respond instead to the potentially damaging presupposition. This is Harris's own version of the *Hey, wait a minute!* response we've seen in several examples thus far in the chapter: i.e. (4), (6), (20), (32), etc.

As we said above, it is often the case that responding to a presupposition rather than the main point of an utterance requires one to stop the flow of conversation. This is something that we as speakers don't normally like to do. It often feels impolite; in any case, it is uncooperative. Consider again Grice's Cooperative Principle, which we discussed above in Chapter 8:

The Cooperative Principle
Make your conversational contribution such as is required, at the stage at which it occurs, by the accepted purpose or direction of the talk exchange at which it occurs, by the accepted purpose or direction of the talk exchange in which you are engaged. (Grice 1989: 26)

A cooperative response in (38), taking into account the "accepted purpose or direction of the talk exchange" would have been for Harris to answer the *yes/no* question with a simple *yes* or *no*. However, doing so would have required Harris to commit to a presupposition that he didn't want to commit to. What is especially interesting here is that the rules of communication can change in a courtroom environment. When we speak in natural, everyday situations, the Cooperative Principle operates in one way; but in the more restricted inquiry or cross-examination environment, where rules of communication are controlled by judges and lawyers, it operates in another. That is, in everyday communication, we expect our interlocutors to be cooperative, and they expect the same of us. This is one reason why questioning attorneys sometimes utilize leading questions and questions that contain suggestive presuppositions: they take advantage of our natural tendency to be cooperative, and can thus be used to elicit information that the witness might not have volunteered otherwise. Let's look at one more example from Mr. Harris's testimony.

Example (39) picks up a few lines after (38) leaves off, and the questioning attorney is still using the factive *regret* to attempt to smuggle in presuppositions that are potentially damaging to Mr. Harris.

(39) Attorney: So you have no **regret** sir?
Harris: I clearly regret what happened in Walkerton, if that's what you're ...
Attorney: Do you **regret** not intervening?
Harris: Ah, well, I didn't say I didn't intervene.
Attorney: Do you **regret** not taking further actions in exploring what the nature of the impacts were which were on that document?
Harris: No. I took every action that you would ever expect, in my view, a Premier to take. And I can honestly tell you that.

Rather than ask Harris directly if or how he had intervened, the attorney tries to presuppose that Harris did not intervene, by packaging this information in the complement of *regret*. It is all further embedded in the *yes/no* question, which requires Harris to either be nonresponsive in his answer or else assent to the unwanted presuppositions.

These examples are useful to us in that they help show the different dimensions of meaning that are present in the sentences we speak. They also help us to see that our responses to our interlocutors often target one dimension or another of our interlocutors' sentences. We can see how Harris could have been cooperative and stayed on topic with the questioning attorney. This would have likely caused him to accept unwanted presuppositions and so appear culpable for the situation. What he actually did though was target his response not to the main topical dimension of meaning but to the backgrounded presuppositional meaning.

9.7 Conclusion

This chapter has taken a close look at linguistic presupposition. This is a dimension of meaning which is incredibly complex and for which there is an immense and ongoing literature. We have looked at basic empirical properties of presupposition and at the kinds of questions that have been asked with respect to them by linguists and philosophers for the last several decades. We have also taken a brief look at the way presupposition is seen to occur in the Non-Indo-European language St'át'imcets, and in the way presupposition triggers are sometimes utilized in courtroom testimony. We have not gone into detail for the various analyses of pre-supposition that have been proposed over the years. Much of this material is highly technical, and is far beyond the scope of this book. We invite you, however, to explore the resources described below in 9.1 if you would like to think more about presuppositions.

9.8 Further Reading

For an intellectual history of presupposition, readers should consult Levinson (1983). Huang (2007) offers a more up to date and concise interpretation of Levinson's treatment of presup-position in general. Birner (2013) is a very good source for the basic landscape of problems surrounding investigation of presupposition as is Beaver and Guerts (2011). An in-depth look at the projection problem can be found in Simons et al. (2010).

CHAPTER 10
Speech Act Theory

We have thus far considered conventional semantic meaning, implied meaning, and meaning that is taken for granted. The topic of this chapter, speech act theory, is concerned with the way speakers perform actions by virtue of speaking. Speech act theory is one of the most widely discussed issues in linguistic and philosophical pragmatics, and it has had implications for virtually every field in the humanities and social sciences since the mid-twentieth century. This chapter will focus primarily on the discussions of speech act theory within linguistics and the philosophy of language, but it also includes sections which explore the significance of speech act theory in real-world situations as well.

10.1 History Of Speech Act Theory

Like the conversational implicature we discussed in Chapter 8, speech act theory was an idea that originated in philosophy. Implicature comes from the work of Oxford philosopher H. Paul Grice, and speech act theory was first proposed by Grice's Oxford colleague, J. L. Austin, in the 1930s. Though Austin presented his ideas on speech acts through the 1950s, they were not published until 1962 in a book entitled *How To Do Things With Words*. Austin, however, had passed away in 1960, and the book was published posthumously by a group of Austin's students, including John R. Searle, who continued to develop Austin's ideas in several important publications in the 1960s and 1970s, and whose work we will consider below in some detail.

Austin first began formulating his ideas in the 1930s, when the central interest in philosophy of language was whether or not a sentence could be judged true or false, a doctrine that was known as logical positivism. The logical positivists believed that if a sentence could not be verifiably proven as true or false, then it in effect had no meaning whatsoever. This idea is known as the "descriptive fallacy". A result of this was that many kinds of sentences that are frequent in all manner of discourses were considered meaningless by the logical positivists— e.g. any sentence that was vague, subjective, evaluative, etc. Austin's work in speech act theory was a direct challenge to this kind of thinking. He showed that contrary to the ideas of logical positivists, many kinds of sentences were not used to make truth-evaluable claims at all; rather, they were used to do things, to perform actions. Further, Austin showed that there were normal declarative sentences that could not be verified as being true or false, and that such sentences were in fact uttered to perform an act rather than to describe the world. These kinds of sentences, which are used to perform actions, Austin referred to as "performatives". He used the term "constative" to refer to sentences whose uses were descriptive: i.e. that were used to describe some aspect of the world. We will turn now to Austin's distinction between these two kinds of sentence.

10.2 Performatives And Constatives

Consider examples (1a-c), which are prototypical performative sentences. In uttering one of these sentences in the appropriate context and situation, the speaker causes an action to occur in the world. If (1a) is uttered during a wedding ceremony, and if it is uttered by someone with the proper authority to do so (i.e. the minister or person conducting the ceremony), and if the addressees of the utterance are participating in the ceremony with the desire to be married, then upon the utterance of (1a) the man and woman become married. The world has changed. They were not married before the utterance of (1a), and they became married after the utterance of (1a).

> (1) a. I now pronounce you man and wife.
> b. I hereby christen this ship the High Noon.
> c. The jury hereby finds the defendant guilty.

Similar descriptions are also true of (1b-c). We might expect to hear (1c) near the end of courtroom trial. Prior to the utterance of (1c), the defendant would be innocent in the eyes of the law, under the idea that those on trial are innocent until proven guilty. However, when the foreman of the jury utters (1c), the defendant becomes guilty in the eyes of the law. As we saw above in the description of (1a), though, there are certain conditions that must hold in order for (1c) to achieve the intended effect. For example, (1c) must be uttered as part of the proceedings of a courtroom trial; it must be uttered by the foreman of the jury; it must be uttered at the appropriate time in the proceedings; and so on. If the statement is made outside of these "felicity conditions", then the action will not be achieved as intended. (We'll talk more about felicity conditions below. Also, see discussion of felicity conditions in Chapter 9 Presupposition.)

The performative sentences like those in (1a-c) are clearly dependent on being embedded in specific institutions, or as Wittgenstein might say, being embedded in "language games". That is, they must occur within the proper ritual framework—a wedding ceremony, the naming of a ship, and a courtroom trial. There are other types of clear performative sentences, though, in which this kind of dependence on the ritual situation is less obvious. For example, consider (2a), which is a run of the mill promise, and (2b), which is a pretty standard apology.

> (2) a. I promise to pick you up at 5:30.
> b. I apologize for saying that.

Consider what happens in a typical utterance of a sentence like (2a). Before the utterance, there is no promise; but, after the utterance of (2a), a promise springs into existence. The utterance of (2a) has caused the world to change by causing a promise to come into existence. The same is true of (2b), *mutatis mutandis*.

In addition to being less dependent on particular ritual situations, the peformatives in (2) are less bound by word choice and syntax as well. That is, the examples in (1) require specific verbs (e.g. *pronounce, christen, find*, etc.) and a formulaic syntax in order to issue the performative. The examples in (2), however, are less dependent in this way. For example, a promise can be conveyed in many different linguistic forms, as in (3a-d).

(3) a. I'll pick you up at 5:30.
    b. Pick you up at 5:30.
    c. See you at 5:30!
    d. 5:30 it is, then!

The examples in (3a-d) do not specifically contain the verb *to promise*, and it is difficult to include the adverb *hereby* without the verb *to promise*. We can see this last claim illustrated by the difference in acceptability between (4a-b).

(4) a. #I'll hereby pick you up at 5:30.
    b. I hereby promise to pick you at 5:30.

There is a wide degree of variation in the form of (3a-d); yet, they can all be used to convey promises, or to cause promises to spring into existence at their mere utterance. The fact that these kinds of sentences can be used to perform the same act, but with such different forms, suggests that we need a way of keeping track of different levels of meaning: i.e. what a sentence literally means, and what a sentence is used to accomplish in a situation. This observation led Austin, the creator of speech act theory, to propose three dimensions of sentence meaning: namely, the locutionary, illocutionary, and perlocutionary meanings. We'll return to these dimensions of sentence meaning below in section 10.3. Meanwhile, let's move on to the second topic of this section, which is the constative sentence.

So, we said that performative sentences "change the world" or cause something to spring into existence by speaking. Constative sentences, on the other hand, describe the world or assert something about the world. Consider the typical constative sentences in (5).

(5) a. The cat is on the mat.
    b. John bought a book from the store.
    c. The boy kicked the ball.

In (5) we see standard, declarative sentences that describe some aspect of the world: a description of a cat being on a mat, the purchase of a book, a boy kicking a ball. These sentences are truth evaluable and verifiable, but they do not cause the world to change in the same way that performatives do. Instead, these constative sentences assert something about the world. They are thus descriptive, and they describe the world rather than change it. We cannot point at an empty mat and say (5a) and expect a cat to appear on the mat. Nor can we say (5b) and expect that event to spring into existence.

Thus, at first blush there seems to be a stark difference between the performative sentences in (1-2), and the constative sentences in (5). However, Austin went on to illustrate that this gap is not as wide as it first seems, and that there were reasons to eventually abandon the distinction he had initially posited between performative and constative sentences.

First, Austin illustrated that it is sometimes difficult to see the difference between performatives and constatives in terms of truth conditions. For example, there are sentences which seem to be constative but which are difficult to evaluate in truth conditional terms, as in (6).

(6) a. France is hexagonal.
    b. John is bald.

The problem with sentences such as those in (6) is that they are vague, and it is not clear at what point they are true or false. A map of France shows a border shape that is roughly hexagonal; though, no one would mistake it for a prototypical geometric hexagon. Similarly, in (6b) it is not clear what exactly constitutes baldness. Example (6b) recalls the problem philosophers have referred to as a sorites paradox:

> *The Bald Man*: Would you describe a man with one hair on his head as bald? Yes. Would you describe a man with two hairs on his head as bald? Yes. ... You must refrain from describing a man with ten thousand hairs on his head as bald, so where do you draw the line? (Hyde 2011)

Thus, it becomes difficult to verify whether a sentence like (6b) is true or not; however, the fact of its simple declarative form suggests it should be a constative sentence with verifiable truth conditions.

A second reason for questioning the performative-constative distinction is that it is straightforward to find sentences that take the form of a performative but which are actually used for asserting claims about the world, as in (7), which is adapted from Levinson (1983: 235).

(7) I hereby state that I am alone responsible.

As Levinson writes, this statement is in the "performative normal form" (it has a verb in the correct form and uses the adverb *hereby*, among other things); however, it is not performative in that it does not cause the event described to spring into existence or to become true.

So far, we have seen sentences in constative form, which are not truth evaluable, and we have seen sentences in performative form, which do not perform actions. A further wedge can be driven in between the performative-constative distinction with the fact that some sentences seem to be both performative and constative, as in (8), which is taken from Levinson (1983: 234).

(8) I warn you the bull will charge.

Use of this sentence would seem to have the performative property of warning as well as the descriptive property with respect to the bull's actions.

A final and important problem for the performative-constative distinction is seen in the fact that sentences in constative form have similar kinds of felicity conditions to what we saw for performative sentences. That is, performative sentences like those in (1) require certain contextual conditions to be in place for the sentence to be used appropriately: i.e. (1a) must be uttered within the context of a wedding ceremony by a person with the proper authority to utter it, etc. But now consider a constative sentence such as (9).

(9) The king of the United States lives in Texas.

As we saw earlier in discussions of presupposition in Chapter 9, use of a definite noun phrase presupposes the existence of what it is used to refer to. However, the United States does not have a king, and so (9) experiences a kind of presupposition failure. As a result of this, (9) cannot be judged true or false. Thus, constative sentences can be seen to have kinds of felicity conditions in place in a way that is similar to those of performative sentences: i.e. the presuppositions of a constative sentence must be satisfied before it can be judged true or false.

A final result here is that the performative-constative distinction cannot be maintained in any kind of distinguished way, and Austin instead proposes to discuss the meaning and use distinctions we have seen thus far in a new way instead: i.e. in terms of locutionary, perlocutionary, and illocutionary acts. We turn to this in the following section.

10.3 Locutionary, Illocutionary, And Perlocutionary

As described briefly above, the same performative act can be achieved with sentences of differing forms. We saw this in the discussion that surrounds example (3). This suggests a need for referring to these different levels of meaning involved in the use of a sentence: i.e. literal meaning, the performative act, etc. Austin (1962: Lecture IX) devised the three-way distinction of locutionary, illocutionary, and perlocutionary as a means of describing these diverse kinds of meaning. We'll discuss them each in turn in this section. In brief, though, here is Austin's own arrangement of the three acts, taken from his Lecture IX (p.108):

> We first distinguished a group of things we do in saying something, which together we summed up by saying we perform a *locutionary act*, which is roughly equivalent to uttering a certain sentence with a certain sense and reference, which again is roughly equivalent to 'meaning' in the traditional sense. Second, we said that we also perform *illocutionary acts* such as informing, ordering, warning, undertaking &c., i.e. utterances which have a certain (conventional) force. Thirdly, we may also perform *perlocutionary acts*: what we bring about or achieve *by* saying something, such as convincing, persuading, deterring, and even, say, surprising or misleading. Here we have three, if not more, different senses or dimensions of the 'use of a sentence' or of 'the use of language'.

Let's begin with locutionary. According to Austin, the locutionary act is essentially the uttering of a meaningful sentence, in a context, with the intention of communicating something. It is not enough here to merely speak the words of a sentence with no communicative intention. For instance, a parrot repeating a sentence over and over would not be an example of a locutionary act. Similarly, singing the lyrics of a song might not constitute a locutionary act either. The locutionary act, then, gives us something like the literal meaning of the sentence in question, based on the words in the sentence and their syntactic combination in a context.

This brings us to the illocutionary act. When a speaker utters a sentence, she usually does so with the intention of communicating something or accomplishing a certain kind of act: i.e. the speaker might want to issue a warning, a promise, a threat, an apology, a joke, a command, or many other possible acts. For instance, Huang (2007) gives the following example, in (10).

(10) The gun is loaded.

On the locutionary level, this sentence conveys the straightforward information that the gun in question, which the speaker expects the hearer to be able to identify, is loaded. This is the extent of the locutionary act. The illocutionary act, though, takes us beyond this and is concerned with the speaker's intention in uttering (10) in the first place. In different contexts (10) could be used to "make a threat, to issue a warning or to give an explanation" (103). For instance, consider a scenario in which a criminal wishes to frighten a person on the street; brandishing her weapon, she might utter (10) as a threat. Or, if a person picks up the gun, not knowing it is loaded, the speaker of (10) might utter it as a warning to take care with the gun. Or, perhaps the addressee of (10) wants to know what has happened to the ammunition that was previously sitting beside the gun on the table. The speaker might then utter (10) as an explanation: i.e. the ammunition is now inside the gun. The sentence in (10) can be used for these purposes and many many others. These intentional acts we discuss in terms of the illocutionary act.

Although there are many kinds of possible illocutionary acts, there have been several attempts over the last few decades to categorize these acts, and systematize them. Austin's student, John Searle, has provided what is perhaps the most influential grouping of illocutionary acts. This categorization, which we have adapted from Curzan and Adams (2009: 255) and Searle (1979), is represented briefly below in (11).

(11)

Type of illocutionary act	Description	Example verbs
Assertives	Illocutionary acts that represent a state of affairs	stating, claiming, hypothesizing, describing, telling, insisting, suggesting, asserting, or swearing that something is the case
Directives	Illocutionary acts designed to get the addressee to do something	ordering, commanding, asking, daring, challenging
Commissives	Illocutionary acts designed to get the speaker (i.e. the one performing the act) to do something	promising, threatening, intending, vowing to do or to refrain from doing something
Expressives	Illocutionary acts that express the mental state of the speaker	congratulating, thanking, deploring, condoling, welcoming, apologizing
Declarations	Illocutionary acts that bring about the state of affairs to which they refer	blessing, firing, baptizing, bidding, passing sentence, excommunicating

So, there are many different kinds of intentions that speakers might hope to communicate, and many actions which they might attempt to perform. In (11), Searle attempts to group this wide range of potential speech acts into a group consisting of five general types. Other researchers have suggested different ways of categorizing the various kinds of speech acts over the years; but, Searle's grouping above is usually the starting point for this kind of project.

The last distinction Austin makes in dimensions of meaning is for the perlocutionary act. As given above, the perlocutionary act describes what actually happens as a result of the utterance—whether the speaker intended it or not. So, speakers utter sentences with the intention of accomplishing something. What they actually accomplish is the perlocutionary act. This might be what the speaker had hoped to accomplish, or it might be something other than that. The perlocutionary act is generally in the hands of the addressee. The speaker utters her sentence with the hopes of achieving a given perlocutionary act, but it is ultimately up to the addressee to respond in the way the speaker has predicted. As you can see, then, this requires quite a lot on the part of the speaker. That is, to achieve her desired perlocutionary act, the speaker must first consider what she knows about the addressee, what the addressee knows about the speaker, how to most effectively structure the sentence, when to say the sentence, how to intonate the sentence, along with many other variables. Once this is done, the speaker sends the sentence out into the world and hopes for the best. If she has guessed correctly on the hows and whens of her utterance, she stands a good chance of achieving her desired perlocutionary act. If she has guessed incorrectly, however, she stands a chance of failing to achieve the desired act.

10.3.1 Direct and indirect speech acts

Now, what the speaker intends to communicate or accomplish might be very close to the locutionary meaning of the sentence, or it might not be close at all. In this latter situation, we speak of indirect speech acts. Consider Doug's response in (12). Tony asks where he can buy some beer, and Doug says that there is a grocery store across the street.

(12) Tony: Where can I buy some beer?
      Doug: There's a Mt. Royal grocery store across the street.

Doug's response can be interpreted along multiple dimensions here. On the one hand, we can discuss the locutionary sense of it, which tells us essentially the location of the Mt. Royal grocery store, and nothing more. On the other hand, we can discuss the further—and likely more important—part of Doug's message, which is that he believes that one can buy beer at the Mt. Royal grocery. This latter message is indirectly conveyed, and it is not close at all to the locutionary meaning of Doug's utterance. We discussed this relation of how implicit messages are conveyed above and beyond what is literally said, above in Chapter 8 in terms of conversational implicature. We will be discussing the same phenomena here, but in terms of speech act theory. Essentially, indirect speech acts can be conveyed via the Gricean mechanism of conversational implicature. (We will return to this relationship below in section 10.3.3.)

Now, consider again the explicit performative sentences from example (1), repeated here for convenience. You can see that there is a direct correlation between the locutionary sense of what is said and the illocutionary sense of what one intends to accomplish by uttering one of these sentences. The examples in (1a-c) are thus direct speech acts.

(1) a. I now pronounce you man and wife.
    b. I hereby christen this ship the High Noon.
    c. The jury hereby finds the defendant guilty.

For example, (1c) is uttered at the conclusion of a jury trial, and the locutionary sense directly reflects what the speaker intends to accomplish with the utterance. There are many such explicit performative verbs in a given language, including promising, threatening, warning, and so on, as you can see from the chart found above in (11).

An interesting problem arises when we return to indirect speech acts. This has to do with the fact that in ordinary speech people tend to speak more indirectly than directly. As a result, there are many different linguistic means of accomplishing what is basically the same indirect speech act. For example, consider the performative verb *to request*. We can use this verb in sentences that are clearly performative, as in (13). Upon uttering this, a request that the door be closed springs into existence.

(13) I hereby request that you close the door.

This is a direct request, but it is a stilted and highly formal means of making the request. It is much more likely that the same request would be accomplished in an indirect manner, as in one of the many possibilities we see in (14a-g), which is adapted from Levinson (1983: 264).

(14) a. I want you to close the door.
       I'd be much obliged if you'd close the door.
    b. Can you close the door?
       Are you able by any chance to close the door?
    c. Would you close the door?
       Won't you close the door?
    d. Would you mind closing the door?
       Would you be willing to close the door?
    e. You ought to close the door.
       It might help to close the door.
       Hadn't you better close the door?
    f. May I ask you to close the door?
       Would you mind awfully if I was to ask you to close the door?
       I am sorry to have to tell you to please close the door.
    g. Did you forget the door?
       Do us a favor with the door, love.
       How about a bit less breeze?
       Now Johnny, what do big people do when they come in?
       Okay, Johnny, what am I going to say next?

In the right situation, each of these sentences (and infinitely many more) could be used to convey a request to close the door. (A good exercise for the reader here is to imagine contexts in which each of these sentences could be used to request that someone close the door. In other words, you are imagining the conditions under which each of these sentences could be used to make a felicitous request. Also, it would be useful to try to imagine contexts in which the various sentences might be infelicitous as well.)

One thing that becomes clear immediately upon considering examples such as (14) is that it would be very difficult to try and associate illocutionary force with a specific type of grammatical form, or even a specific word. That is, it would be difficult to try and make illocutionary force a conventional part of the meaning of a sentence. For example, following the chart in (11), we might say that the many examples in (14) are types of directive. However, there is little consistency in form across these examples. There are a wide range of statements and questions used to achieve the same basic act. As a result of these kinds of observations, many researchers have assumed that illocutionary force is likely not part of the grammar of a sentence but that is something that speakers must get their hearers to recognize by the fact that they chose to utter a given sentence in a given context. This is very much like the process we described above in Chapter 8 with respect to speaker intentions and conversational implicatures, and which we will return to below in the discussion on felicity conditions in section 10.3.3.

In addition to conversational context, we generally offer our addressees many kinds of guidance in how they are to interpret our utterances. For example, (14g) literally is a question about whether the addressee has forgotten a given door. In context, though, the speaker might point to the open door, or nod to the open door, or use some other paralinguistic means of drawing the addressee's attention to the open door.

We also frequently employ what have been called illocutionary force indicating devices (IFID) to help guide interpretation of our speech acts. For example, we might use the adverb *please* to mark a request, or performative verbs such as *promise, request, command*, etc. Searle also mentions other IFIDs such as word order, mood of the verb, and intonation. Can you think of other ways speakers might indicate what the illocutionary force of their statement is meant to be?

In the next section we move from how we guide interpretation of speech acts to the kinds of conditions that must be in place for speech acts to occur. We refer to these conditions as "felicity conditions".

10.3.2 Felicity conditions

We mentioned felicity conditions above in section 10.2 in the discussion of performative and constative sentences. We also discussed them above in Chapter 9 Presuppositions. We want to return to them now to illustrate in more detail the importance of felicity conditions to speech acts.

Much discussion has been given over the years to felicity conditions of performative sentences. Austin (1962: 14-15) proposed a list of felicity conditions that he argued must be satisfied for a performative to occur successfully. Austin's set of conditions was later elaborated upon by Searle (1969), which resulted in a more concise and direct representation of Austin's ideas, and which Searle argued should hold for all felicitous speech acts. We reproduce Searle's conditions here as well as illustrating along the way how they pertain to different kinds of performative acts—i.e. promising, requesting, threatening. In what follows, *S* stands for "speaker", and *T* stands for an uttered sentence, *H* stands for "hearer", *p* stands for "promise", and *A* stands for "act". According to Searle, then, the speech act of promising is successfully performed if "a speaker *S* utters a sentence *T* in the presence of a hearer *H*, then, in the literal utterance of *T*, *S* sincerely and non-defectively promises that *p* to *H* if and only if the following conditions 1-9 obtain" (1969: 57-61).

1. *Normal input and output conditions obtain.*

This pertains to the basic conditions of a speech situation; it requires that both participants speak the same language, do so clearly, with no impediments, etc. Essentially, both participants need to be able to understand one another clearly. Further, Searle excludes here what he terms "parasitic communication", like telling jokes or play-acting.

2. *S expresses the proposition that p in the utterance of T.*

The idea here is that in uttering a performative sentence, we must be able to isolate the primary content of it from the rest of the utterance. We must be able to understand what the speech act is primarily about.

3. *In expressing that p, S predicates a future act A of S.*

This condition is concerned further with the propositional content mentioned in *2*. Essentially, if a speaker makes a promise, then that promise must be a future act. It is impossible to make a promise about the past. Further, the future act must be of the speaker: i.e. a promise that the speaker will perform some act. The closely related speech act of requesting is also made with respect to a future act; however, with this speech act, the future act belongs to the hearer. So, when a request is made, it is made of the hearer. When a promise is made, it is made with respect to the speaker.

4. *H would prefer S's doing A to his not doing A, and S believes H would prefer his doing A to his not doing A.*

This condition basically says that the hearer would like for the speaker to do the action described in the promise and that the speaker is aware of this. Here, Searle makes an interesting comparison between promises and threats. The former is something that the hearer desires; while the latter, is something that the hearer does not desire. That is, if you "promise" to do something to someone that they do not want done to them, then you have likely issued a threat to them rather than a promise.

5. *It is not obvious to both S and H that S will do A in the normal course of events.*

As Searle writes, the act must have a point to it. That is, it makes no sense to promise to do something for someone that you were already planning to do anyway, and that your hearer knew you were already planning to do. Similarly, we do not normally request that people do things that they are already in the middle of doing, or are already planning to do, or that we do not believe they are capable of doing. This would be a flawed kind of request.

6. *S intends to do A.*

Searle refers to this point as "the sincerity condition", and it basically requires that the speaker of a promise is sincere in her promise, that she intends to carry out her promise.

7. *S intends that the utterance of T will place him under obligation to do A.*

This is Searle's " essential condition", and it basically requires the speaker have the intention to actually do what she has promised to do. Thus, when one promises something of herself, she puts herself under the obligation of the person she makes a promise to, and it is necessary for the recipient of that promise to recognize this. Similarly, with a request, the speaker must make clear to the hearer that the speaker wants something from the hearer. If this essential condition fails, then the speech act is unsuccessful.

8. *S intends to produce in H the knowledge (K) that the utterance of T is to count as placing S under an obligation to do A. S intends to produce K by means of the recognition of his intention, and he intends his intention to be recognized in virtue of (by means of) H's knowledge of the meaning of T.*

This condition reads in a very complicated way, and this is necessary to include all of the facets of meaning that Searle is concerned with; however, we can simplify it immensely for our purposes. Essentially, this condition is about recognition. The speaker creates her desired effect by causing the hearer to recognize the speaker's intention to create that effect. This sounds circular and convoluted, to be sure, but it makes very good sense. Here is a useful analogy: consider an event where people are expected to dress nice: where men are required to wear suits, etc. Now, consider a person who tries very hard to dress nicely, and puts on a suit, but who does not look good in the suit. Perhaps the colors do not match, or it does not fit properly, etc. This person will still count as being "dressed nicely" because others at the event will recognizes his intention to dress nicely. The fact that he might not look good in the suit doesn't change the fact that he has attempted to dress nicely and that others have recognized that intention. It is similar with a speech such as promising. If a speaker can make the hearer recognize that she is trying to convey a promise, then the speaker will have succeeded in conveying that promise, if the other conditions described above also hold.

9. *The semantical rules of the dialect spoken by S and H are such that T is correctly and sincerely uttered if and only if conditions 1-8 obtain.*

This condition basically holds that S and H speak the same language, and that the rules of that language are what cause the meaning of the promise to be available from the sentence in question. This condition, then, is closely related to conditions *1* and *8* above. Searle mentions specifically that this condition—in conjunction with condition *8*—allows us to rule out potential counterexamples to the conditions such as (15), which is quoted from Searle (1969: 44).

(15) Suppose that I am an American solider in the Second World War and that I am captured by Italian troops. And suppose also that I wish to get these troops to believe that I am a German soldier in order to get them to release me. What I would like to

do is to tell them in German or Italian that I am a German soldier. But let us suppose I don't know enough German to see through my plan. Let us suppose I know only one line of German which I remember from a poem I had to memorize in a high school German course. Therefore, I, a captured American, address my Italian captors with the following sentence: *Kennst du das Land wo die Zitronen blüben*? [Knowest thou the land where the lemon trees bloom?] [...] I intend that they should think that what I am trying to tell them is that I am a German soldier. But does it follow from this account that when I say *Kennst du das Land... etc.*, what I mean is, "I am a German soldier"? I find myself disinclined to say that when I utter the German sentence what I mean is "I am a German soldier".

Thus, by speaking a random sentence of German to the Italian captors (who presumably don't understand German) the American captive hopes to convince them that he is a German soldier; however, this doesn't mean that the American has actually said that he is German, and it doesn't mean that *Kennst du das Land...* means anything like "I am a German soldier". The idea here is that it is not enough for a speaker to cause a hearer to comprehend her intentions, as in condition *8*. The language itself, and the semantic meaning of the language, plays an important role as well.

According to Searle, then, these conditions, or something like them, need to hold for the speech act of *promising* to be felicitous (or as Austin would say, for the speech act to be "happy"). However, Searle goes on to say that these rules are generalizable across all speech acts. So, modulo certain act-specific changes, these conditions should hold for all speech acts, especially conditions *1*, *8*, and *9*. For example, even though a promise requires something of the speaker and a request requires something of the hearer, both acts will still have the propositional content condition, preparatory conditions, sincerity conditions, and essential conditions listed above.

Now, an interesting thing about indirect speech acts is that they can often be accomplished by the speaker's merely pointing out a felicity condition for performing the act in the first place. Consider, for example, a situation where you notice that your friend's shoe is untied. You are worried that she will trip over her shoelace, so you want to tell her that she should tie her shoe. But, you don't want to tell her directly because that could be considered rude, awkward, etc., as in (16).

(16) Will you tie your shoe, please?

It could be awkward to phrase a request this way to someone who is your social peer, such as a friend, or even worse, to someone who is somehow in a position of greater power than you, or with whom you have a formal relationship. In doing so, you seem to suggest that you are in a position to make this kind of direct request of the addressee. Even though it is phrased as a question or request, it still has the effect of implying that you are somehow in a position of power. (Compare how it would feel to ask (16) of your friend as opposed to asking it of a young child who was in your care.) So, we are very often indirect in our speech. As Tannen (1982: 218) writes:

Indirectness is a necessary means for serving the needs for *rapport* and *defensiveness* [...]. *Rapport* is the lovely satisfaction of being understood without explaining oneself, of getting what one wants without asking for it. *Defensiveness* is the need to be able to save face by reneging in case one's conversational contribution is not received well—the ability to say, perhaps sincerely, 'I never said that', or 'That isn't what I meant'.

Thus, in many situations, we would like to convey the content of (16) in an indirect way. One way that we can do this is by pointing out, or making apparent, a felicity condition for making the request in the first place. The obvious way of doing this for (16) would be to point out that the addressee's shoe is untied, as in (17).

(17) Hey man, your shoe's untied.

Taken literally, (17) expresses only the observation that the addressee's shoe is untied. There is no request here for the addressee to tie his shoe. However, one condition that must be in place in order to make a request such as (16) felicitous in the first place would be that the addressee's shoe must in fact be untied. So, by pointing out this condition to the addressee, we can convey our request that he tie his shoe, but we have done so indirectly, and this is a very normal way of conveying requests in our society. And in accord with the Tannen quote above, the speaker of (17) could most likely qualify her statement if the addressee were to object: perhaps as in (18)

(18) I'm not TELLing you to tie your shoe! I'm just sayin'...

However, notice that it would be much more difficult for person A in (19), who makes a more direct request for person B to tie her shoes, to qualify what she has said in the same way. Consider the infelicity of A's rejoinder. Even though (19a) is grammatically phrased as a question, it can easily feel like it is an order to person B to tie her shoe. As a result, it is more difficult for person A to qualify her statement in the way that she did in (18).

(19) A: Will you tie your shoe, please?
     B: Excuse me?
     A: #I'm not TELLING you to tie your shoe! I'm just sayin'...

Thus, a speaker can perform an indirect speech act just by demonstrating that one of the conditions for making the speech act in the first place is already satisfied, as in (17). This way, the speaker is not on record as making a direct request, or seeming as if she is giving an order, and this can be a good thing for the speaker who hopes to accomplish something in speaking.

In (17), for instance, the speaker merely wants the addressee to tie his shoe so he doesn't trip, etc. So, it can be in the speaker's interest to do this indirectly and not be seen as issuing an order. Depending on the speaker-addressee relationship, it can be easy for addressees to interpret an order as a kind of insult or slight, as it suggests that the speaker views her relationship with the addressee as such that she is in a position to hand down orders to the addressee. In other words, it might seem as if the speaker views the addressee as being a kind of subordinate, someone who can be given orders or direct requests. This can be insulting to the addressee if she does not agree that the relationship is indeed that way. This can have the further damaging effect for the speaker that she doesn't accomplish her goal in making the order in the first place. Imagine if someone told you *Close the door!* and you didn't view that speaker as being in the position to give orders to you. Most likely, you wouldn't close the door at all but would respond in some way that let the speaker know she was out of order in issuing the command that way. On the other hand, if the request is more indirect, as in (14), it is more likely that the speaker will achieve her goal without causing offense.

Similarly, as we saw in (18), the speaker can go on to qualify her indirect speech act if need be. This is less possible in the direct request, and this is undoubtedly one of the reasons why speakers tend to make indirect requests more frequently than directly. (A good exercise for the reader here is to listen closely to the way people around you make requests. Do they do so indirectly, like in (17), or in a more direct manner? And if the latter, what is the nature of the speaker-addressee relationship?)

10.3.3 Indirect acts and conversational implicatures

As we mentioned in the previous section, there is a close relation between Grice's conversational implicature (which we studied in Chapter 8) and indirect speech acts. Namely, we can rely on a Gricean account of inferential meaning to get from the locutionary meaning of a speech act to the kinds of indirect meanings we saw above in the previous section. For example, the locutionary meaning of (17) does not entail a request by the speaker for the hearer to tie her shoe. Yet, the hearer easily understands this request as part of what the speaker intends to convey. Since the request is not part of the semantic meaning of what the speaker has said in (17), it must be inferred by the hearer. We can talk about this inferential process in much the same way we discussed it in Chapter 8 with respect to conversational implicatures. This is actually a move (with some minor changes) that Searle (1969: Ch. 2) makes in his elaboration upon Austin's original program. Recall, John Searle was one of Austin's students, and he was most responsible for developing Austin's ideas on speech acts after Austin's untimely death. Searle's use and adaptation of Grice's ideas in this area does not answer all of the questions with respect to the gap between locutionary meaning and what the speaker intends to convey in indirect speech acts, but it does do considerable work. In what follows, we will not go into the details of Searle's adaptation of Grice, but will instead provide a general account of how the Cooperative Principle as discussed in Chapter 8 can inform our understanding of indirect speech acts.

As a reminder, we provide Grice's Cooperative Principle here for you.

The Cooperative Principle
Make your conversational contribution such as is required, at the stage at which it occurs, by the accepted purpose or direction of the talk exchange at which it occurs, by the accepted purpose or direction of the talk exchange in which you are engaged. (Grice 1989: 26)

The idea is that speakers of a language assume that something like the Cooperative Principle is in place. That is, they can assume that those involved in a speech situation are being cooperative in the way the principle describes and they can thus infer meaning based on what is said, the situation and context, what they believe the speaker's intention to be, and so forth.

Let's consider briefly an indirect speech act of the kind we discussed above in section 10.3.2, where the speech act involves the speaker acknowledging one of the necessary felicity conditions for performing the act in the first place. Consider (20).

(20) [Context: John and Mary walking through a crowded bar, looking for a place to sit.]
 John: There's an empty table.
 Implicature: *We should sit at the table in question.*

In this context, John and Mary are looking for a place to sit down in the bar. John makes a simple statement about the existence of an empty table. Nowhere does he say that they should actually sit at the empty table; yet, this is what Mary most likely infers. Mary is able to do this by assuming that John is being cooperative, and that he is saying something informative and relevant. (It isn't necessary to rehearse Mary's entire calculation process here; for examples of this process, see Chapter 8.2.4.)

Consider, then, what happens in (20). In stating that there is an open table, John directly acknowledges one of the conditions that must be met in order for them to sit at the table: i.e. that it is not occupied. In stating the felicity condition in this way, John does not TELL Mary that they should sit at the table, but he in effect leads her to draw that conclusion on her own by anchoring his indirect statement to one of the principal conditions for their sitting at the table. This manner of anchoring ensures that his statement is directly relevant to their task at hand. Thus, John has performed an indirect speech act, and thereby conveyed a conversational implicature. The implicature is not equivalent to the indirect speech act, but it is conveyed as a result of the act.

We have been looking in detail thus far at the mechanisms of indirect speech acts, and have claimed that indirect speech acts are very frequent in normal speech. In the next section, we will go on a brief tangent from the discussion of speech acts, *per se*, in order to discuss politeness theory, which allows us to be more specific about what it means to be "indirect" as well as about our motivations for being so in the first place.

10.3.4 More on indirectness: politeness theory

In the previous section we discussed the tendency to use indirect speech acts as opposed to direct ones. This idea can be clarified somewhat in terms of a theory of social and linguistic interaction called politeness theory. With the term "politeness", we are not referring to the everyday sense of using proper manners, minding your p's and q's, and so forth; rather, we are referring to a linguistic theory that has as its basis the idea of "saving face", or saving "self-esteem". The classic work on politeness theory is Brown and Levinson (1987). In this work, Brown and Levinson introduce their understanding of face, which they adapt from work by the sociologist Erving Goffman. The idea is that speakers' concern for face—both their own and those of their interlocutors—has serious consequences for how utterances are constructed, and this then plays an important role in our tendency toward speaking indirectly.

According to Brown and Levinson (1987: 66):

[face] is something that is emotionally invested, and that can be lost, maintained, or enhanced, and must be constantly attended to in interaction. In general, people cooperate (and assume each other's cooperation) in maintaining face in interaction, such cooperation being based on the mutual vulnerability of face.

Thus, part of what occurs in cooperative communication is that interlocutors work together to maintain face, by, among other things, speaking indirectly, not making direct requests, etc.

This basic notion is behind much of what we do in terms of conversational implicature and indirect speech acts.

Now, Brown and Levinson assume that there are two halves of each person's face. These they refer to as positive face and negative face. *Positive* face is generally considered to be a person's desire to be thought well of, to be considered a peer, or to have solidarity with others. On the other hand, *negative* face is a person's desire to be left alone, or to be autonomous. So when formulating an utterance, speakers can appeal to their interlocutor's positive or negative face, and so protect or maintain the face of their interlocutor. Speakers who are uncooperative can also attack the positive or negative face of their interlocutor. Let's look at examples of these now, starting with an appeal to positive face in (21). In (21), the speaker addresses the hearer as *my friend*, which suggests she views the addressee as a peer or equal. Similarly, the colloquial tone of the second clause: *can you break a $1* as opposed to something like *do you have change for a $1* also suggests familiarity or a kind of social equivalence with the speaker.

(21) Hello, my friend! Can you break a $1?

On the other hand, a speaker can also attack the positive face of her addressee, by formulating her utterance in such a way that suggests she and the addressee are not peers. Consider (22). Most obviously, the term of address here is condescending, or at least suggests an imbalance in the social relationship. Further, there is the use of the direct request to fetch change, which suggests that the speaker believes the addressee is somehow subordinate to her.

(22) Hello boy. Please fetch me change for this $1.

Thus, (22) can be seen as an attack on the positive face of the addressee. Let's turn now to appeals and attacks on negative face. Recall, a person's negative face is the desire to be left alone, or to be autonomous. We can appeal to a person's negative face, then, by appearing to minimize the impact of our statement or request upon the person. Consider (23), in which a student at the university library asks a person at the next table to watch her books, laptop, etc., while she goes to the restroom. It is unlikely that the trip to the restroom will last only a second, and the addressee knows this. At the same time, the speaker has appealed to the negative face of the addressee by appearing to minimize her request of the addressee: after all, she is only asking for a second of the addressee's time.

(23) Would you mind watching my things for a second while I run to the bathroom?

Imagine now that the speaker phrased her request as in (24). The 15-minute time estimate in this sentence is probably more realistic than the second that the speaker asks for in (23), and the addressee undoubtedly knows this is the case. Still, the more realistic request seems more invasive, and it seems to place a larger burden upon the addressee's negative face.

(24) Would you mind watching my things for 15 minutes while I go to the bathroom?

We can magnify the feeling of this pressure on the negative face by making the request seem even more burdensome, as in (25).

(25) Will you watch my computer, books, backpack, and writing supplies for 15 minutes while I go to the bathroom to wash my face and use my phone to call my friend?

In reality, in terms of watching the speaker's things, (25) places no more of an actual burden on the addressee than does (23). However, you can imagine that the addressee of (25) is much more likely to feel burdened by the request than the speaker of (23). This is because (25) more directly threatens the negative face of the addressee.

From this point it is straightforward to see the connection to indirectness, especially as it relates to minimizing the burden a speaker places on the negative face of her addressee. That is, if a request, say, can be downgraded such that it is conveyed indirectly, it would seem to be much less of a burden on the negative face of the addressee. Consider (26), in which a student is in line with her friend at the coffee shop. In this example, the student has just realized that she does not have her wallet and so cannot pay for her coffee. She could either ask her friend directly to loan some money to her; or, she could perform the act indirectly, as in (26).

(26) Oh no. I forgot my wallet!

Chances are here that the friend will offer to pick up the tab for her friend's coffee. The speaker of (26) has not made a direct request for her friend to cover the cost of the coffee, but she has drawn attention to one of the felicity conditions of doing so—namely, that she has forgotten her wallet and so has no money. This example, then, is similar to those we discussed above in section 10.3.2. The idea with respect to politeness here is that the indirect means of requesting puts less of a burden on the negative face of the addressee. As a result, the speaker hopes, she will be able to achieve her desired result more effectively.

There is much more to Brown and Levinson's theory of politeness, and it has been extended into many areas. However, what we have covered thus far suffices for our purposes here with respect to speech act theory and indirectness. In the next section, we will turn to a related area, which considers the effects of imbalances of power on the interpretation of certain kinds of speech acts.

10.4 Requests And Power Dynamics

As we have seen in previous sections, the nature of the speaker-addressee relationship can have a serious effect on how speech acts are interpreted. There are many dimensions to personal relationships, and each can play a role in how speech acts are formulated and interpreted. In this section, though, we want to look particularly at the way that the power inherent in the position of a law enforcement officer affects interpretation in dealings with the general public. The examples below are taken from an excellent book by Lawrence Solan and Peter Tiersma, entitled *Speaking of Crime: The Language of Criminal Justice*. Solan and Tiersma are both linguists and lawyers, and they write about many aspects of language having to do with the courts and criminal justice. These particular examples come from a chapter entitled "Consensual Searches", and they have to do with the manner in which police officers obtain consent to search property, vehicles, etc.

10.4.1 Legal background

The US Bill of Rights prohibits against unreasonable searches by law enforcement officers. As Solan and Tiersma (2005: 36) write:

> The Fourth Amendment's prohibition against "unreasonable searches and seizures" generally requires the police to obtain a warrant issued on a showing of probable cause unless there are extraordinary circumstances, such as evidence that a crime is in progress. Although the Supreme Court has recognized an "automobile exception" to the warrant requirement, probable cause that a crime has been committed is also required to trigger the exception. Neither the lack of a driver's license nor a hunch or vague suspicion is enough to overcome the probable cause requirement.

In other words, police are not authorized to search a vehicle or property unless they witness a crime in progress (i.e. they have probable cause) or unless they are given consent to search the property by a person with authority to give that consent, such as the owner or driver of a car that has been pulled over. So, it is common for police officers to request to search a property when they do not have a warrant to do so. If consent is granted, then the police officers can conduct a legal search. The question for Solan and Tiersma, and for us in this chapter, is to what extent the imbalance of power in the relevant relationships (i.e. between police officer and a member of the general public) affect interpretation of the request to search. In other words, how does power affect the interpretation of a speech act? Let's look at a couple of examples.

10.4.2 Interpreting requests as commands

The first example comes from a 2002 decision by the US Supreme Court, entitled *United States v. Drayton* (1966), and is described in Solan and Tiersma. The defendants in this case had been sitting on a bus, when the bus was boarded by police officers. The officers asked the first defendant if he had any luggage, and then asked if they could check the luggage, as in (27a). The defendant then allowed the police officer to check the luggage. The police officer then asked (27b), to search the physical person of the defendant.

(27) a. Do you mind if I check it? [the luggage]
      b. Do you mind if I check your person?

The defendant then agreed that the police officer could search his person. There, the officer found drugs strapped to the defendant's body. The defendants were then arrested, and the court found that even though the officer had had no warrant, the defendants had given their consent to be searched.

One question that Solan and Tiersma ask of this case is why, given the fact that the defendants knew that they were carrying illegal goods, did they allow themselves to be searched? Their answer to this question is because the defendant didn't know he could refuse the search. He didn't have knowledge of the law. As a result of this lack of knowledge, there was a substantial imbalance of power between the officer and the defendant. Thus, when the officer "requested" consent to search the defendant, the defendant interpreted that request as a command, and so complied with it.

Consider a more mundane imbalance of power from a non-legal context: for instance, that of a parent and child. When a father requests that his son take out the trash, this is generally interpreted as a direct order, not as a request that can be refused. Consider a scenario like in (28).

(28) Father: Do you mind taking out the trash?
      Son: Yes, I do mind. I'd rather not take out the trash.
      Father: Oh, okay. Just thought I'd ask.

Even though the father's request is phrased indirectly, we understand that it is most likely meant as a direct order. This is directly related to the fact that the parent is in a position of power over the child.

Another example illustrating the effect of power on interpretation, which originates with John Searle, and which is quoted by Solan and Tiersma, is a request made by a military general to a private, as in (29).

(29) If the general asks the private to clean up the room, that is in all likelihood a command or order. If the private asks the general to clean up the room, that is likely to be a suggestion or proposal or request, but not an order or command.

In this example, then, we are to imagine a general making a request of a private to clean up a room; and, the private, who holds a very low military rank, naturally interprets that request as a command. This is due in part to the wide imbalance in power in that particular of the relationship. Now, this imbalance of power is completely dependent on the situation; we can imagine other contexts where the private might have more power than the general. Suppose, for example, the private has caught the general doing something illegal, and is blackmailing the general. In this situation, along this dimension, perhaps the private would be in a position of greater power than the general, in which case requests like the one in (29) might be interpreted as a command by the general.

Returning to the defendants described above in (27), the problem there was that they did not understand the law, and so were in a position of lesser power than the police officer. As Solan and Tiersma make clear, this apparent imbalance in power is made especially salient by the appearance of the officer, by the fact that he is asking to search and so on. Consider further, for example, if a police officer has pulled a car over for a traffic infraction. The officer is already exercising a kind of power, and to a person not well-versed in the law it might appear that that power extends to areas like property searches. Conversely, however, we can imagine a scenario where the same officer makes a request like (27) to a judge or a lawyer who is well-versed in that aspect of Fourth Amendment law. In this case, the imbalance in power between the two would be much less, and it seems less likely that the judge or lawyer would consent to the police officer's request. The judge, knowing full well the extent of the law, would probably not interpret the police officer's request as a command, but rather as a request that could be refused.

Let's turn away from power and speech act interpretation now, and look at another area of communication in which speech act theory is highly informative. In the next section we will consider what it means *to lie*, and how speech act theory can help us understand this a little better.

10.5 The Composition Of A Lie

In everyday usage, we are pretty sure of what it means *to lie*, and we're pretty sure that we can recognize a lie when we hear one: i.e. someone says something that is not true. When we look a little bit closer, though, it becomes less clear what this means, and it becomes less clear that it means the same thing from person to person. Linguists Linda Coleman and Paul Kay take up this question in a 1981 article, entitled "Prototype Semantics: The English Word *Lie*", which is also discussed in Solan and Tiersma (2005).

Coleman and Kay suggest that a prototypical lie contains three elements. In a situation where a speaker (S) asserts some proposition (P) to an addressee (A), a prototypical lie consists of the elements found in (30) [Coleman and Kay (1981: 28)].

(30) a. P is false.
     b. S believes P to be false.
     c. In uttering P, S intends to deceive A.

A prototypical lie, then, has a speaker uttering something that she believes to be false, with the intention of deceiving her addressee. Thus, a lie that is unquestionably a lie should contain these three components. The question is, however, what do we say about a speech act that contains only one or two of the components of (30)? And, what can speech act theory tell us about this? That is the topic of this section.

Consider (31), which is taken from Coleman and Kay, page 31.

(31) John and Mary have recently started going together. Valentino is Mary's ex-boy-friend. One evening John asks Mary, "Have you seen Valentino this week?" Mary answers, "Valentino's been sick with mononucleosis for the past two weeks." Valentino has in fact been sick with mononucleosis for the past two weeks, but it is also the case that Mary had a date with Valentino the night before. Did Mary lie?

The issue here is that Mary has answered John in a way that is literally true; however, she has not responded directly to his question. Mary's statement fulfills two of the prototypical elements of a lie found in (30): namely, (30a) and (30c). But it does not fulfill (30b). Mary knows that Valentino has been sick with mononucleosis, so she clearly does not believe her utterance to have conveyed a false proposition. As a result, it is more complicated here to decide whether or not Mary has "lied" to John in her utterance.

Now, what if Mary had responded to John as in (32)?

(32) John: Have you seen Valentino this week?
     Mary: No.

In this case, we would have no trouble in identifying Mary's statement as a lie. Mary's statement would fulfill all three of the elements of (30), and it would also meet our everyday understanding of what it means to lie. Mary clearly said something false, which she knew was false, and which she said with the intent to deceive.

An interesting problem here is that in both (31) and (32) Mary has convinced (or at least tried to convince) John to believe something false. On the first count, though, she tried to convince John to believe something false by uttering something that was literally true.

In terms of speech act theory, we can discuss this in a very clear way by returning to Austin's three dimensions of a speech act that we discussed above in Section 10.3. These were the locutionary, illocutionary, and perlocutionary dimensions of a speech act. As a reminder, we defined these three dimensions as the following. A *locutionary* act is roughly equivalent to uttering a certain sentence with a certain semantic meaning. An *illocutionary* act can be roughly considered how we intend our statement to be understood: i.e. as a warning, threat, promise, request, etc. Finally, there is the *perlocutionary* act, which is the result of our speech act. It is what we bring about in having uttered our speech act. Recall that we said above that the perlocutionary act was ultimately out of the hands of the speaker. We can try to cause the speaker to act in a certain way as a result of our utterance, but it is ultimately not up to the speaker if this happens or not.

So, we can say that in (31) and (32) Mary achieved (or attempted to achieve) the same perlocutionary effect in her responses to John. In both cases she caused him to believe something false. These differ, though, at the level of the illocutionary intention. In (31) Mary intended to convey something true to John, with the ultimate intention that he believe something false as a result of her statement. In (32), Mary intended to convey something false to John, with the intention that he also believe something false. Speech act theory, then, and especially Austin's three dimensions of a speech act, gives us a clear means of grappling with the difficulty we sometimes experience in situations of truth and truthiness, and in situations where a statement is true but misleading.

10.6 Conclusion

In this chapter we have looked closely at speech act theory and the way that we can perform acts with our words. This way of thinking about language, which grew out of J. L. Austin's work at Oxford in the 1930s, has been incredibly influential in philosophy and linguistics, and as we mentioned in the introduction, it has had an impact in essentially every area of the humanities and social sciences—extending into literary criticism, rhetoric, gender and racial studies, psychology, sociology, anthropology, and many others. This chapter has stayed mostly within the realm of linguistic questions, but it will still be very useful for students who will be taking coursework in these other disciplines. We have thus considered the basic framework of speech act theory, as proposed by Austin and extended by Searle, as well as a couple of real-world applications of speech act theory, such as the law enforcement scenarios mentioned in section 10.4. We also considered the relation between H. Paul Grice's ideas of conversational implicature and indirect speech acts, and the manner in which the two understandings of language use inform each other. Lastly, we considered the theoretical notion of "politeness" and what this can tell us about our tendencies toward indirectness and accomplishing our speech goals with indirect speech acts.

We did not address the question of speech acts in cross-cultural situations, although there are many interesting questions to be considered here and much research has been done in this area. For instance, there is a very large literature comparing apologies and comparing requests across languages. While most languages allow for these kinds of speech acts, it is not the case that they do so in the same way as English. That is, the language and grammar might obviously differ, but what is less obvious at first blush is that the felicity conditions for performing apologies and requests can differ too. This has interesting implications in many areas of life:

from communication in international settings to learning a second language. The latter case is especially interesting for us in this course. So, a student might learn the grammatically correct way of saying an apology in a foreign language, but she might not understand WHEN it is appropriate to do so. Thus, learners of second languages are faced with learning the grammatical systems of the target language, but they also must learn how the target language is USED in different situations. As this book has focused mainly on English, though, to this point, we have left aside the wider question of speech acts in cross-cultural contexts.

10.7 Further Reading

Students who would like to read more about speech act theory would do very well to go to the original source, which is Austin's (1962) book *How to Do Things with Words*. Like his Oxford colleague, H. Paul Grice, Austin's prose is extremely readable for the non-specialist. Also, like Grice's prose style, readers will find Austin's prose charming and witty at the same time as being extremely thought-provoking. Beyond Austin, the next step for the interested reader is to consult the work of Austin's student, John Searle, who is really the person most responsible for formalizing and for bringing speech act theory to the wide audience that it enjoys today. Searle's (1969) book, entitled simply *Speech Acts*, is an excellent place to start. For criticisms of speech act theory readers will find Levinson (1983) very useful. Levinson discusses many problems that have been raised with respect to speech act theory over the years. He also discusses solutions that have been proposed to those problems. Another aspect of Levinson's work that readers might find interesting is his coverage of an attempt from the 1970s to embed illocutionary force into the syntactic structure of sentences. This movement was known as generative semantics, and Levinson discusses it and problems that were raised against it at some length. For a current overview of many of these issues and of Austin's program in general, readers can consult the Stanford Encyclopedia of Philosophy's online entry for speech act theory, which is written by Mitchell Green. Readers interested in what speech act theory can tell us about the law and courts will do well to read Solan and Tiersma's (2005) book. This book is very informative (and readable), and it discusses the application of speech act theory and linguistics in general to legal concerns.

CHAPTER 11
Phonetics

Phonetics is the subfield of linguistics that deals with describing speech sounds, the patterns of these sounds, and the changes sounds undergo in different speech environments. While phoneticians can describe every sound in every language of the world, as well as many of their changes and patterns, our main concern here is simply describing the sounds, patterns, and changes found in the English language. We won't cover every single topic in English phonetics, but by the time you finish this chapter, you will have a good understanding of how speech sounds function.

11.1 How Speech Is Made

Most of us probably have never thought about our ability to speak. How are speech sounds produced? The starting point of speech is the respiratory system. We breathe in, we breathe out; this process alone can account for the production of all English sounds. Air starting in the lungs and moving up the windpipe, or trachea, travels through the larynx. At this point, the air makes contact with our vocal cords. The position of the vocal cords at the time of the air passage is what determines the resulting sounds. If the air travels through open vocal cords, as is the normal position when one breathes out, the air has free passage through the remaining vocal organs, the pharynx and the mouth. If the air travels through constricted vocal cords, or rather vocal cords that have been adjusted by the potential speaker for the purpose of speaking, the air can travel only through a narrow path. The volume of air traveling through the narrow passage causes the vocal cords to vibrate, producing a distinctive type of sound.

breathing + talking

The sound made with vibrating vocal cords is called a voiced sound. In the previously described situation, where the air traveled through relatively relaxed or open vocal cords, it produces a sound called a voiceless sound. Both voiced and voiceless sounds are important parts of our speech. Consider the sounds of the letters *f* and *v* in the words *fan* and *van*. Can you tell which one is voiced and which one is voiceless? Draw out the sound for the letter *f*. We will use the notation [fff] for this long, drawn-out sound. Can you feel your vocal cords moving? Probably not. Do the same with the letter *v*, drawing it out as [vvv]. Clearly, the sound for the letter *v* requires vibrating vocal cords, whereas the sound for *f* does not.

Let's keep in mind that we are talking about *sounds* and not the alphabetic letters themselves. After all, think about the letter *g* in the words *general* and *gnome*. Is the letter *g* pronounced the same way in both instances? Not at all. In fact, in *gnome*, the letter *g* is silent. This means that we must be clear in our descriptions of what we are talking about. We will expound on this idea more when we talk about the International Phonetic Alphabet (IPA) later in the chapter. For now, we will continue our discussion of the vocal organs.

11.2 The Vocal Tract

When we discussed the production of sounds earlier in this chapter, we mentioned several organs that pertain to the making of sound. Of these, several are air passages that are located above the vocal cords and larynx, such as the pharynx, the mouth, and the nose. These organs are generally referred to as the *vocal tract*.

Within the vocal tract are several articulators, or parts that are capable of adjusting to tweak airflow and modify the sound produced. In this chapter, we will talk only about the articulators that are pertinent to the sounds we have in the English language. When we talk about the location of the articulators, we generally think of them as being either on the upper half of the vocal tract—toward or on the roof of the mouth—or on the lower half—closer to where the tongue rests. If you say the word *lovely* slowly, you will feel your tongue move up and down in your mouth, touching the upper articulators on the letter *l* and moving back down for the vowel sounds. While this is a very basic way to test the existence of upper and lower half articuators; it is also important to be able to relate to this distinction as we move through our study of articulation.

Figure 11.1 depicts the articulators that are located on the upper half of the vocal tract: the upper lip, upper front teeth, the alveolar ridge (a small, bony protrusion just behind the upper front teeth), the palate and the velum. The palate and the velum are sometimes referred to as the hard and soft palate, respectively. The articulators located on the bottom half of the vocal tract are the tongue, which is typically divided into the tip, blade, and body; the lower front teeth, and the bottom lip. The tongue is clearly the most mobile of the articulators. As you will soon see, it plays a crucial role in the formation of many English words.

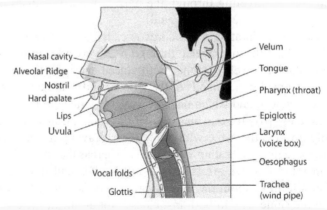

FIGURE 11.1 A diagram of articulators

11.3 Articulation Of Consonants

Articulation is the process of using the articulators to manipulate speech sounds by way of obstructing or constricting the airflow during speech. Articulation is a two-fold process in the formation of English consonants (we will get to vowels later in our discussion). Both the place and manner of articulation are important concepts for consonants, along with the notion of the sound being voiced or voiceless, which we discussed in the previous section.

Before going into a detailed discussion of the place of articulation, make sure you are very familiar with the diagram in Figure 11.1. This diagram will help you understand the locations of various articulators, which in turn will help you understand the place of articulation more accurately.

11.3.1 Place of articulation

We have discussed several articulators briefly in our discussion so far. Each major articulator has a corresponding place of articulation. The names for the places of articulation are strikingly similar to the articulators they correspond to, thus easing understanding of the process. We will discuss in detail each place of articulation; refer to the diagram in Figure 11.1 at any time because understanding this diagram will help you greatly.

11.3.1.1 Place of articulation: bilabial

Can you guess where bilabial sounds are made? If you take the word *bilabial* and break it down, it provides a clue. *Bi* means "two," and if you have taken Spanish or Latin, you know that lips is either *labios* or *labiae*, respectively; so the *labi* of *bilabial* is likely to mean "lips." Finally, the *-al* suffix generally changes a noun to an adjective. In this case, this polymorphemic word, *bilabial*, describes the place where the sound is made—the space between the lips. When both lips are pressed together, sounds like [b], [p], and [m] can be made. Say each of these sounds. Your lips should come together when you say them. In fact, [p] and [b] are the same sound, essentially, as far as having the same place and manner of articulation. The only difference is voicing: The [b] is voiced and the [p] is voiceless. The sound [m] is a little different because of its manner of articulation, but that is a topic we will save for later in the chapter because our main concern at the moment is the place of articulation. For now, all you need to know is that [b], [p], and [m] are the three English sounds made in the bilabial position.

To be consistent in our description of sounds, we denote the various sounds by showing a letter between brackets, like these [ ]. Recall that there is not always a correlation between the spelling of a word and the sounds it contains, and that a single letter in different environments may represent different sounds. Therefore, we will use the International Phonetic Alphabet (IPA) to describe sounds. For a chart containing all the consonant sounds in IPA, as well as examples of the corresponding sounds, see Figure 11.A2 in section 11.8. You will need to consult both charts in section 11.8 frequently throughout this chapter to make sure the sound we show within brackets is the same as the sound you have in mind. We will explain the IPA symbols as we continue through this chapter, so the chart will be of use as you read the chapter. For place of articulation, we are discussing the columns of the chart. Disregard the rows until we begin the discussion of manner of articulation. At the end of this chapter, you will see how place and manner of articulation work together with voicing to describe the sounds of the English consonants.

11.3.1.2 Place of articulation: labiodental

This place of articulation is even easier to guess. You already know *labi(o)* from the previous description if you didn't know it already. Surely you already know *dental*, so the result is a place of articulation that involves teeth and a lip. In this case, it would be the top front teeth and the bottom lip that comprise this place of articulation. Air flowing through the vocal tract and exiting through this place of articulation has a distinctive sound. Position your teeth and lip in the labiodental position, as in the sounds for [f] and [v]. Like [p] and [b] from the last section, [f] and [v] share the same place and manner of articulation, and they are the same sound except for voicing. Can you guess which one is voiced and which is voiceless?

11.3.1.3 Place of articulation: interdental

As we continue with our discussion of places of articulation, we progress farther back in the mouth. We began with the outermost place of articulation, the lips, and we continued with the lip and teeth combination that is the labiodental place of articulation. Entirely behind the lips is the interdental position, or the position where the tongue is between (the meaning of *inter*) the upper and lower rows of the front teeth. In this position, air flows in such a way to produce the interdental sounds of English.

Sounds like the voiced and voiceless *th* sound are produced in this position. These sounds are denoted by the [ð] and [θ] symbols, respectively. Like the previous examples, these sounds form a pair that shares the same place and manner of articulation. Remember to look at the examples in Figure 11.A2 to make sure you have the correct sounds in mind when learning these symbols.

11.3.1.4 Place of articulation: alveolar

The alveolar ridge is the bony protrusion just behind your upper front teeth, near the gum line. The alveolar place of articulation accounts for many of our English sounds. When the tip of the tongue makes contact with the alveolar ridge, air is constricted in such a way to produce some of the following sounds (keep in mind that their manners of articulation differ in some cases): [d], [t], [z], [s], [n], [l], and [r]. Pairs of sounds, like [d] and [t], as well as [z] and [s], are sounds that share the same places and manners of articulation, with the only difference being voicing.

11.3.1.5 Place of articulation: alveopalatal

English is a language that doesn't have any true palatal sounds. However, when the tongue makes contact with the place between the alveolar ridge and the hard palate, it constricts the air to form four sounds in English. The [tʃ] and the [dʒ] sounds, along with the [ʃ] and [ʒ], are pairs of sounds produced in the alveopalatal place of articulation. We refer again to voicing to explain the differences between the sounds. [ʃ] and [tʃ] are the voiceless sounds, and [ʒ] and [dʒ] are the voiced sounds, as you may well have guessed.

11.3.1.6 Place of articulation: velar

Recall that the velum, located toward the back of the oral cavity, is often called the soft palate. It is also the part of the vocal tract that moves up and down to block airflow to the nasal cavity, preventing nasal and allowing velar sounds. The body of the tongue makes contact with the velum, obstructing the airflow and producing sounds like [g], [k]; and the *ng* sound, which is denoted by [ŋ].

11.3.1.7 Place of articulation: glottal

The last place of articulation we will discuss in this book is the glottal place of articulation. The glottis is located the farthest back in the oral cavity of all the articulators we have discussed. If you say the sound for the English letter *h*, denoted by [h], you can feel the constriction where the glottal place of articulation resides: near the throat. There are two glottal sounds in the English language. One, which we already discussed, is [h]. The other is [ʔ], which is called simply a glottal stop. This name refers to both the place and manner of articulation of this sound, which is the total constriction of airflow at the glottis. The glottal stop can be found in words such as *button*. Chances are, you don't pronounce the [t] sound in this word, but rather use the [ŋ] instead. Glottal stops can be found in other words as well, such as *cotton* and *sentence*.

11.3.1.8 Summary of places of articulation

So far in this chapter, we have discussed all the places of articulation applicable to the English language. Obviously, there are more articulators in the oral cavity and more places of articulation that apply to other languages, but for the purposes of this book, you only need to be familiar with those mentioned here. Bilabial, labiodental, interdental, alveolar, alveopalatal, velar, and glottal places of articulation are the concepts you need to know before reading the next part of the chapter, which focuses on manners of articulation. If you are unsure about anything thus far, reread section 11.3.1. The concept of place of articulation is a basic building block of both phonetics and phonology, and you need solid knowledge of this concept for the next chapters, too.

11.3.2 Manner of articulation

We will discuss six manners of articulation in this chapter. Manner of articulation deals with the *how* of the pronunciation, as opposed to the *where* (the place of articulation we just discussed). The manners of articulation we cover in this chapter are the ones that apply only to English sounds.

11.3.2.1 Manner of articulation: stop

Stops, which are also called plosives, are very distinctive sounds because the airflow during production of stops is completely obstructed, or stopped, hence the name. English sounds that are stops include [p], [t], [k], [b], [d], [g], and [ʔ]. Keep in mind that all of these sounds pertain to two other categorizations in addition to being stops: voiced/voiceless and place of articulation. For example, [p] is a voiceless bilabial stop, and [g] is a voiced velar stop. From now on, when you describe a sound, you should describe it in a way similar to how we described [p] and [g]: first, voicing. Is it voiced or voiceless? Next, say the place of articulation, and finally, the manner of articulation. Now that you know how to describe sounds correctly and know something of stop sounds, can you tell which sound is a voiced bilabial stop? How about which sound is a voiceless alveolar stop? Before reading the next section, see if you can describe the voicing, place, and manner (which, in this case, is stop for all) of the sounds listed. If you get stuck, make sure to consult the chart in Figure 11.A2.

11.3.2.2 Manner of articulation: nasal

Almost every language in the world features at least one nasal sound. In English, only three sounds have the nasal manner of articulation. The nasal sounds are produced when the oral cavity is blocked at a particular place of articulation, and air flows partially through the nasal cavity instead. For example, the airflow is blocked at the bilabial place of articulation for [m]. You can say the [m] sound with your mouth completely closed, with no air coming out. This is because the air is routed through the nasal cavity instead. Because we can feel the vocal cords vibrating for [m]—put your hand on your throat to feel it if you are unsure—we can now officially be sure of its description: voiced bilabial nasal.

There are two other nasal sounds in English. One is [n] and the other is [ŋ]. Which is a voiced velar nasal? How about the voiced alveolar nasal? If you are unsure, double-check the chart in Figure 11.A2. A better way, though, is to attempt to make the sound based on the description given. To do this, you must simply use the articulators described in the place of articulation and produce a voiced or voiceless sound in the given manner of articulation, depending on the description. You can try this test in the next section (and later sections) if you find it helpful.

11.3.2.3 Manner of articulation: flap

The English language has one flap sound, denoted by [ɾ]. Consider the words *udder* and *butter*. The sound you make on the double consonant in both words is the same sound, the flap. The tongue taps the alveolar ridge, blocking air for just a brief moment, which may explain why flaps are sometimes called *taps*. Some linguists make a distinction between *taps* and *flaps*, but for the purpose of this course, you may use either term. As for our one English flap sound, it is described as a voiced alveolar flap.

11.3.2.4 Manner of articulation: fricative

Fricatives are the biggest group of all the manners of articulation in English. Fricatives are caused by constrictions of airflow that produce noisy sound at the place of articulation. Sounds like [f] and [v] are examples of fricatives; in this case, both sounds represent almost the same sound, with the slight difference of voicing. Both [f] and [v] are labiodental fricatives: [f] is voiceless and [v] is voiced. There are many such pairs of similar fricatives, and they span several places of articulation. For example, [s] and [z] are both alveolar fricatives. Can you tell which is voiced and which is voiceless? Consult the chart in Figure 11.A2 to see a complete list of English fricatives.

11.3.2.5 Manner of articulation: affricate

Affricates comprise an interesting group of sounds because they begin like a stop and end like a fricative. That is, airflow starts in the blocked position of a stop and is then released when the articulators move into the fricative position. This blending of the two manners makes the distinctive affricate manner of articulation possible. The English language has two affricates: [tʃ] and [dʒ]. As you probably remember from our discussion of the alveopalatal place of articulation, [tʃ] and [dʒ] correspond to the sounds made by the *ch* in *chase* and the *j* in *jasmine*. Can you describe both sounds using voicing, place of articulation, and manner of articulation?

11.3.2.6 Manner of articulation: approximant

Approximants are sounds made with very little obstruction of airflow. Sounds like [w], [ɹ], and [j] are all approximants found in English. Check the latter two sounds, [ɹ] and [j], on the list of IPA symbols so that you are sure of which sounds they stand for. To explain briefly, the [ɹ] is the sound at the beginning of the words *really* and *righteous*. The [j] is the sound that starts the following words: *yellow* and *yourself.* Even if these sounds are explained in a general manner here, you should still consult the IPA symbol list for more words containing these sounds. It never hurts to have many examples to create a clear picture.

11.3.2.7 Manner of articulation: lateral (lateral approximant)

The last manner of articulation that we will discuss in this chapter is what is referred to as a lateral manner of articulation (sometimes it is called a lateral approximant because of its close ties to the approximant category). There is only one sound in English that belongs to the lateral category: [l]. In this manner of articulation, the sides of the tongue, not the body, cause a slight obstruction of airflow, producing the lateral sound. The airflow is also slightly obstructed at the alveolar ridge, making [l] a voiced alveolar lateral.

11.3.2.8 Summary of manners of articulation

Manner of articulation answers the question of *how* the sound is produced. Previously in the chapter, we addressed voicing and the *where* of sound production, which is known as the place of articulation. In the section on manner of articulation, we combined these three concepts to give a three-part description of sounds, referring first to voicing, then place, and then manner of articulation. For example, we said that [g] was a voiced velar stop. We went through the stop, nasal, flap, fricative, affricate, approximant, and lateral manners of articulation, we discussed how each of these types of sounds are found in English.

We have now finished our discussion on the manners of articulation found in the consonants of English. Naturally, many other manners of articulation exist in other languages, but for the purposes of this introductory course, we keep our conversation to the concepts that focus on English. If you find that you like the study of articulatory phonetics and wish to learn more about the sounds found in other languages, refer to section 11.7 for some books on that topic.

11.4 Articulation Of Vowels

In our discussion of consonants, we focused on three characteristics to define each sound: voicing, place of articulation, and manner of articulation. Vowels are defined with different characteristics, however. Vowels, unlike consonants, are not sounds produced by the constriction or obstruction of airflow. Instead, they are produced with an open vocal tract, and they are manipulated by the height of the tongue (high, mid, or low), and the backness of the tongue at the time of pronunciation (front, central, or back). Another feature linguists use to describe the vowel sounds is called rounding, which refers to the rounding of the lips during sound production. Our study of vowels in this book will not extend to rounding, but it is important to recognize that it is one of the distinctions used to categorize vowels. In fact, a few other characteristics can be used to further define vowels, but again, in this introductory textbook, we will try to hit the major points only so that we have time for broad coverage of topics.

11.4.1 Vowels and dipthongs

Before we continue, we should make the distinction between simple vowels and complex vowels (dipthongs) because both will be discussed in the following chapters. The simple vowels of English include all of the following: [i], [ɪ], [e], [ɛ], [æ], [u], [ʊ], [o], [ɔ], [ɑ], [ʌ], [ɝ], and [ə]. Each of these sounds is a simple vowel of the English language. Dipthongs, however, are the blending of two vowel sounds. They are described including both vowel sounds in brackets. The English dipthongs are [aɪ], [aʊ], [ɔɪ], [oʊ], and [eɪ]. A list with sample words for each of the sounds in English is provided in Figure 11A.1 in section 11.8. To get a real feel for the sounds and the symbols of the International Phonetic Alphabet (IPA), consult this list several times. While we will provide information about the height and backness of the simple vowels, we will not go into these details about dipthongs for the sake of simplicity.

11.4.2 Vowel height

Vowel height is a key component in describing vowels. Vowel height refers to the relative height of the tongue in the oral cavity when a particular vowel is produced. For example, if you say the words *hot* and *heat*, you will notice that your tongue is substantially higher in your mouth when you say the vowel sound in *heat* as opposed to *hot*. We can say that *heat* contains a higher vowel than *hot*.

Three major tongue positions are related to tongue height: low, mid (or middle), and high. Some linguists use *open*, *mid*, and *closed* instead to refer to how much of the airflow is restricted. While you should know these terms if you plan to continue your study of linguistics, we will use *low*, *mid*, and *high* for this book. As you may have guessed, linguists tend to be very detailed in their descriptions, and they use several more categories to describe vowel height. For our purposes, however, we will cover the main three. We will begin our discussion with low vowels and work our way higher in the oral cavity throughout our discussion.

11.4.2.1 Low vowels

The lower vowels of the English language are [ɑ] and [æ]. If you don't know which sounds these symbols stand for, refer to the list in Figure 11A.1. This list will give you some sample words containing the sound that the symbols describe. The sounds [ɑ] and [æ] are all pronounced with the tongue rather low in the oral cavity (mouth). Remember the *hot* and *heat* test from the vowel height section? These sounds are pronounced with the tongue in the same low position as in *hot*.

11.4.2.2 Mid vowels

Somewhere between the tongue positions of *hot* and *heat* lies the mid position, where the tongue is roughly halfway between the low and high vowel positions. English mid vowels include [e], [ɛ], [o], [ɔ], [ʌ], [ə], and [ɝ]. The last vowel mentioned, [ɝ], is called a rhotic vowel, or sometimes, an "r-colored vowel." Rhotic vowels are mid-height, central vowels that are immediately followed by an [r] sound. You will find this sound in the middle of the IPA vowel chart in Figure 11A.1.

11.4.2.3 High vowels

High vowels are analogous to the tongue height of *heat*. The tongue is in its highest position in the oral cavity, while not directly touching the roof of the mouth and obstructing airflow. High English vowels include [i], [ɪ], [u], and [ʊ].

11.4.3 Vowel backness

The backness of a vowel is simply how far back in the mouth the tongue is moving up to pronounce the vowel sound. For example, if you take the words *beat* and *boot*, you will notice that they both have high vowels. The difference between these two sounds lies in the backness. *Beat* is a front vowel, whereas *boot* is certainly a back vowel. If you say both words in succession, you will note how your tongue moves up in the front for one, and in back for the other.

Front, central, and back are the main backness categories that we will discuss in this book. While linguists use more distinctions to be more specific, for this introductory text, we will focus on these three only. Let us begin with front vowels.

11.4.3.1 Front vowels

If you consult the IPA vowel chart in Figure 11A.1, you will see that several vowels fall into the category of front vowels: [i], [ɪ], [e], [ɛ], and [æ] are the English front vowels. If you say a word with each of the aforementioned front vowel sounds, you will notice that your tongue moves up and down in the front part of the oral cavity to make these sounds.

11.4.3.2 Central vowels

The sounds [ɝ] and [ə] are the central vowels of English. This means that the tongue rises between the front and back positions to form these two vowel sounds. You use many words with central vowels in them throughout the course of your day. Can you think of any now? If so, say them and note the position of your tongue. That position is the central position, and should exist in your mouth somewhere between the positions of the vowels in *beat* and *boot*.

11.4.3.3 Back vowels

The sounds [u], [ʊ], [o], [ɔ], [ʌ], and [ɑ] are all back vowels, meaning the tongue rises relatively far back in the oral cavity to produce these sounds. The word *boot* is representative of back vowels.

11.4.3.4 Describing vowels

Now that you know that vowels are classified on both height and backness, it is time to check your knowledge. What are high front vowels? Try to remember both the IPA vowel chart in Figure 11A.1 and the symbols representing sounds. If you can, make the sounds based on what you know of the tongue position. If you made the [i] or [ɪ] sounds, you would be correct. How about a low back vowel? If you guessed [ɑ], you'd be right.

Before moving on, make sure you can describe a vowel simultaneously by its height and backness (memorizing the IPA vowel chart would help in this task). Knowing these things by heart will prepare you for the general skill of IPA transcription, which will be discussed briefly in the next section.

11.5 Transcription Of Words

One of the skills that students often learn while studying phonetics is that of transcription. We have talked in detail about the sounds of the IPA. As you may recall, we use the International

Phonetic Alphabet because we need a one-to-one mapping of sound and form; one symbol per sound. Using the alphabet doesn't work because a single letter can often represent many sounds. Also, different dialects of English use the same spelling but have different pronunciations. Therefore, we use the IPA to talk about sounds, like we did throughout the consonant and vowel sections of this chapter.

If you have been keeping up with the chapter discussion thus far, you have probably memorized (or almost memorized) the sound and symbol concepts demonstrated in the charts in section 11.8. Now, it is time to write out words in IPA instead of individual sounds. If you haven't completely memorized the information in section 11.8, you may refer to it while you learn to transcribe. Remember, to transcribe, you must think of how a word sounds, not how it is spelled. Write one symbol per each sound in the word. Just like when we show a sound, all IPA-transcribed words must appear in brackets. We will start with a simple transcription: *cat* [kæt]. We transcribed each sound in the word *cat*, resulting in [kæt]. Remember that we are dealing with sounds, not the number of letters. Just because *cat* has three letters does not necessarily mean that three IPA symbols would be used when transcribing the word. In this case, though, the same number of letters in the word matches its number of sounds in its English transcription, but this is only because the word has three distinct *sounds* that must be transcribed.

Let's move on to a more challenging example where the number of English alphabet letters and the number of sounds do not match. Let us take the English word *enough*. We will transcribe it into IPA. Either [ɛnʌf] or [inʌf] could be your transcription, depending on how you pronounce the first vowel in the word, but in either case, the result is a four-sound, four-IPA-letter transcription. The English word *enough* has six letters, but only four sounds. One other point of interest in this transcription is the use of [ʌ]. If you look on your sound description list, you may have noticed that [ʌ] and [ə] are almost the same sound. Even though there is a slight difference in tongue height between the two, the sounds seem so close. So why would we not use [ə] instead? Could it also work for this answer? The answer, simply put, is no. The [ə] is for unstressed syllables, where the tongue is slightly higher. The [ʌ] is for stressed syllables, and the tongue is slightly lower. Even though they sound very similar, they are not interchangeable.

Now that we have done two examples together, it's time for you to see what you can do on your own. Take the words *scissors* and *rebate*. See if you can transcribe them; then check your answer in the next sentence. (The answers to this exercise are [sɪzɚz] and [ɹibeɪt], respectively.) You will likely find that vowels are the most difficult to transcribe. While consonants are usually straightforward, each person may have a slightly different pronunciation of vowels, as seen in our *enough* example. Surely you have heard the word pronounced both ways, thus making it difficult to transcribe. The best way to avoid confusion is to transcribe a word like you say it, unless you are making a transcription of someone else's speech. While there might be more than one correct transcription for a given word, there are definitely incorrect transcriptions. The best way to become a good transcriber is to practice frequently and check your answers.

11.6 Summary

We have discussed many concepts in this chapter on phonetics, beginning with how speech is made and the vocal tract itself, and later moving into specific sounds. During our discussion on articulation, we talked about the articulators that we use when producing the sounds of the English language. We also discussed how consonants can be classified according to place and manner of articulation, as well voicing, which simply means whether or not our vocal cords are vibrating. Each consonant we described also had a distinct symbol to go with the particular sound. The symbols we used were from the International Phonetic Alphabet (IPA). After consonants, we talked about vowels, characterizing them by vowel height and backness. We defined dipthongs and gave IPA symbols to all English vowel sounds. Each IPA symbol, whether consonant or vowel, corresponded to one and only one sound. Then we continued with the fundamentals of transcription. While the discussion on transcription was brief, it provided a few examples and encouraged you to practice and check your own work.

11.7 Further Reading

Peter Ladefoged and Keith Johnson's *A Course in Phonetics* (Ladefoged and Johnson 2010) is a classic on the subject of phonetics. The other book of Ladefoged's, *Vowels and Consonants* (Ladefoged 2005), is another authoritative introduction to phonetics. Both books have companion CDs, so readers can hear the sounds discussed in the readings.

11.8 Appendix: IPA Charts

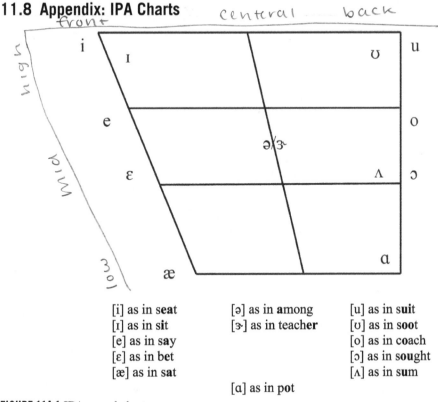

[i] as in seat   [ə] as in among   [u] as in suit
[ɪ] as in sit   [ɚ] as in teacher   [ʊ] as in soot
[e] as in say   [o] as in coach
[ɛ] as in bet   [ɔ] as in sought
[æ] as in sat   [ʌ] as in sum

[ɑ] as in pot

FIGURE 11A.1 IPA vowel chart

		Bilabial	Labiodental	Interdental	Alveolar	Alveopalatal	Velar	Glottal
		Place of Articulation						
MANNER		Bilabial	Labiodental	Interdental	Alveolar	Alveopalatal	Velar	Glottal
Stop	voiceless	p pill			t till		k kill	ʔ uh-oh
	voiced	b bill			d dill		g gill	
Flap	voiceless				ɾ butter			
Fricative	voiceless		f fine	θ thin	s sip	ʃ pressure		h hill
	voiced		v vine	ð then	z zip	ʒ pleasure		
Affricative	voiceless					tʃ choke		
	voiced					dʒ joke		
Nasal	voiced	m simmer			n sinner		ŋ singer	
Liquid	voiced	w wore			ɹ roar	j your		
Lateral	voiced				l lore			

FIGURE 11A.2 IPA consonant chart

CHAPTER 12

Phonology I

Now that you have completed your study of phonetics, we will continue with the study of phonology in this chapter. Phonetics is the study of speech sounds themselves, but phonology takes a deeper look into the interaction between speech sounds and certain environments, as well as the distribution of sounds within a language. You may need to review phonetics in Chapter 11. Before starting this chapter, you will need a solid knowledge of articulators, place and manner of articulation, voicing, and all the individual sounds that we have already covered in our study of English sounds in Chapter 11.

12.1 Phonemes And Allophones

How many sounds are pronounced for the English letter *t*? Most English native speakers will answer, "One, of course!" But the field of linguistics, and especially phonology, sees things differently. Compare the *t* sound in the words *mitten* and *stop* in natural speech. You could even compare the *t* in *top* and *stop*. Don't change your normal pronunciation; just say the words normally, in a sentence if it helps. If you have the opportunity, record your voice saying the two words naturally. Do you hear a difference? Ideally, you should. Both sounds are represented by the letter *t*, but they are actually two different sounds. We account for this easily without abandoning our dream of a one-to-one mapping of International Phonetic Alphabet (IPA) symbol to sound.

Where the IPA gives us a one-to-one mapping of "ideal" sounds, it says nothing of how sounds actually manifest themselves in different environments. To see how we treat slightly different sounds in English, let's consider an analogy. Imagine a person named Jenny. When she is with her two children at their home, which is 65% of the time, she functions as their mother. When she visits her own mother, she acts as a daughter, and when she is alone with her husband, she acts as his wife. Speech sounds are very much the same. We can say that Jenny, who has many functions in various environments but is primarily a mom, is similar to our concept of a *phoneme*. A phoneme is the standard or most frequently occurring form of a particular sound. Variations thereof are much like Jenny's functions in her alternate environments, and we can compare them to our concept of *allophones*. Allophones are simply variations of phonemes. If we think about the *t* we talked about earlier, you can see how the pronunciation changes based on the environment it is in. Based on the manner and place of articulation of the sounds surrounding it, *t* takes on different sounds, becoming more similar or different from the sounds around it. By looking at speech data and transcribing it into IPA, we can take a deeper look at phonemes and allophones.

12.1.1 Contrastive and noncontrastive phonemes

As we continue our discussion of phonemes and allophones, we must remember that each language has its own set of phonemes and allophones, and these vary from language to language. For example, Spanish does not have /θ/ as a phoneme, whereas English does. Korean has both /t/ and /tʰ/ as phonemes, whereas English has /t/ as a phoneme and /tʰ/ as an allophone. Note the slashes used instead of the brackets we saw in the last chapter. Slashes are used to indicate phonemes. By contrast, brackets denote actual speech forms.

In the case of Korean sounds, both /t/ and /tʰ/ are phonemes, and thus we call them *contrastive sounds*. Contrastive sounds are sounds that are both considered phonemes of a language, thereby making them *different sounds* from each other. In English, for example, /t/ and /tʰ/ are not considered to be different phonemes, but allophones of the form /t/. Therefore, changing the pronunciation of [stɑp] to [stʰɑp] does not change the meaning of the word. To most native speakers, they would be treated as the same word. In Korean, however, changing the pronunciation of /t/ to /tʰ/ in a given word could change the meaning of the word. To see this in action, consider the words /tal/ "daughter" and /tʰal/ "mask." Note how one change alters the entire meaning of the word. This happens because there are two different phonemes, each representing a sound entirely different from the other, to the ears of a Korean native speaker. For English, one of the sounds is an allophone, and English speakers would consider the sounds to be *noncontrastive* because they are not similar in type (one is a phoneme, the other an allophone). If one is interchanged with the other, in the given language, the meaning of a word would not be changed, though the pronunciation would seem odd to the listener. This might sound confusing, but think about a person with a foreign accent: Despite her or his different pronunciation of words, you probably still understand what she or he is saying. Unless the person with the accent commits an error having to do with a contrastive pair—say, a Korean person says *cold* instead of *cord*, where /l/ and /ɹ/ are contrastive phonemes in English but not Korean—you likely won't have trouble understanding him or her.

Korean is very interesting in terms of its phonemes and allophones, as we have already discussed. Let us continue our study of Korean. In English, /l/ and /ɹ/ are a contrastive pair, but in Korean, they are noncontrastive, meaning that a Korean person hears /l/ and /ɹ/ as the same phoneme. The result? Korean people who learn English often use /ɹ/ when they should use /l/, and vice versa. This phenomenon is not limited to Korean alone—in fact, many languages have contrastive phonemes where other languages do not. This makes learning a new language a little more difficult when it comes to conversation and speaking. Whether the speakers are Korean, French, Dutch, or Portuguese, this type of pronunciation difficulty is something that most language learners have to struggle with at one point or another. If you've ever taken a foreign language, you know that your pronunciation is not the same as a native speaker's. Now you know why: The phonemes in your native language are different from those in the language you are learning.

12.1.2 Minimal pairs

Think about how the words *cold* and *cord* are related phonetically. When they are transcribed into IPA, only one sound differs between them. The sounds that differ between the words are both phonemes in English. In the word *cold*, there is clearly an /l/, and in *cord*, there is definitely an /ɹ/. When two words have a difference of only one phoneme between them, we call those words a *minimal pair*. To be a minimal pair, the two words must differ by only one sound, and they must have distinctly different definitions. The sounds that differ between the two words of the minimal pair must both be phonemes, as opposed to allophones, in the language of the two words. Why is this distinction important? Most native speakers of a language do not distinguish among various allophones of a phoneme, but they *can*, in fact, distinguish among different phonemes.

When it comes to phonemes, you must remember that one sound, not necessarily the spelling of the words, must be different. In fact, spelling doesn't matter at all, as you may have already guessed. How about the words *though* and *sew*? Are they a minimal pair? Yes, of course. The meanings are clearly different, and once you transcribe them into IPA, you can clearly see that the sounds differ by the word-initial phoneme only, the phoneme that starts the words. Let's take a look: [ðoʊ] & [soʊ]. What other minimal pairs can you think of?

12.2 Phonological Rules

Have you ever noticed that sometimes when we speak, we say words differently? Once we are talking, whether talking fast or slow, words seem to run together and take on different sounds. Often, when we pronounce a word, it changes slightly based on a nearby sound.

Of course, many of our endeavors so far in this book have been to identify the patterns found in human language. Phonology is no different. In this section, you will learn how to formulate rules to describe correctly changes in sound based on environmental factors. We will go from the rather abstract concept of phonemes to describing actual speech phenomena with the rule formation process. Before we begin, let us review the concept of phonemes again.

A phoneme is a speech sound that is found in a particular language. It is perceived as one single, distinctive sound to native speakers, and represents a sound on a more ideal or abstract level because it is the "base sound" for its allophonic counterparts. Allophones, on the other hand, are the actual manifestation of a speech sound in a given speech environment. Let us look at data set (1). This set is comprised of English language data. The brackets surrounding the sentences transcribed in IPA represent the actual speech sounds.

(1) I ran around.   [aɪ ɹæn əɹɑ ʊnd]
    I ran slowly.   [aɪ ɹæn sloʊli]
    I ran briskly.   [aɪ ɹæm bɹɪskli]
    I ran past.   [aɪ ɹæm pæst]
    I ran gracefully.   [aɪ ɹæŋ gɹeɪsfəli]
    I ran quickly.   [aɪ ɹæŋ kwqɪkli]

What assumptions can be made about the pronunciation of the /n/ in *ran* in this data? To consider this, we must first look at the IPA transcriptions. Note how the pronunciation of /n/ in *ran* changes in some instances. Because the entire word *ran* is a constant in each phrase, this means the sound before the /n/ does not change from example to example. The pronunciation of /n/ does differ though, so we must assume that the sound *following* /n/ in speech is affecting it. What do the sounds following the /n/ have in common, in the cases when the sounds change?

The /n/ pronunciation remains the same (as [n]) for *I ran around* and *I ran slowly*. We can save this for later because there is no change in pronunciation. In the case of *I ran briskly* and *I ran past*, both /n/ pronunciations become an [m]. What do the sounds following /n/ have in common? Both /b/ and /p/ are bilabial stops, so we can say that /n/ becomes [m] when it appears before a bilabial stop. Keep in mind that brackets around a letter, as in [x], denote an *actual speech sound*, whereas slashes, as in /x/, denote a phoneme, or conceptual sound. If you are still having problems thinking in terms of phonemes versus allophones, think of a phoneme as analogous to a lexeme. A phoneme is the conceptual form of a sound, whereas a lexeme is the conceptual form of a word. Allophones, then, are similar to word forms because they are the actual realization *in speech* of the conceptual form.

For our last two sentences, *I ran gracefully* and *I ran quickly*, the /n/ sound changes to an [ŋ]. What do the /g/ and the /k/ sounds following the /n/ in *ran* have in common? If you said that both /g/ and /k/ are velar stops, you are correct! This means that the pronunciation of /n/ changes to [ŋ] when /n/ comes before a velar stop.

Let us begin a more scientific representation of speech change: rule formulation. Because we can generalize sound changes based on their environmental factors as seen in the example in (1), we can also formulate some equations (rules) to show these changes. Let us formulate some rules to describe what happens to /n/ in (1).

One change we noted was that /n/ changes to [m] when the sound following it is a bilabial stop. The way we would show this as a rule is shown in (2):

(2) /n/ → [m] / ___ [+ bilabial, + stop]

If you were to read (2) out loud, it would read something like, "Phoneme /n/ changes to pronunciation [m] in the environment where /n/ comes before a bilabial stop." Here, the notation [+ bilabial, + stop] means that the following sound has the qualities of being both a bilabial and a stop. This means, in the case that we added the sentence *I ran more* to our data set, we could easily remove the [+ stop] to reveal that /n/ is pronounced as [m] when it precedes a bilabial sound in general, and not specifically only bilabial (oral) stops, because [m] is a member of the bilabial group and is not an (oral) stop. However, rules are formulated to show instances of change in the data set *only*. You may only write rules based on the data sets given.

Let us formulate a rule, as seen in (3), for the [ŋ] pronunciation, too:

(3) /n/ → [ŋ] / ___ [+ velar, + stop]

This one can be read as "Phoneme /n/ changes to pronunciation [ŋ] in the environment where /n/ comes before a velar stop." Again, [+velar, +stop] means that something exhibits the properties of being both velar in the place of articulation and a stop in the manner of articulation.

We can now make a bigger generalization: an "everywhere else" rule, or what is often called a *default rule*. Our data set showed that /n/ changes in two specific environments, as seen in (2) and (3). However, as we recall, /n/ did not change when it came before a mid central vowel or an alveolar fricative. Mid central vowels and alveolar fricatives have nothing in common. They do not share the same manner or place of articulation. While all vowels are voiced, the alveolar fricative /s/ is not, thereby confirming that there are no similarities between the two. Another way to say this is that they cannot be generalized together using phonetic features such as place or manner of articulation. When there is no change in the phoneme pronunciation in a particular environment that cannot be generalized in this way, we can generate a rule that we will call an everywhere else rule because it applies everywhere else outside the instances we described in (2) and (3). Our "everywhere else" rule for data set (1) can be seen in (4).

(4) /n/ → [n] / ___ [everywhere else]

One last important thing to keep in mind is that the position of the underline in the equation will switch sides of the bracketed items if the data set reveals that the sound before (and not after, like in our previous examples) changes the pronunciation of the sound to follow. For example, if there were a data set that had the pronunciation of /s/ changing to /z/ when the sound before /s/ was a voiced sound, the equation would look like (5).

(5) /s/ → [z] / [+ voiced] ___

Note that the line is now *following* the bracketed items. The line stands for the sound that is making the change from phoneme to actual pronunciation, so it is only logical that the line is before the bracketed items when the sound is affected by the sounds that follow. Conversely, when the sound is affected by a sound coming before it, the line follows the bracketed items. Again, the bracketed items indicate the things making the phoneme change into an allophone, and the line itself stands for the speech manifestation of the conceptual phoneme.

12.3 Feature Structures

In this section, we will discuss in more depth the equations we just learned to make and the implications they have. We will also use one analogy to better understand the plus and minus features within the bracketed segments of the equations.

12.3.1 Natural class

Do you remember the equation we wrote for (3)? Within the brackets, we had two features: [+ velar] and [+ stop]. That meant that changes were induced on any /n/ preceding a velar stop. In English, the group of oral velar stops is small, comprised of only /k/ and /g/. Both /k/ and /g/ share some obvious common factors: Both are velar in their place of articulation and both are oral stops. When two sounds share any one (or more) common feature, they are called a *natural class*. The sounds /k/ and /g/ belong to the natural class of oral velar stops. As you can see, natural classes are comprised of sounds that share specific features, the features of voicing, place, and manner of articulation.

Again, for something to be a natural class of sounds, it must share *at least* one feature (voicing, place, and/or manner of articulation). Large natural classes share only one feature, such as fricative sounds, which have nine phonemes in the English language. The more features a natural class shares, the fewer phonemes exist within it because it becomes more specific. If we talk about the natural class of alveolar fricatives, our class becomes smaller, with only two members. If we talk about the natural class of voiced alveolar fricatives, we have become so specific that, in English, only one phoneme exists: /z/.

The next subsection will continue our discussion about features and natural classes, and we will introduce an analogy to help you remember how features and natural class work together to make larger or smaller generalizations in your equations.

12.3.2 An online dating site

In the previous subsection, we talked about how features are used to delineate natural classes. The more features the members of a natural class share, the smaller the group will be. The fewer features it shares, the larger the group of phonemes will be.

Think about an online dating site. If you were to fill out a profile for a potential date, what would you want him or her to be like? We can think of this in terms of the bracketed parts of the equations we wrote. Perhaps, you'd like your ideal date to be a businessperson. You would then want to add [+ businessperson] to your brackets. Let us say the group of businesspeople online is approximately 1,000 people. What else do you want in a potential date? How about a nonsmoker? Your brackets now look like this: [+ businessperson, − smoker]. By adding [− smoker] to your brackets, your group just became more specific. Now, instead of looking at the 1,000 potential people you could have dated when you specified only "businessperson," you can now choose from only 750 people, which is the group of businesspeople who don't smoke. If you aren't comfortable choosing from a group of 750 people, you can narrow down the options even more. Perhaps you'd like to date someone who likes sushi. Your brackets would become more full with an additional feature, and your group of potential dating partners would become a bit smaller: [+ businessperson, − smoker, + sushi lover]. Now, you have narrowed the group down to 100 potential dates.

For some people, having more options is a good thing. For others, it is not. The same is true for equations. The more features included in the brackets, the smaller the natural class of sounds will be. The fewer the features, the bigger the group. When we included only [+ businessperson], our group was large, with 1,000 potential dates. The more specific we got, the fewer options we had. Whether we added a + feature or a − feature, the result was still more specific than the previous. Natural classes are exactly the same: The natural class of alveolar sounds in English has eight phonemes, the natural class of alveolar fricatives has two phonemes, and the natural class of voiceless (denoted as [− voiced]) alveolar fricatives has just one phoneme. We can see this in bracket notation, as we would in an equation, in (6).

(6) [+ alveolar]   /t/, /d/, /s/, /z/, /ɾ/, /n/, /l/, /ɹ/
       [+ alveolar, + fricative]   /s/, /z/
       [+ alveolar, + fricative, − voiced] /s/

As we stated above, the relation between the number of items in the brackets is directly related to the size of the natural class of sounds, as you can see. The more bracketed items, the smaller the group.

12.4 Case Studies

Now that you have a better grasp of the concept of natural class and its relation to phonetic features, it's time to practice our new skills in rule formulation by considering the first three sets of data and instructions, taken from the textbook *Language Files,* Tenth Edition. The fourth set of data introduced in section 12.4.4 deals with English plural alternations.

12.4.1 Case study: Sindhi

The following data are from Sindhi, an Indo-European language of the Indo-Aryan family, spoken in Pakistan and India. Examine the distribution of the phones [p], [pʰ], and [b]. Determine if the three are allophones of separate phonemes or allophones of the same phoneme. What is your evidence? Is the relationship among the sounds the same as in English? Why or why not?

(7) a. [pənu]   leaf   g. [təru]   bottom
     b. [vədʒu]   opportunity   h. [kʰəto]   sour
     c. [ʃeki]   suspicious   i. [bədʒu]   run
     d. [gədo]   dull   j. [bənu]   forest
     e. [dəru]   door   k. [bətʃu]   be safe
     f. [pʰənu]   hood of snake   l. [dʒədʒu] judge

How can we deal with this data set? Here, we'll break down the process step by step, so you can see how we will solve the problem.

Step 1: Identify any information that is irrelevant. We are focusing on three phonemes and those three phonemes *only.* If a word in the list does not contain a [p], [pʰ], or [b], it is not relevant to our study. Cross out words that don't apply. Letters b, c, d, e, g, h, and l do not contain the phonemes we are looking for.

Step 2: Our task is to identify whether the sounds [p], [pʰ], and [b] are all distinct phonemes, or whether some are allophones of the same phoneme. How can we do this? Our first inclination should be to look for any minimal pairs. Remember that, for two words to be a minimal pair, they must differ by only one phoneme and have distinctly different meanings. Because minimal pairs revolve around the concept of phonemes, finding a minimal pair would give us solid evidence of phonemes. Look at letters a, f, and j. No matter how you divide them up, they all form minimal pairs with each other, the only difference being the sounds we are exploring. [pʰənu] "hood of snake" is different from both [pənu] "leaf" and [bənu] "forest" in meaning. In fact, all the meanings are distinctly different from each other, and the words all differ by one phoneme. This is our evidence that [p], [pʰ], and [b] are all phonemes, *not* allophones of the same phoneme.

Step 3: Our final task is to decide whether [p], [pʰ], and [b] are all distinctive phonemes in English, or if they differ from our Sindhi data in that way. We can start by trying to identify some minimal pairs in English that contain these sounds and see if they have distinct meanings. Let's use the words *pat* and *bat*. If we pronounce [pæt] as [pʰæt], there is really no difference in meaning. A native speaker would identify both as the word *pat*. However, if we compare [pæt] and [bæt], we are now dealing with two distinctly different meanings. One is a verb, meaning "to gently make contact with the palm of the hand several times," and the other is a nocturnal animal. Clearly, *pat* and *bat* form a minimal pair, meaning that [p] and [b] are actually phonemes in English. Because we can make no distinction between [pæt] and [pʰæt], however, we see that [pʰ] is an allophone of the English /p/. To provide even more evidence, we could list several English words where the pronunciation of [p] and [pʰ] doesn't affect the meaning of the word. For your assignments, you should provide ample evidence. In light of the amount of time allotted for this chapter and the space in the book, however, we will stop here and move on to the next case study.

12.4.2 Case study: Korean

In the following Korean words, you will find the sounds [s] and [ʃ]. Determine whether the sounds [s] and [ʃ] are allophones of the same phoneme or separate phonemes. If the sounds are allophones of the same phoneme, write a rule to show how the sound changes based on environmental factors.

(8) a. [ʃi]   poem   j. [sɑl]   flesh
    b. [miʃin]   superstition k. [kɑsu]   singer
    c. [ʃinmun]   newspaper   l. [sɑnmun]   prose
    d. [tʰaksɑŋʃige] table clock   m. [kɑsəl]   hypothesis
    e. [ʃilsu]   mistake   n. [miso]   smile
    f. [oʃip]   fifty   o. [susek]   search
    g. [pɑŋʃik]   method   p. [tɑpsɑ]   exploration
    h. [kɑnʃik]   snack   q. [so]   cow
    i. [kɑʃi]   thorn

Step 1: Our first step in completing the task of determining whether [s] and [ʃ] are both phonemes or if they are instead allophones of the same phoneme is to see if there is any irrelevant data, or rather words that do not contain [s] or [ʃ]. It looks like all data are relevant, so we should continue.

Step 2: We should now see if there are any minimal pairs in the data set. Remember how the minimal pairs helped us to crack the code in the first case study. Here, however, there do not seem to be any minimal pairs. This might be a hint that the two sounds are allophones of the same phoneme. To continue, we must provide evidence of this hypothesis.

Step 3: Because we think that the sounds are both allophones of the same phoneme, it might be valuable to see if we can write a rule (equation) to explain the change in the sound. We must determine which sound is found in which environment. Look at the sounds before and after [s] and [ʃ] in each piece of data to see if there is a pattern. It looks like [s] is found in a variety of phonological environments. It can start a word, or appear in the middle of a word. It appears before and after a variety of vowels, and there is seemingly no pattern. Now, let us consider [ʃ]. For all items of data containing [ʃ], it is evident that [ʃ] comes directly before [i].

This is a substantial pattern. Clearly, we can now see that [ʃ] is an allophone of [s] because [s] is found in a wider variety of settings. Because [ʃ] appears in one specific place only, there is an environmental factor that is changing [s] to [ʃ], meaning that [ʃ] is an allophone of [s].

Step 4: Now, let us write a rule to finalize our argument. We will begin with a rule for the [s] change to the [ʃ] allophone, and end with an everywhere else rule to describe the phoneme pronunciation.

For the first rule, we know that [s] becomes [ʃ] when the sound following [ʃ] is [i]. We must now describe [i] according to the position and tongue height that is standard in describing vowels. [i] is a high front vowel, meaning its two bracketed features should be [+ high, + front], based on what we learned about phonetic features in the last section.

(9) /s/ → [ʃ] / ___ [+ high, + front]

This rule should read: "The phoneme /s/ becomes the sound [ʃ] in Korean when it precedes a high front vowel." While this rule is perfectly fine and would suffice as an answer in itself, now is the perfect time to consider why a change like this would take place. We will discuss types of phonological changes in detail in the next section; now we will briefly cover the motivation for this phonological change.

We know that /s/ changes to the pronunciation [ʃ] when the following sound is [i]. If we want to know precisely why this happens, we need to consider what kind of sound [s] is versus what kind of sound [ʃ] is. Let's look at the phonological features of [s]. It is a voiceless alveolar fricative. If we were to write that in the bracketed notation that we use for equations, it would look like this: [− voiced, + alveolar, + fricative]. How does [ʃ] differ? [ʃ] is a voiceless alveopalatal fricative, meaning its pronunciation is slightly farther back in the oral cavity than that of [s]. If we used the bracketed notation, [ʃ] would look like this: [− voiced, + alveopalatal, + fricative] Like we said before, the pronunciation of [ʃ] is slightly farther back than that of [s]. However, when we consider that [i] is a [+ high, + front] vowel, things start to make sense. High front vowels are pronounced closer in position to [ʃ] than they are to [s]. Remember that vowels deal with tongue height and frontness only (and *not* place or manner of articulation), and something that raises roughly the front third of the tongue is considered front. Just the tip of the tongue touches the alveolar ridge for [s], and as for the pronunciation of [i], a front vowel would likely raise the tongue *slightly* farther back than that of the pronunciation of [s]. If [s] changes to [ʃ] in the presence of a high front vowel, then our logical assumption is that the two sounds are trying to become similar to each other. It is an example of assimilation. Assimilation is where two sounds become more alike in pronunciation, with one sound taking on a phonological feature of the other.

Let us look at this phenomenon written as a rule to show the assimilation motivation for the change:

(10) [− voiced, + alveolar, + fricative] →
      [− voiced, + alveopalatal, + fricative] / [+ high, + front]

Now our rule shows the phonological motivation for change. Naturally, sounds can undergo many kinds of changes, and not all are this simple to grasp. We will leave those changes for a later section in this chapter and continue answering the question that was asked at the beginning of this chapter subsection. Without making our everywhere else rule, our job is not yet finished.

Our next rule is a bit more simple. It is the everywhere else rule we talked about before.

(11) /s/ → [s] / ___ [everywhere else]

We write the rule this way because there is no other good way to generalize where the [s] pronunciation takes place. It literally occurs in a wide variety of environments, where the [ʃ] pronunciation was found in an extremely limited environment.

We have now answered the question completely and are ready to move on to our next case study.

12.4.3 Case study: English

English is an Indo-European language of the Germanic family. In the following dialect of English, common in Canada and parts of the United States, there is a predictable variant [əɪ] of the diphthong [ɑɪ]. What phonological environments motivate the change?

(12) a. [bəɪt]   bite   i. [fɑɪl]   file
      b. [tɑɪ]   tie   j. [ləɪf]   life
      c. [ɹɑɪd]   ride   k. [tɑɪm]   time
      d. [ɹɑɪz]   rise   l. [təɪp]   type
      e. [ɹəɪt]   write   m. [nɑɪnθ]   ninth
      f. [fəɪt]   fight   n. [fɑɪɹ]   fire
      g. [bɑɪ]   buy   o. [bəɪk]   bike
      h. [ɹəɪs]   rice

Step 1: In this case, we already know that [əɪ] is an allophone for the phoneme [ɑɪ]. Our task is to identify the environment that motivates this change, meaning we will write an equation to describe it. We must first observe the environment in which [əɪ] occurs. Remember to identify patterns in the sounds before and after the [əɪ] pronunciation. This will give us some clues as to why this pronunciation occurs. One thing that is easily noticeable is that the sound coming before the [əɪ] sound doesn't seem to matter. Often, as in (12d) and (12e) of the data set, the same sound can occur before both pronunciations. This means we should instead focus on the sounds following the [əɪ] pronunciation to look for patterns. If we look at data items (12a), (12e), (12f), (12h), (12j), (12l), and (12o), we can see that the sounds that follow the [əɪ] pronunciation differ greatly in place and manner of articulation. Some of the following sounds are fricatives, while others are stops. Some are velar, and others are alveolar. What could they possibly have in common? We cannot ignore the third phonetic feature that can define a natural class of sounds: voicing. In all instances of the [əɪ] pronunciation, the sound following [əɪ] is a voiceless sound. We have now identified the factor that changes the [ɑɪ] pronunciation to the [əɪ] pronunciation.

Step 2: It is now time to write a rule for the change. We should also include an everywhere else rule for the base sound.

(13) /aɪ/ → [əɪ] / ___ [− voiced]

(14) /aɪ/ → [aɪ] / ___ [everywhere else]

The first equation should read: "The diphthong /aɪ/ changes to pronunciation [əɪ] when it comes before a voiceless sound." The second equation should read: "The diphthong /aɪ/ remains pronounced as /aɪ/ in all other environments (everywhere else)."

12.4.4 Case study: English plurals

In English, regular nouns have several pronunciations of the plural morpheme *s*, as in *beets* [bit + s], *cabs* [kæb + z], and *fuses* [fjuz + əz]. Let's look at the data set to determine what factors affect the pronunciation of the /s/ that denotes pluralization.

(15) a. [pɛts]   pets   i. [kʊks]   cooks
      b. [pɛnz]   pens   j. [æʃəz]   ashes
      c. [kæps]   caps   k. [fjuzəz]   fuses
      d. [kæbs]   cabs   l. [paiz]   pies
      e. [tʃɝtʃəz]   churches   m. [dægɝz]   daggers
      f. [dʒʌdʒəz]   judges   n. [pɪts]   pits
      g. [θɪŋz]   things   o. [bɝθs]   births
      h. [bʌsəz]   buses   p. [bits]   beets

Step 1: We should start by identifying the patterns for the different pronunciations. We have three distinct pronunciations of the *s* morpheme: [s], [z], and [əz]. We will assume that the base sound here is /z/. We can certainly explain the data under the assumption that the base form is either /s/ or /əz/. However, positing /z/ as the base form yields the most natural explanation of the data presented in (15). We will leave the question of why this is as an exercise for the reader. Because the three possible sounds of the plural morpheme occur at the end of the word, the only logical choice is to look at the sound occurring before the plural morpheme, or rather the final sound in the singular form of the word.

Here, it looks like the [s] pronunciation occurs when the last sound of the singular noun form is [− voiced], or voiceless. The pronunciation with the insertion of the [ə] sound, the [əz] pronunciation, occurs when the final sound of the singular noun form is a fricative, [+ fricative]. The [z] pronunciation is observed everywhere other than the aforementioned cases of [− voiced] and [+ fricative].

Step 2: Now, it is time for rule formulation. Here are the rules for the [s] pronunciation:

(16) /z/ → [s] / [− voiced] ___

If we'd like to show some phonological motivations for these changes, again we can describe each sound individually, as in the next equation.

(17) [+ voiced, + alveolar, + fricative] → [− voiced, + alveolar, + fricative] / [− voiced] ___

The next rule gets slightly more complicated because we have to account for the addition of a sound, [ə], as in the [əz] variation of the plural marker. One of the phonological changes you will learn about in the next section is that of insertion. Sometimes, when two sounds are very similar, the insertion of a new sound between the similar sounds occurs to avoid a difficult pronunciation. There are other motivations for insertion as well. However, the similarity of the fricative sounds in this example is the motivating factor. In this case, the neutral sound [ə] was added to the /z/ plural marker, resulting in [əz]. Below, you will find a rule to describe this.

(18) /z/ → [əz] / [+ fricative] ___

Finally, the everywhere else rule is formulated as in (19). Remember that the everywhere else rule must be applied after the other two rules previously formulated.

(19) /z/ → [z] /[everywhere else] ___

12.5 Types Of Phonological Changes

You now have some experience in making phonological rules for several different languages. The changes you show in your rules may describe the many kinds of phonological changes that sounds undergo. In the next subsection, we will take an in-depth look at the kinds of changes sounds can make.

12.5.1 Assimilation

Think back to the Korean case study in the last section. [s] became [ʃ] because its neighboring sound was [i]. Assimilation is the process where a sound becomes more like a neighboring sound in regard to its manner or place of articulation, or its voicing. Assimilation is ubiquitous, and can be found in every language.

12.5.2 Dissimilation

Dissimilation occurs when a sound becomes more different from a neighboring sound. An example of this would be the pronunciation of *etcetera*. Often, the word [ɛtsɛtəɹə] is pronounced as [ɛksɛtəɹə] because /t/ and /s/ are both voiceless alveolar sounds. This might be a difficult sound combination to produce, so the [t] becomes [k] in pronunciation. /k/ is a voiceless velar sound, and different in its place of articulation from /t/, thereby allowing for an easier pronunciation.

12.5.3 Insertion

Insertion occurs when a sound that is not part of a word is inserted as a result of a phonological process. An example of this would be the [ə] insertion that we saw in the English plurals case study in the previous section. Because the fricative sounds ending the singular form of the noun are close to the plural marker /z/, [ə] is inserted to make the pronunciation easier. As a result, where there was originally no sound, there is now an inserted [ə].

12.5.4 Deletion

Deletion is another common phonological process. It occurs when one sound that is ideally present in a word is deleted in pronunciation. There are many examples in English: the pronunciation of [laɪbɛɹi] for [laɪbɹɛɹi] and the pronunciation of [səpɹaɪz] for [səˑpɹaɪz]. While the deletion of /ɹ/ (written here as ə + ɹ, or ɚ, in the above example) is a very specific kind of deletion, any sound can potentially be targeted for the process of deletion if the proper circumstance presents itself within a word.

12.5.5 Metathesis

Metathesis is the last phonological process we will cover in this chapter. Through this phonological process, sounds are rearranged within a word. Take, for example, the word *cavalry*. If we transcribed it into IPA, we would write [kævəlɹi]. In actual pronunciation, however, many people say [kælvəɹi]. The sounds /l/ and /v/ are clearly switched. A similar process occurs with the word *nuclear*. A common pronunciation of the word is [nukilɝ], though many people agree that the "correct" pronunciation is actually [nukliɝ]. While metathesis is not as common as some of the other phonological changes in English sounds, it is definitely one of the more interesting phenomena.

12.6 Summary

Throughout this chapter, you have expanded your knowledge of phonemes and allophones, as well as your knowledge of how sounds interact with each other. In the first half of the chapter, we discussed the importance of natural class and how phonemes are a crucial concept in terms of minimal pairs. We demonstrated how some sounds change based on the influences of their neighboring sounds, and how these changes can be easily accounted for through writing rules (equations). Next, we discussed some phonological changes that sounds undergo and the motivations for these changes. These were illustrated in the case studies via examples from several languages and individual examples in the last section of the chapter. You have completed your coursework on phonology and are now ready to move on to the next step up from the phoneme: the syllable. Please make sure you understand all the concepts in this chapter before you move on to the final chapter of this book.

12.7 Further Reading

There are many outstanding textbooks on introductory phonology. The two books we cited in this chapter are The Ohio State University's *Language Files*, Tenth Edition. Kenstowicz and Kisseberth (1986) is a classic introduction to generative phonology. More serious readers should consult Kenstowicz's (1994) *Phonology in Generative Grammar*. This book contains a significant amount of data and analysis. An introductory text that focuses on the English language only is Giegerich (1992). Odden (2005) and Roca and Johnson (1999) would be great companions to this book as well.

CHAPTER 13
Phonology II: syllables

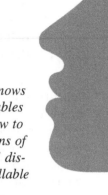

In this last chapter, we will discuss various syllable structures. Everybody knows what the word syllable *means. Most students remember learning about syllables from elementary school English class. By clapping our hands, we learned how to determine the number of syllables in a word. Nonetheless, technical definitions of what a syllable actually is have proven challenging. In this chapter, we will discuss how we define syllables, followed by some discussions about English syllable structures.*

13.1 What Is A Syllable?

Syllables seem to be an easy concept for many students to grasp. Without any further linguistics training, everybody can easily figure out that the word *syllable* contains three syllables, while the word *the* has only one syllable. Although figuring out the number of syllables within a word is relatively straightforward, that does not mean it is easy to say what, exactly, a syllable is. As already addressed, answering this question systematically is very challenging, and as far as we are aware, there is no unanimous agreement among linguists. In attempting to define what a syllable is, we will adopt the sonority theory, which is widely known compared to other theories. The theory also provides us with nice generalizations on the syllable structures of English.

13.1.1 Sonority scale

To understand the sonority theory, we have to discuss the notion of sonority. As you might have guessed, the word contains two morphemes, one being *sonor-*, and the other *-ity*. The morpheme *sono* is coming from the Latin word *sonor* meaning "sound," and *-ity* is an affix that makes the stem into a noun. Literally speaking, as a result, sonority means "sound." In actuality, however, the word is used in relation to loudness. The sonority of a sound is its relative loudness compared to other sounds, everything being equal. Without much difficulty, we can figure out that not every sound is equally loud. Some sounds are louder than other sounds, and some sounds are quieter than other sounds. Naturally, voiceless sounds are not as loud as their voiced counterparts, for instance. Consider the example in (1). Let's assume that you have a leg muscle cramp while you are swimming in the university pool. Although the lifeguard at the pool is very attentive, you cannot draw her attention by saying (1) because there are many people chattering in the pool area. Now, what you have to do is to make (1) louder. How can you achieve the goal? Perhaps the only possibility is to scream like in (2). If you try to make (1) louder by emphasizing the consonants in *help* like in (3), (4), and (5), you may not end up being loud enough to draw the lifeguard's attention.

    (1) Help me!
    (2) Heeeeeeelp me!
    (3) Hhhhhhelp me!
    (4) Hellllllllllp me!
    (5) Helppppp me

It is very easy to make (1) louder by emphasizing the vowel in *help*, as in (2), but the goal is hard to achieve when you emphasize consonants. In particular, (5), where [p] is emphasized, seems to be almost impossible to pronounce. This observation leads to the conclusion that vowels are louder than consonants. In other words, vowels have higher sonority. Among the consonants, each has a different value on the sonority scale. Stop sounds are least sonorous because stop sounds require complete stoppage of the airstream before their release, mostly with the help of vowels. Fricatives are more sonorous than stops because the airstream is not completely blocked. Nasals are more sonorous than fricatives. Although nasal sounds require complete contact between the tongue and other articulators, the airstream should still come out of the nose. As a result, the sonority of the sounds is higher than it is in stops and fricatives. The sonority of liquids is higher than nasals because the airstream proceeds along the sides of the tongue in articulating laterals. The sonority of approximants falls between liquids and vowels. Because approximants are often called semivowels, it is not surprising to see a high sonority that almost reaches the level of vowels. The information discussed here is summarized as a chart in (6).

(6)

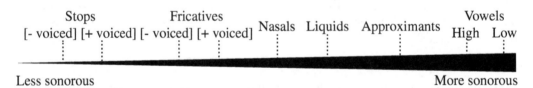

What the chart in (6) illustrates is that speech sounds can be ranked in terms of their relative sonority. Stops are the least sonorous sounds, while vowels are the most sonorous sounds. All other sounds are ranked between these two extremes on the sonority scale.

13.1.2 Sonority peak and sonority sequencing

Based on the sonority scale provided in the previous section, let's consider the monosyllabic word *plan*. First, transcribe the word into IPA before we discuss the syllabicity of the word: The notion of syllable is based on sounds, not on letters. The sonority chart illustrated in (7) shows that there is one and only one peak in the monosyllable word *plan*. In other words, the sonority continuously increases until it reaches the peak, then it drops, which is a phenomenon dubbed sonority sequencing.

(7) The sonority chart for /plæn/

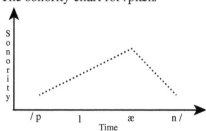

This one peak–one syllable hypothesis can explain quite a bit of English data. Consider words such as *cat*, *dog*, *school*, *desk*, and so on. All of these monosyllable words have one and only one peak, and the sonority within these words continuously increases until the vowel sound, then it decreases. Consider the words *and* and *sea*. Both of them are monosyllabic, but *and* begins with a vowel, and *sea* ends with a vowel. The sonority charts for these words are illustrated in (8) and (9), respectively.

(8) The sonority chart for /ænd/

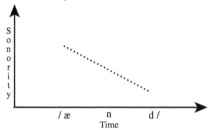

(9) The sonority chart for /si/

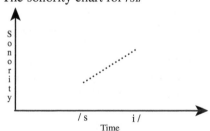

Although the dotted lines in (8) and (9) look different from that of (7), there is a visible peak in (8) and (9), both of which are represented by the vowel sounds. In other words, these monosyllabic words still have one peak, making them felicitous syllables in English. The simplest monosyllabic word is composed of only one vowel. Think of the English indefinite article *a*, as in *a book*. Although the sonority chart for *a*, illustrated in (10), shows neither an increasing nor a decreasing pattern, there is one and only one peak, which is notated by • in (10).

(10) The sonority chart for /ə/

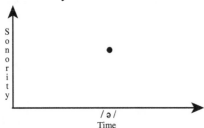

Now that we discussed some examples of monosyllabic words, we can consider some bisyllabic words, which are words that contain two syllables, in order to see if our explanation is still valid. As everybody knows, *planner* is a bisyllabic word. Based on the sonority scale provided in (6), the sonority chart for *planner* looks like (11). In (11), two peaks are clearly visible: One is made by the vowel /æ/, and the other by /ə/. Because there are two visible peaks, we clearly see that there are indeed two syllables in the word *planner*.

(11) The sonority chart for /plænəɹ/

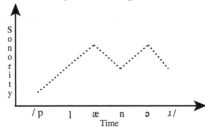

The one peak–one syllable hypothesis can also explain possible words in English. The words listed in (12) are all *possible* words in English, although they are not attested either in dictionaries or in actual speech. If you ask native speakers of English if they are possible words in English, most native speakers will answer yes, although they have never heard of these words. By contrast, when we switch the two initial consonants of each word in (12), the results are not possible words; this is shown in (13). Most native speakers will agree that the words in (13) are not possible English words and are extremely difficult, if not impossible, to pronounce.

(12) pling, srug, klog, slulp, knimp, and so on
(13) lping, rsrug, lkog, lsupl, nkimp, and so on

The question is, How do we know which words are possible words and which are not? The one peak–one syllable hypothesis provides us with a reasonable answer for this question. The words listed in (12) are possible words because they do not violate the sonority scale we discussed. Although the words in (12) are not actually used by speakers, they follow the sonority pattern observed in actual English words: Each of these monosyllabic words has only one peak. On the other hand, the words listed in (13) do not follow that pattern by yielding two peaks, although they are putative monosyllabic words in English. We will illustrate, with the impossible word *lpring* in (14), why the words in (13) do not follow the one peak–one syllable pattern. In (14), there are two visible peaks: One is made by /l/ and the other by the vowel /ɪ/. As a result, the one peak–one syllable assumption is violated, yielding a word not felicitous in English.

(14) The sonority chart for /lpɪŋ/

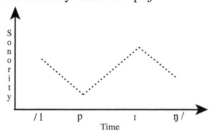

Now that we discussed one word listed in (13), we encourage readers to check their own understanding by drawing a sonority chart for each word in (12) and (13). By doing so, readers will easily understand why some combinations of sounds can never make a potential (or possible) English word.

13.1.3 *Some apparent counterexamples*

The sonority chart in conjunction with the sonority scale provided in (6) seems to account for the syllabicity of English words. However, we cannot explain several counterexamples using the hypothesis we have discussed. First, some English syllables are completely acceptable, although they do not fit the required sonority pattern. For instance, the monosyllabic words in (15a) do not conform to the sonority pattern we have discussed. Nonetheless, they are all legitimate English syllables and words.

(15a) spit, stop, skid, and so on

They do not conform to the pattern we illustrated because there are two visible peaks in those words, one made by /s/, the other by the vowel /ɪ/, as illustrated in (15b). To make our hypothesis more robust, we have to explain why /spit/ is an acceptable syllable, although it does not conform to the sonority sequencing pattern.

(15b) The sonority chart for /spit/

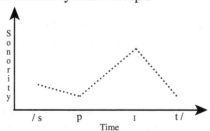

The second problem concerns the number of phonemes within a syllable. That is, how many phonemes can a syllable contain? Let us assume the hypothetical word /pljɑʊlmp/. Although the sonority sequencing pattern illustrated in (16) is perfect with one and only one visible peak, the syllable is not considered acceptable for most native speakers of English.

(16) The sonority chart for /pljɑʊlmp/

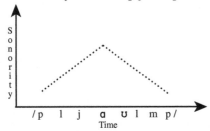

The reason why the hypothetical word /pljɑʊlmp/ is considered unacceptable for most native speakers of English is that there are two many phonemes in one word. This observation raises one question, How many phonemes are allowed in one word?

The third problem concerns syllabification of words. Let us consider the two phrases in (17) and (18). When these two phrases are uttered naturally, the two phrases sound identical in their pronunciations. Both of them are ideally represented as /hidneɪmz/. Nonetheless, most native speakers will agree that *hidden aims* contains three syllables, while *hid names* contains only two syllables. We have to answer the question, Where does the difference come from?

(17) hidden aims
(18) hid names

Finally, although the sonority sequencing can explain many words, many examples cannot be accounted for by the sonority sequencing we discussed earlier. In English, words cannot start with certain combinations of sounds like /kn/, /ps/, and /bn/, as shown in (19). Therefore, our hypothetical words listed in (20) are all unacceptable and treated as impossible words in English by most native speakers. Note that what we are dealing with are sounds, not letters. Though *kn* is a possible letter combination in English, it is not an acceptable sound combination.

(19) *kn, *ps, *bn
(20) */knip/, */psoʊl/, */bnɪŋ/

Before we solve the four problems introduced in this chapter, we have to discuss the structure of English syllables in more detail. The next section will deal with this topic.

13.2 Structures Of Syllables

In explaining the syllable structures of English, we might simply assume that all phonemes are directly connected in a flat structure, as shown in (21) for the English word *bat* /bæt/. The syllable is notated by the Greek letter σ. In (21), the three phonemes, /b/, /æ/, and /t/ constitute one syllable, forming a flat structure.

(21)

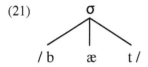

One problem with the structure in (21) is the inability to explain the rhyming structure in English. Within an English syllable, a vowel and the following consonant(s) form one unit called a rhyme. In each pair of words in (22), the combination of a vowel and its following consonant(s) is viewed as one unit by native speakers.

(22) bat versus pat, man versus ran, milk versus silk, cop versus top, and so on

By contrast, in each pair in (23), the first consonant and its following vowel is *not* considered one unit by most native speakers.

(23) pat versus pal, bat versus bang, cool versus cook, and so on

What this observation reveals about English syllable structures is that the vowel and its following consonant(s) in a syllable must form one unit. We may thus propose a revised syllable structure, like the one in (24). The structure provided in (24) is reminiscent of the X′ structure we discussed in Chapter 5: Both structures now have an intermediate node. In (24), the rhyme forms a separate unit to include only nucleus and coda, while the onset, or starting consonant(s) are left separate.

(24)

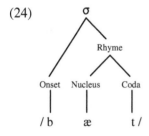

In (24), the nucleus means the peak of the syllable denoted by a vowel. The nucleus may be preceded by one or more consonants. The consonants that precede the nucleus are called the onset. Following the nucleus may be more consonants; they are referred to as the coda.

13.2.1 The onset

As briefly explained in the previous section, the onset can contain one or more consonant sounds. In (24), we have just illustrated the case where only one consonant occurs in the onset position. When there are two consonants appearing in the onset position, the syllable diagram would look like (25), which is illustrated with the English word *flat*.

(25)

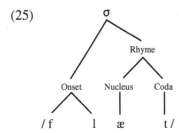

In (25), two consonants /f/ and /l/ are associated with the onset. Other than this, the structure in (25) is identical to that of (24).

To represent the number of phonemes within one syllable, we might revise (24) slightly, as in (26), where X simply represents a position occupied by a single phoneme. In (26), there are three X marks, which means that the word *bat* in English has three phonemes.

(26)

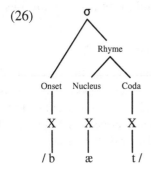

Naturally, the revised structure of (25) with the X marks would look like the one in (27). As we can tell from the structure in (27), the English word *flat* has four phonemes. Two of the phonemes among the four are associated with the onset.

(27)

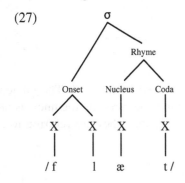

We have shown that the onset may contain two Xs. At this point, let's assume that the maximum number of Xs appearing in the onset position is two. This issue will be revisited in sections 13.3.1 and 13.3.2.

13.2.2 The Nucleus

Just like the case of the onset, the natural question we may raise here is, How many X positions are allowed in the nucleus? It seems that a maximum of two X positions are allowed in the nucleus position, as illustrated in (28). Each component of /aɪ/ (/a/ and /ɪ/) occupies one X position, and /ɪ/ in /bɪt/ occupies one X position in (28).

(28) /aɪ/ (for *I*) , /bɪt/ (for *bit*), /bi/ (for *bee*)

The syllable structures of /aɪ/ and /bɪt/ are illustrated in (29) and (30), respectively. Note that the onset and coda positions are not shown in (29) because there are no onset and coda for the English word *I*. The English word *I* is a monosyllable composed solely of a vowel.

(29)

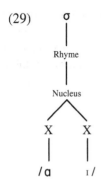

(30)

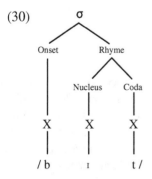

Let us now compare the vowels /i/ in /bit/ (for *beat*) and /ɪ/ in /bɪt/ (for *bit*). /ɪ/ is clearly shorter than /i/. The difference in the vowel quality between /i/ and /ɪ/ can be explained by the structure in (31), where the nucleus has two X slots and both of them are associated with the vowel /i/. Note that the coda consonant /t/ is ignored for the simplicity of exposition in (31).

(31)

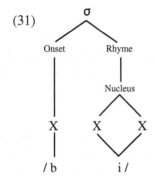

In fact, a syllable that contains a stressed vowel without a coda consonant must have two X slots associated with the vowel. If there is only one X slot associated with a stressed vowel without a following consonant, the syllable is not felicitous in English. For example, /bɪ/, where /ɪ/ is associated with one X slot, as illustrated in (32), is not an acceptable syllable in English.

(32)

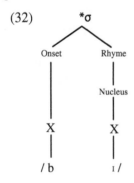

This observation leads us to the generalization that all stressed syllables are heavy syllables, where a heavy syllable is defined as a rhyme with two X slots. That is, /bi/ (for *bee*) is a heavy syllable because there are two X slots in its rhyme. Similarly, /bɪt/ is a heavy syllable because there are two X slots in the rhyme structure of /bɪt/, one being associated with /ɪ/, the other with /t/. A closer examination reveals that monosyllabic *lexical* or *content* words in English, words with conceptual meanings, must be stressed and therefore they must be heavy syllables. Therefore, /tʊ/ and /ðə/ are not possible lexical words, although they are actual *function* words, words that serve a grammatical purpose only. Note that the vowels in /tʊ/ and /ðə/ are not stressed and therefore yield a one-X rhyme structure, which is not felicitous for the lexical words in English.

13.2.3 The coda

The coda is the consonant(s) following the nucleus. Just like the onset, the coda is optional, as you can see in (33). The coda also may contain more than one consonant, as illustrated in (34).

(33) /paɪ/ (for *pie*), /su/ (for *Sue*), /ki/ for (*key*), and so on

(34) /bæt/ (for bat), /kæmp/ (for *camp*), /plænt/ (for *plant*), and so on

Because we have already illustrated a syllable structure where the coda does not appear (see section 13.2.2), we will not demonstrate the syllable structure for the words in (33). To demonstrate a complex-coda syllable, however, the word *camp* is illustrated in (35). Not surprisingly, /m/ and /p/ are associated with the X slots in the coda position.

(35)

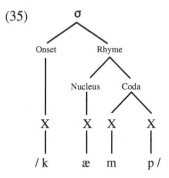

In (35), the rhyme has three X slots, one associated with the nucleus, and the other two associated with the two coda consonants /m/ and /p/ individually.

13.3 Answers

Armed with the information on the English syllable structures discussed above, we can now revisit the problems we discussed in section 13.1.

13.3.1 The status of /s/ in the onset

The first problem we discussed in section 13.1 concerns the status of /s/ in the onset. As illustrated in (15), /spit/ is a completely acceptable syllable, even though it apparently violates the sonority sequencing requirement. The problem can be solved by adopting the notion of appendix. Appendix is defined as a phoneme that is not part of the core syllable. In other words, in the syllable structure /spit/, the core onset is /p/ only. We may argue that the appendix /s/ may precede the core onset. This solution sounds like an ad hoc solution at first, but it actually provides a convenient generalization without breaking the assumption that the maximum number of Xs appearing in the onset is two. To explain this, consider the two monosyllabic words *strip* and *spring* in (36). These two words apparently have three consonants in the onset position. However, by treating the first /s/ as an appendix, we can explain the syllable structures of these monosyllabic words without violating our assumption about the maximum number of consonants in the onset.

(36) /strɪp/ (for *strip*), /spɹɪŋ/ (for *spring*)

The syllable structure of /strɪp/ would look like (37), where /s/ is an appendix to the core onset /tr/. The appendix property here is depicted with a dotted line.

(37)

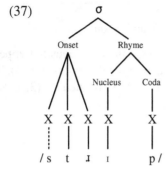

The structure provided in (37) accounts for the two-peak problem demonstrated in (15) when we are dealing with sonority sequencing. Because /s/ is not part of the core onset, /s/ is exempt from the sonority sequencing requirement. Excluding /s/, the syllable shown in (37), /stɹɪp/, conforms to the sonority requirement we discussed: The sonority increases until the peak and then it decreases.

13.3.2 The maximum number of phonemes in one syllable

As we discussed, /pljɑʊlmp/ is not a possible syllable in English, although it meets the sonority sequencing requirement. Simply put, the reason why /pljɑʊlmp/ is not acceptable is that there are too many phonemes in one syllable. Previously, we assumed that there are two X positions allowed in the onset. When we dealt with the rhyme, we also discussed three possibilities for lexical words, as seen in (38), (39), and (40). (38) shows the case when the two Xs are associated with a single nucleus phoneme; (39) illustrates a heavy syllable that contains one nucleus and one coda consonant; (40) shows the case where the coda contains two X positions.

(38)

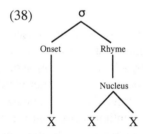

(39)

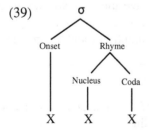

(40)

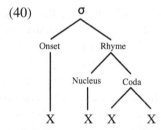

These three possible rhyme structures yield the generalization that the maximum number of Xs in the rhyme is three. However, this generalization is still not quite right. Consider the syllables listed in (41).

(41) /loʊbd/ (for *lobed*), /tɛkst/ (for *text*), /maɪnz/ (for *minds*), /koʊks/ (for *coax*), and so on.

All monosyllabic words in (41) need more than three Xs in the rhyme. All of them also violate the sonority sequencing requirement. To illustrate these two problems, let's look at the syllable /koʊks/. If we apply the same ideas from the previous discussion to this example, we would have the structure in (42), where there are four X positions in the rhyme.

(42)

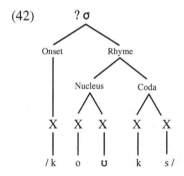

The sonority chart for the syllable /koʊks/ would look like (43), which violates the sonority sequencing. In (43), there are two visible peaks instead of one required for a felicitous syllable.

(43) The sonority chart for /koʊks/

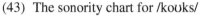

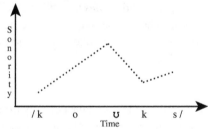

To solve these two problems, we can adopt the same notion of appendix that we discussed in explaining the /s/ phoneme in the onset. Although /s/ is the only appendix found in the English onset, the English coda has several appendixes. The final phoneme of each syllable listed in (41) can then be treated as an appendix. Because the final phoneme of each syllable is an appendix, it is not really part of the core coda. As a result, we can still maintain the assumption that the maximum number of Xs allowed in the rhyme is three. The problem with the sonority sequencing is naturally resolved as well. Once again, the /s/ phoneme in /koʊks/ is an appendix, and it is therefore exempt from the sonority sequencing requirement.

13.3.3 Syllabification

The third problem we encountered concerns syllabification of a phrase. Recall the two examples we discussed in (17) and (18): *hidden aims* versus *hid names*. Most native speakers analyze *hidden aims* as a three-syllable phrase, and *hid names* as a two-syllable phrase. As far as the pronunciation is concerned, however, the two phrases are pronounced the same: / hɪdneɪmz/. As a result, the two phrases are illustrated with one sonority chart, shown in (44).

(44) The sonority chart for /hɪdneɪmz/

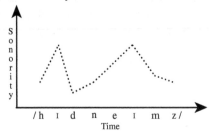

What this observation reveals is a general property of the rules that govern the way in which strings are divided into syllables, which is often referred to as the rules of syllabification. Judging from our observations in this chapter, we may conclude that syllabification happens at the single-word level. That is, words are syllabified individually, and later, they are combined to form phrases and sentences. To explain this syllabification rule, consider the phrases *hidden aims* and *hid names* once again. Though they sound identical in speech, the way they are interpreted in terms of syllables differs between the phrases. In the phrase *hidden aims, hidden* and *aims* are syllabified individually, yielding two syllables for *hidden*, and one for *aims*. These two words are put together to form a phrase. Because the syllabification of each word is inherited in the new phrase *hidden aims*, the phrase is syllabified as a three-syllable phrase. By contrast, in syllabifying *hid names, hid* and *names* are syllabified individually, yielding one syllable for *hid* and one for *names*. When these two words are put together to form the phrase *hid names*, the syllabification of each word is inherited in the phrase *hid names*; hence the phrase is interpreted as a two-syllable phrase.

13.3.4 Negative onset conditions

The last problem we discussed in section 13.1.3 concerns some phoneme combinations that are considered impossible in English by native speakers. The examples are reintroduced in (45).

(45) */knip/, */psʊʊl/, */bnɪŋ/, and so on

The phoneme combinations found in the onset of the words in (45) are all unaccept-able in English. Nonetheless, the combinations /kn/, /ps/, and /bn/ illustrated in (45) do not violate the sonority sequencing or the number of X slots in the onset. One way to solve this is to formulate negative onset conditions by individually listing unacceptable onset clusters. For example, the clusters listed in (46) are not acceptable onsets in English, although they all meet the sonority sequencing requirement. Remember, these are IPA transcriptions of speech sounds, not spellings, that are unacceptable.

(46) */kn/, */bn/, */pm/, */pn/, */pw/, */ps/, */stw/, */skŋ/, among others

To explain the unacceptability of the onsets in (46), we can list all ill-formed onset clusters individually. Although this negative onset condition describes the ill-formed onset clusters quite well, the criticism of this type of condition would be the lack of explanatory power of the condition. In other words, the question of why these clusters are not unacceptable is not clearly explained in this type of condition. To fix this problem, some linguists proposed that a statement of the possible syllable onsets of English consists of a positive template amended by a set of negative conditions. What this means is that there are some templates that can generate possible onsets in English. These possible onsets generated by the templates are later filtered out by a set of negative onset conditions. Because this approach requires in-depth discussion of more detailed feature structures of phonemes, we will not discuss the issue in this book. Nonetheless, the general idea is very close to that of the X′ theory discussed in Chapter 5. In dealing with X′ theory, we generated sentence structures by X′ rules. The generated structures were later filtered out by a set of constraints. We hope that readers see the similarities between these two approaches that are not directly related.

13.4 Summary

We examined English syllable structures in this chapter. We started by discussing the notion of syllable based on the notion of sonority. Sonority scale and sonority sequencing were dis-cussed, and various examples were provided. In doing so, we included a number of sonority charts that illustrate the sonority sequencing of the syllables in question. After pointing out four problems with the sonority sequencing, we discussed the syllable structure of English in detail, which is made up of the onset and the rhyme. We also discussed that the rhyme consists of the nucleus and the coda. Based on the schematic syllable structure provided, we solved the problems raised at the beginning of the chapter and provided some necessary modifications of that structure.

13.5 Further Reading

The books recommended in Chapter 12 are also valuable in understanding syllable structures. Giegerich (1992) and Roca and Johnson (1999) are particularly useful in understanding English syllable structures.

CHAPTER 14
Envoi

With this book, we have tried to open the door to you to the study of human language, which is ultimately the study of what it means to be a human being. We use our language to communicate our thoughts and feelings with our fellow human beings, to pass along information but also to create and maintain bonds with family, friends, and loved ones. We also use our language to do things and to identify ourselves as belonging to a certain group or as hailing from a certain part of the world. We do all of this with our language on a daily basis, and we do it so automatically that we take it for granted, much like we take for granted our ability to smile, breathe, love, or go for a walk in the park. It comes to us naturally as we grow from newborn babies through the first few years of our lives, and it is something that is so much a part of us that we rarely give it a conscious thought, and even less often think about it in a scientific way!

This is exactly what we wanted to show you in this book. Even though we take it for granted, our language is a system, and it can be the object of scientific questions. And in posing and trying to answer these kinds of questions, we can learn a lot about language and the way the system is put together, the way the different parts of it interact with one another and come together to compose the complete system. There are an infinite number of questions that one can ask about language, and there are many many approaches to answering those questions. We can ask, for instance, where is language located in the brain or mind? How does it interact with other components of our mental faculty, such as vision, hearing, musical ability and appreciation? How do we acquire language in the first place, and what does it mean to do so? Why does it happen so effortlessly and playfully for children, yet so painstakingly and inefficiently for adults learning a second language in a high school classroom? What is the difference here? Why can we so easily learn multiple languages when we are children but not when we are adults? And how can we have intuitions about whether a sentence in our language is grammatical, if we have never heard that sentence before? These are some kinds of questions that linguists hope to answer. But there are more. Where does language come from? How does language change over time? Why do languages vary across regions and social groups, and why do people have such strong opinions and attitudes about their language and the language of others? What are the implications of these attitudes?

All of these kinds of questions and many more are the subject of linguistics. And as such, they can be approached in a scientific fashion. The basic formula goes like this: make a hypothesis about data; test the hypothesis; reformulate the hypothesis to account for new observations; rinse and repeat as necessary. So knowledge about language is discovered in this kind of fashion, and the field moves forward through this kind of argumentation. The result of all of this is that we end up with a picture of a language and of language users that is faithful to the world as we find it; we have a scientific account of an actual thing as it exists in the world. This seems infinitely more satisfying than taking for granted, for instance, that we cannot split infinitives or that we should not end a sentence in a presupposition simply because that is what we have always been told. Those things may or may not be true in a given language, but what we do in this book is to provide a way of testing those claims and arguing for whether or not they are true. A big difference!

Which brings us to our final point. Beyond what we have just described with respect to accruing knowledge in linguistics, this book offers a model for accruing knowledge about the world in general. The methods of direct and indirect argumentation that linguists use are generalizable, much like the kind of arguments used in running a proof in geometry. So, whether you are asking questions about word meaning or syntactic order, phonological structure, or something beyond, with the argumentation-style used in this book you have a means of asking those questions. This is true of linguistic questions just as it is true of questions beyond linguistics, to understanding facts about the world in general. The means of arguing we have illustrated here provides a scientific way of asking and answering questions.

RECOMMENDED READING

Aronoff, Mark and Kristen Fudeman. 2011. *What Is Morphology*, 2nd ed. Malden, MA: Wiley-Blackwell.

Austin, J. L. 1962. *How to Do Things with Words*. Cambridge, MA: Harvard University Press.

Baker, Mark. 2003. *Lexical Categories: Verbs, Nouns, and Adjectives*. Cambridge: Cambridge University Press.

Beaver, David I. and Bart Geurts. 2011. Presupposition. *The Stanford Encyclopedia of Philosophy* (summer 2011 ed.), Edward N. Zalta (Ed.), http://plato.stanford.edu/archives/sum2011/entries/presupposition/.

Bloomfield, Leonard. 1933. *Language*. Chicago, IL: University of Chicago Press.

Booij, Geert. 2007. *The Grammar of Words: An Introduction to Linguistic Morphology*, 2nd ed. Oxford: Oxford University Press.

Carnie, Andrew. 2007. *Syntax: A Generative Introduction*, 2nd ed. Malden, MA: Blackwell.

Carnie, Andrew. 2008. *Constituent Structure*. Oxford: Oxford University Press.

Chomsky, Noam. 1957. *Syntactic Structures*. Berlin: Mouton de Gruyter.

Chomsky, Noam. 1965. *Aspects of the Theory of Syntax*. Cambridge, MA: The MIT Press.

Chomsky, Noam. 1970. Remarks on nominalization. In Jacobs, R. and Rosenbaum P. (Eds.) *Readings in English Transformational Grammar*. Waltham, MA: Ginn, 184–221.

Chomsky, Noam. 1981. *Lectures on Government and Binding: The Pisa Lectures*. The Hague: Mouton.

Coleman, Linda, and Paul Kay. 1981. Prototype semantics: The English word *lie*. *Language* 57, pp. 26–44.

Croft, William and Alan Cruse. 2004. *Cognitive Linguistics*. Cambridge: Cambridge University Press.

Curzan, Anne, and Michael Adams. 2011. *How English Works: A Linguistic Introduction*. New York: Longman.

Ehrlich, Susan, and Jack Sidnell. 2006. I think that is not an assumption you ought to make: Challenging presuppositions in inquiry testimony. *Language in Society* 35, pp. 655–676.

Evans, Vyvyan, and Melanie Green. 2006. *Cognitive Linguistics: An Introduction*. Mahwah, NJ: Lawrence Erlbaum Associates.

Finegan, Edward. 2008. *Language: Its Structure and Use*, 5th ed. Boston: Thomson Wadworth.

Gamut, L. T. F. 1990. *Logic, Language, and Meaning: Introduction to Logic*, Volume 1. Chicago, IL: University of Chicago Press.

Giegerich, Heinz. 1992. *English Phonology*. Cambridge: Cambridge University Press.

Goldberg, Adele. 1995. *Constructions: A Construction Grammar Approach to Argument Structure*. Chicago, IL: University of Chicago Press.

Goldberg, Adele. 2006. *Constructions at Work: The Nature of Generalization in Language*. Oxford: Oxford University Press.

Green, Mitchell. 2009. Speech acts. *The Stanford Encyclopedia of Philosophy* (spring 2009 ed.). Edward N. Zalta (Ed.). http://plato.stanford.edu/archives/spr2009/entries/speech-acts/.

Greenbaum, Sydney. 1996. *The Oxford English Grammar*. Oxford: Oxford University Press.

Grice, H. Paul. 1989. *Studies in the Way of Words*. Cambridge, MA: Harvard University Press.

Grundy, Peter. 2008. *Doing Pragmatics*. London: Hodder Education.

Haegeman, Liliane. 1994. *Introduction to Government and Binding Theory*, 2nd ed. Oxford: Blackwell.

Horn, Laurence. 1972. *On the Semantic Properties of Logical Operators in English*. Ph.D. Dissertation, University of California at Los Angeles.

Horn, Laurence. 1984. Toward a new taxonomy for pragmatic inference: Q-based and R-based implicature. In Deborah Schiffrin (Ed.), *Meaning, Form, and Use in Context: Linguistic Applications*. Washington, DC: Georgetown University Press.

Horn, Laurence. 2004. Implicature. In Laurence Horn and Gregory Ward (Eds.), *The Handbook of Pragmatics*. Malden, MA: Blackwell.

Huang, Yan. 2008. *Pragmatics*. Oxford: Oxford University Press.

Huddelston, Rodney, and Geoffrey Pullum. 2002. *The Cambridge Grammar of the English Language*. Cambridge: Cambridge University Press.

Hyde, Dominic, 2011. Sorites paradox. *The Stanford Encyclopedia of Philosophy* (winter 2011 ed.). Edward N. Zalta (Ed.). http://plato.stanford.edu/archives/win2011/entries/sorites-paradox/.

Jackendoff, Ray. 1977. *X-Bar Syntax: A Study of Phrase Structure*. Cambridge, MA: The MIT Press.

Kadmon, Nirit. 2001. *Formal Pragmatics*. Malden, MA: Blackwell.

Katamba, Francis. 2006. *Morphology*, 2nd ed. New York: Palgrave Macmillan.

Kenstowicz, Michael. 1994. *Phonology in Generative Grammar*. Malden, MA: Wiley-Blackwell.

Kenstowicz, Michael, and Charles Kisserberth. 1986. *Generative Phonology: Description and Theory*. New York: Academic Press.

Ladefoged, Peter. 2005. *Vowels and Consonants*, 2nd ed. Malden, MA: Wiley-Blackwell.

Ladefoged, Peter, and Keith Johnson. 2010. *A Course in Phonetics*, 6th ed. Boston: Wadsworth Publishing.

Langacker, Ronald. 1987. *Foundations of Cognitive Grammar*, Volume 1. Stanford, CA: Stanford University Press.

Langacker, Ronald. 1991. *Foundations of Cognitive Grammar*, Volume 2. Stanford, CA: Stanford University Press.

Langacker, Ronald. 2008. *Cognitive Grammar: A Basic Introduction*. Oxford: Oxford University Press.

Larson, Richard. 2010. *Grammar as Science*. Cambridge, MA: The MIT Press.

Levinson, Stephen. 1983. *Pragmatics*. Cambridge: Cambridge University Press.

Levinson, Stephen. 2000. *Presumptive Meanings: The Theory of Generalized Conversational Implicature*. Cambridge, MA: The MIT Press.

Lewis, David.1979. Scorekeeping in a language game. *Journal of Philosophical Logic* 8, pp. 339–359.

Lobeck, Anne. 2000. *Discovering English Grammar: An Introduction to English Sentence Structure*. Oxford: Oxford University Press.

Matthews, P. H. 1991. *Morphology*, 2nd ed. Cambridge: Cambridge University Press.

Matthewson, Lisa. 2006. Presuppositions and cross-linguistic variation. *Proceedings of NELS* 26, pp. 63–76

Napoli, Donna. 1993. *Syntax: Theory and Problems*. Oxford: Oxford University Press.

Newmeyer, Frederick. 1986. *Linguistic Theory in America*, 2nd ed. New York: Academic Press.

Nida, Eugene. 1949/1965. *Morphology: The Descriptive Analysis of Words*. Ann Arbor, MI: University of Michigan.

Odden, David. 2005. *Introducing Phonology*. Cambridge: Cambridge University Press.

Ohio State University. 2008. *Language Files*, 10th ed. Columbus: The Ohio State University Press.

Partee, Barbara, Alice ter Meulen, and Robert Wall. 1990. *Mathematical Methods in Linguistics*. Norwell, MA: Springer Verlag.

Pinker, Steven. 1994. *The Language Instinct: How the Mind Creates Language*. New York: Harper Collins.

Quine, W. van Orman. 1963. *Set Theory and Its Logic*. Cambridge, MA: Harvard University Press.

Quirk, Randolph, Sydney Greenbaum, Geoffrey Leech, and Jan Svartvik. 1985. *A Comprehensive Grammar of the English Language*. New York: Longman.

Radden, Gunter and René Dirven. 2007. *Cognitive English Grammar*. Amsterdam: John Benjamins Publishing Company.

Radford, Andrew. 1988. *Transformational Grammar: A First Course*. Cambridge: Cambridge University Press.

Roca, Iggy, and Wyn Johnson. 1999. *A Course in Phonology*. Malden, MA: Wiley-Blackwell.

Searle, John R. 1969. *Speech Acts*. Cambridge: Cambridge University Press.

Simons, Mandy, Judith Tonhauser, David Beaver, and Craige Roberts. 2010. What projects and why. *Proceedings of SALT* 20, pp. 309–327.

Soames, Scott, and David Perlmutter. 1979. *Syntactic Argumentation and the Structure of English*. Berkeley: University of California Press.

Solan, Lawrence, and Peter Tiersma. 2005. *Speaking of Crime: The Language of Criminal Justice*. Chicago, IL: University of Chicago Press.

Spencer, Andrew. 1991. *Morphological Theory: An Introduction to Word Structure in Generative Grammar*. Malden, MA: Wiley-Blackwell.

Spencer, Andrew, and Arnold Zwicky. 2001. *The Handbook of Morphology*. Malden, MA: Wiley-Blackwell.

Sperber, Dan, and Deirdre Wilson. 1995. *Relevance: Communication and Cognition*. Malden, MA: Blackwell.

Tannen, Deborah. 1982. Ethnic style in male-female conversation. In John Gumperz (Ed.), *Language and Society*, pp. 217–231. Cambridge: Cambridge University Press.

Ungerer, Friedrich, and Hans-Jorg Schmid. 2006. *An Introduction to Cognitive Linguistics*, 2nd ed. London: Longman.

Wall, Robert. 1972. *Introduction to Mathematical Linguistics*. New York: Prentice Hall.

INDEX

CPSIA information can be obtained
at www.ICGtesting.com
Printed in the USA
LVHW021721300420
654621LV00001B/1